365 Special Pasta Recipes

(365 Special Pasta Recipes - Volume 1)

Vicky Roy

Content

365 Awesome Pasta Recipes

***

1. 3 Ingredient Fettuccine Alfredo Recipe

Serving: 4 | Prep: | Cook: 30mins | Ready in:

Ingredients

- 2 sticks butter
- 1/2 pound grated parmesan cheese, plus more for serving
- salt to taste
- 1 pound fettuccine

Direction

- Using an electric mixer, beat butter and Parmesan until creamy.
- In a large pot of boiling salted water, cook fettuccine according to package instructions until al dente, about 12 minutes.
- Reserve about 1/2 cup of cooking water; drain pasta.
- Return fettuccine to warm pot.
- Toss pasta with 1/2 teaspoon salt, cheese mixture, and 1/4 cup of the pasta water.
- Add more pasta water, as needed.
- Serve with additional cheese.

2. All You Need To Know About Making Russian Pierogis Recipe

Serving: 6 | Prep: | Cook: 10mins | Ready in:

Ingredients

- For The Dough (makes about 6 dozen):
- 1 tsp. salt
- 3 eggs
- 1 cup warm (not hot) water
- 4-1/2 cups all-purpose flour
- extra flour for rolling the dough
- For The potato Pierogi Filling:
- 6 medium potatoes (I like to use red)
- 8 tbsp. butter, softened
- 6 oz. cream cheese, softened
- 1 onion, chopped and sauted until soft
- salt and pepper to taste
- 2 onions+ 4 tbsp. butter for the butter sauce (optional)
- For The Meat Pierogi Filling:
- 2 tbsp. butter
- 1 tbsp. oil
- 1/2 cup finely chopped onions
- 6 oz. lean groun beef
- 6 oz. ground pork
- 1 tsp. salt
- 1/2 tsp. pepper
- 1/2 cup cold water
- For The cabbage Pierogi Filling:
- 1 can (15 oz.) souerkraut, drained
- 1 small head of cabbage, shredded
- 1/2 package of bacon, cooked, drained on paper towels and crumbled
- 1 onion, chopped
- 1 tsp. sugar
- 4 tbsp. sour cream
- salt and pepper to taste
- 2 onions, chopped+4 tbsp. butter for the onion butter sauce(optional)
- For The cheese Pierogis:
- 2 lbs. ricotta chesse
- 4 tbsp. sugar (add more sugar if you prefer them sweeter)
- 2 egg yolks
- 2 tbsp. melted butter, cooled
- 1/2 tsp. salt
- 1 cup sour cream

- For The fruit Filled Pierogis:
- Use your favourite fruit pie filling, like cheery, blueberry, etc., or make your own.

Direction

- To Make The Dough:
- In a large mixing bowl, combine flour and salt and make a deep well in the center. Drop in the eggs and warm water.
- Here comes the fun part. I like to mix the dough with my hands, rather than utensils. This helps you "feel" the dough and mixes it a lot better. Take off any hand jewellery and mix the flour into the liquid ingredients, until the mixture can be gathered into a compact ball.
- Transfer the dough to a lightly floured surface and knead it by pressing it down and pushing it forward with the heel of your hand. Sprinkle the dough with extra flour if necessary to prevent it from sticking to the board. Knead for about 10 minutes, or until the dough is smooth and elastic. Shape it into a ball, cover loosely with Saran wrap and let rest for about 10 minutes.
- Divide the dough in 2 parts. On a lightly floured surface, roll the dough into a rough circle, about 1/8-inch thick. Flip the dough over and roll on the other side as well.
- Using a 2-1/2 to 3-inch cookie cutter, cut out rounds of dough. Do not stack the cut outs, as they may stick together. The same goes for the shaped dumplings. Place them in a SINGLE layer, on a FLOURED surface and keep covered with wax paper to prevent from drying.
- When ready to fill, stretch a circle cut out with your fingers and place a little less than a tbsp. of chosen filling in the middle. (Recipes for fillings are included on this page). Also note that you only need to use one stuffing per batch of dough. Fold the dough over the filling. Seal the edges with your fingers first, then go over them with the prongs of a fork. This adds a decorative touch as well. *Note: For the meat pierogies, a traditional fold is to

also lift the two corners, pinching them together to form a circular pouch.
- Bring 3 quarts of water to a boil over high heat. Add a small amount of oil to the boiling water (this will help dumplings not to stick during cooking). Add 1 tsp. salt to the boiling water. Drop about a dozen of pierogies into the water. Gently stir and reduce the heat to a light boil.
- Cook, uncovered, for about 5 minutes. Generally, they are ready when rise to the surface. With a slotted spoon, transfer them to a bowl and immediately coat with some olive oil or butter.
- I usually make an onion butter sauce by sautéing 2 chopped onions in 4 tbsp. of butter and then lightly brown the cooked dumplings in non-stick skillet in this sauce. This will keep them from sticking when cooled.
- If you don't want to cook all the pierogies at the same time, place uncooked dumplings in a single layer on a floured cookie sheet and sprinkle with extra flour. Then put in the freezer for about 30 minutes. Take out and place in a zip lock. Store in the freezer until ready to use. When ready to use, just add the frozen dumplings to the boiling water.
- For The Potato Pierogi Filling:
- Boil the peeled potatoes in water until soft. Drain the water, mash the potatoes. Stir in 8 tbsp. softened butter, cream cheese, sautéed onion, salt and pepper. Mash again until smooth.
- Note: After dumplings are cooked, sauté 2 chopped onions in 4 tbsp. butter and fry the dumplings lightly in this sauce.
- For The Cabbage Pierogi Filling:
- Sauté shredded cabbage and onion in some oil and butter until soft, reduced in bulk and lightly caramelized. I like to add 1/3 cup water to the cabbage while it's cooking and cover it with lid. This helps it to cook faster.
- When cabbage is cooked, add a can of sauerkraut and cook for 8 minutes longer.
- Stir in sugar, salt and pepper to taste and crumbled bacon. Cook for 3 more minutes. Take off the heat and stir in 4 tbsp. sour cream.

- Note: When dumplings are cooked, sauté 2 chopped onions in 4 tbsp. butter and fry the dumplings lightly in this sauce.
- For The Meat Pierogies:
- In a skillet, melt butter in the oil and sauté the chopped onions until they are soft, about 3-4 minutes.
- Scrape the onions into a large mixing bowl. Add the raw meats, salt, pepper and 1/2 cup cold water. Mix with a large spoon or your hands until well combined and the mixture is smooth. *Note: this filling doesn't get cooked prior to boiling. The ground meat cooks fast in boiling water.
- For The Sweet Cheese Pierogies:
- Beat the sugar into the Ricotta cheese. Then beat in the egg yolks, melted butter and salt. Stir in the sour cream. If you prefer sweeter filling, add more sugar. These dumplings are served with extra sour cream or maple syrup when cooked.
- For The fruit Filled Pierogies:
- Just use your favourite fruit pie filling such as cherry, blueberry, etc. These are served with sour cream or maple syrup when cooked.

3. Amish Haystacks Recipe

Serving: 810 | Prep: | Cook: 20mins |Ready in:

Ingredients

- 2 pounds ground beef
- One 1/4-ounce package taco seasoning mix
- One 14-ounce jar (or 1 1/2 cups) spaghetti sauce
- Two 9-ounce bags tortilla chips, crushed
- 2 cups hot cooked rice, prepared as label directs
- 1 head lettuce, thinly sliced
- 2 cups diced tomatoes
- 1 cup grated carrots
- 1 cup chopped green onions
- 1 cup sliced pitted ripe olives
- 1 cup diced green pepper
- 1 cup diced celery
- 1 1/2 cups shredded cheddar cheese
- 1 cup crumbled cooked bacon
- 1 cup sunflower seed kernals
- One jar salsa

Direction

- In large skillet, brown ground beef with taco seasoning over medium-high heat. Add spaghetti sauce; heat to boiling. Reduce heat to low; simmer, uncovered, until most of liquid evaporates.
- Mix crushed crackers and tortilla chips in a bowl. Place ground-beef mixture, rice, and remaining ingredients in individual bowls.
- Allow guests to serve themselves, layering as suits each individual: lettuce, chips, meat mixture, rice, tomatoes, carrots, onions, olives, pepper, celery, cheese, bacon, sunflower seeds, and salsa.

4. Andouille Cajun Fettuccine Recipe

Serving: 5 | Prep: | Cook: 20mins |Ready in:

Ingredients

- l lbs. of cooked Al Dente fettuccine
- 3 tablespoons olive oil
- 3 tablespoons minced garlic
- 1 medium julianne cut onion
- 1 small julianne cut red bellpepper,
- 1 small julianne cut green bellpepper
- 1 cup thinly sliced andouille sausage
- 1/2 cup white wine
- 1 cup heavy cream
- 1/4 cup parmesan cheese
- McCormick's cajun seasoning to taste
- black pepper to taste

Direction

- Heat a large sauté pan on high heat
- Add olive oil, garlic, bell peppers and sausage cook till sausage is done stirring constantly
- Deglaze pan with white wine
- Add heavy cream bringing to a boil
- Add parmesan cheese and cooked pasta stir and season with McCormick's Cajun seasoning to taste
- Add black pepper to taste. (Lots of love in this dish)

5. Andouille And Chicken Creole Pasta Recipe

Serving: 8 | Prep: | Cook: 30mins | Ready in:

Ingredients

- 1/2 pound andouille sausage, sliced
- 3 skinless, boneless chicken breasts-cut into strips
- 1-3 tablespoons of creole seasoning, start with one and add to taste
- 2 tbs. diet margarine
- 2 bell peppers, cut into strips
- 8 oz. of fresh mushrooms, sliced (can use canned, drained)
- 4 chopped green onions
- 1 can (14oz.) fat free chicken broth
- 1 cup skim milk or regular milk
- 2 tsp. lemon pepper
- 2 tsp. garlic powder
- 1/4 cup cornstarch
- 1/2 cup cold water
- 1 16 oz. pkg thin spaghetti

Direction

- Cook spaghetti according to package
- Heat a large skillet over med-high heat. Cook sausage and chicken with the creole seasoning until the meat is halfway done.
- Add mushrooms, green onion, and bell pepper.

- Sauté over med. heat about 10 mins.
- Stir in the chicken broth, milk, lemon pepper, and garlic powder.
- Reduce the heat to low.
- Mix together the corn starch and cold water until it's dissolved.
- Stir into the skillet
- Bring to a boil and boil for 1 min.
- Remove from heat
- Serve over cooked pasta. Enjoy!

6. Angel Hair And Three Onion Soup Recipe

Serving: 4 | Prep: | Cook: 90mins | Ready in:

Ingredients

- 4 Tbsp olive oil
- 1/2 lb baby (pearl) onions, fresh (or ½ frozen bag, thawed)
- 1 medium red onion, sliced thin
- 1 medium vidalia onion (or other sweet onion), sliced thin
- 6 cups (48 fl oz) chicken stock
- salt (to taste)
- 1/4 tsp red pepper flakes
- 1/2 lb angel hair pasta, broken in 2-inch pieces
- 1/4 cup chopped flat leaf parsley
- 4 tsp grated romano cheese

Direction

- PLACE oil and all onions in a large sauce pan over low heat and sauté, stirring occasionally, about 20 minutes, until onions are golden.
- Add stock and salt to taste.
- Sprinkle with red pepper flakes and simmer for about 1 hour.
- ADD pasta and parsley and cook until pasta is just al dente.
- LADLE into soup bowls.
- Sprinkle with grated Romano cheese

7. Angel Hair Pasta With Creamy Mushroom Sauce Recipe

Serving: 4 | Prep: | Cook: 20mins | Ready in:

Ingredients

- 4 ounces angel hair pasta
- 1-1/2 cups sliced fresh mushrooms
- 1 medium white onion chopped
- 1 teaspoon butter
- 3 ounces cream cheese cut into cubes
- 1/4 teaspoon salt
- 1 teaspoon freshly ground black pepper
- 1-1/3 cups milk
- 2 tablespoons chives snipped

Direction

- Cook pasta according to package directions then drain well.
- In a medium saucepan cook the mushrooms and onion in the butter until vegetables are tender.
- Stir in cream cheese, salt and pepper then cook and stir over low heat until cheese is melted.
- Gradually stir in milk and chives and heat through.
- Pour sauce over pasta and toss to coat.
- Serve immediately.

8. Angel Hair Pasta With Shrimp Scampi And Broccoli Recipe

Serving: 4 | Prep: | Cook: 20mins | Ready in:

Ingredients

- 1-1/4 pounds medium shrimp shelled deveined rinsed and patted dry
- 3 large garlic cloves minced
- 1/2 teaspoon salt
- 1 teaspoon freshly ground black pepper
- 6 tablespoons olive oil
- 4 tablespoons butter at room temperature
- 1 bunch broccoli cut into medium florets
- 9 ounces fresh angel hair pasta

Direction

- Combine shrimp, garlic, salt, pepper and 4 tablespoons olive oil in medium bowl.
- Cover and let marinate in refrigerator for 1 hour or up to 4 hours.
- Remove shrimp from marinade and reserve marinade.
- Remove garlic pieces adhering to shrimp with small rubber spatula and return garlic to marinade.
- Put 4 tablespoons butter in a large warm bowl for tossing with pasta.
- Add broccoli to a large saucepan of enough boiling salt water to cover generously.
- Cook uncovered over high heat for 5 minutes then drain broccoli well and return to saucepan.
- Cover and keep warm.
- Heat remaining olive oil and 2 tablespoons butter over medium in large heavy skillet.
- Add shrimp and sauté tossing often for 2 minutes.
- Reserving fat in skillet transfer shrimp with a slotted spoon to a large bowl.
- Cut some of larger shrimp into thirds.
- Cover and keep warm.
- Bring a large pot of water to a boil then add salt then pasta.
- Cook uncovered over high heat separating strands occasionally with a fork about 2 minutes.
- Drain well then add angel hair to the bowl containing butter pieces and toss well.
- Add about 2/3 of shrimp and 1/2 of broccoli flowerets and toss.
- Add shrimp marinade to skillet used to cook shrimp.
- Cook over medium heat stirring until garlic is tender but not brown.
- Immediately pour mixture over pasta and toss until blended.

- Mound pasta mixture on a large heated platter and encircle with remaining shrimp and broccoli.

- Sprinkle with basil.
- NOTE: Tomato mixture can stand at room temperature up to 2 hours.

9. Angel Hair Pasta With Fresh Tomato Sauce Recipe

Serving: 6 | Prep: | Cook: 20mins | Ready in:

Ingredients

- 1 small garlic clove
- 3 lb tomatoes
- 2 tablespoons fresh lemon juice
- 1 teaspoon salt
- 1 teaspoon sugar (optional)
- 1/2 teaspoon black pepper
- 1 lb dried capellini (angel-hair pasta)
- 1/2 cup chopped fresh basil
- ****
- Accompaniments:
- finely grated parmigiano-Reggiano
- extra-virgin olive oil for drizzling (optional)
- fresh Mozzarella broken into pieces (optional)

Direction

- Mince garlic and mash to a paste with a pinch of salt using a large heavy knife.
- Core and coarsely chop two thirds of tomatoes. Halve remaining tomatoes crosswise, then rub cut sides of tomatoes against large holes of a box grater set in a large bowl, reserving pulp and discarding skin. Toss pulp with chopped tomatoes, garlic paste, lemon juice, salt, sugar (if using), and pepper. Let stand until ready to use, at least 10 minutes.
- While tomatoes stand, cook pasta in a 6- to 8-quart pot of boiling salted water, uncovered, until al dente, about 2 minutes.
- Drain in a colander and immediately add to tomato mixture, tossing to combine. (Add fresh mozzarella at this point if you go that route).

10. Apple Lasagna Recipe

Serving: 8 | Prep: | Cook: 45mins | Ready in:

Ingredients

- 8 pieces lasagna uncooked
- 2 cans apple pie filling
- 1 cup ricotta cheese
- 3 eggs
- 1 teaspoon almond extract
- 1/4 cup white sugar
- 6 tablespoons flour
- 1/2 teaspoon cinnamon
- 3 tablespoons butter
- 6 tablespoons brown sugar
- 1/4 cup quick cooking oats
- 1/4 teaspoon nutmeg
- 1 cup sour cream
- 1/3 cup brown sugar

Direction

- Prepare lasagna according to package directions then drain well.
- Spread one can apple pie filling in a greased rectangular pan slicing any extra thick apples.
- Layer four pieces of lasagna over apples.
- Mix together cheese, eggs, extract and sugar then spread evenly over lasagna.
- Top with remaining four pieces of lasagna.
- In small bowl combine flour, cinnamon, butter, brown sugar, oats and nutmeg until crumbly.
- Sprinkle over apple filling then bake at 350 for 45 minutes.
- Let stand 15 minutes then cut into serving pieces.
- Combine sour cream and brown sugar then dollop over top of lasagna when serving.

11. Asiago Ranch Pasta Recipe

Serving: 8 | Prep: | Cook: 22mins | Ready in:

Ingredients

- 3 cups uncooked gemelli noodles or cellentani noodles
- 1 can (5 ounces) evaporated milk
- 1 cup Hidden Valley Original Ranch with garlic
- 2 eggs, slightly beaten
- 3 cups finely shredded asiago cheese
- 1/2 cup unseasoned dry breadcrumbs
- 2 tablespoons butter, melted

Direction

- Cook pasta according to package directions; rinse and drain. Combine evaporated milk, Hidden Valley Garlic Ranch and eggs in medium bowl.
- Stir in shredded cheese.
- Add cooked pasta; mix well.
- Spoon pasta mixture into sprayed 1 1/2 quart casserole.
- Combine breadcrumbs and melted butter.
- Sprinkle on top of casserole.
- Bake 20 to 22 minutes, or until heated through.

12. Asian Noodle Salad Recipe

Serving: 4 | Prep: | Cook: | Ready in:

Ingredients

- 4 oz (uncooked) thin spaghetti (angel hair, vermicelli etc...)
- 2 tablespoon peanut or canola oil
- 2 tablespoon soy sauce
- 2 tablespoon hoisin sauce
- 2 tablespoon lemon juice
- 2 gloves of garlic minced

- 2 teaspoon sesame oil
- 1 teaspoon finely grated ginger
- handful of snow peas (I do not like snow peas, so I use about 1/2 cup of peas)
- 1 cup baby corn — rinsed and drained
- 1 red pepper sliced
- 2 green onions — thinly sliced
- 1 1/2 cups shredded savoy cabbage (or even a bag of coleslaw mix might work)
- 1-2 tablespoon sesame seeds
- 1 -2 tablespoon finely chopped fresh cilantro (coriander)
- ***I kinda fiddled with the measurements for the sauce,(I did not make this up myself, just changed the amounts) so you may like a little more or a little less of something****

Direction

- COOK the noodles, then rinse under cold water and drain.
- MIX together the oil, soy and hoisin sauce, lemon juice, sesame oil, garlic and ginger in a bowl until well combined.
- PUT the noodles and all remaining ingredients, except the dressing, in a salad bowl. POUR the dressing over the salad and toss gently to combine.

13. Asparagus And Lemon Cream Pasta Recipe

Serving: 4 | Prep: | Cook: 11mins | Ready in:

Ingredients

- 1 14 ounce box of whole grain pasta (or fresh or regular)
- 1 lb asparagus, cleaned, ends snapped and cut into 1 1/2 pieces or so
- 1 Tbsp butter
- 1 1/2 cups of heavy cream
- 1 1/2 cups vegetable stock
- 1 lemon, for juice and zest

- fresh cracked pepper or lemon pepper - to taste (i use a ton)
- garlic salt - to taste (again, i'm a salt fiend so I use alot)
- 3/4 cup of fresh grated parmesan
- chopped flat-leaf parsley to sprinkle on top
- fresh parmesan shavings for top

Direction

- Bring your pasta water to a boil
- Shallow boil your asparagus - put all it in a pot and cover with 1/2 cup vegetable stock, boil until tender, then add butter, set aside
- While waiting for that pour your heavy cream into a deep frying pan
- Add your remaining 1 cup of stock and microplane the full lemon for zest, bring to a rolling simmer.
- Whisk in about 3/4 the juice from the lemon
- Add the fresh grated parmesan and reduce heat, stir until melted and every so often for around 8 minutes or until thickened.
- Back to the pasta, your water should be boiling, toss the pasta in and boil to al dente according to box
- When sauce thickens add asparagus, cracked pepper and garlic salt.
- When pasta is done, drain it and toss it into the pan, Use tongs to turn the sauce into the pasta
- Top with chopped parsley and fresh shaved parmesan
- If you are me, add more salt and lots more pepper because you're a freak like that.
- Get that last squeeze of lemon over your pasta to add brightness
- Enjoy!

14. Asparagus Lasagna Recipe

Serving: 9 | Prep: | Cook: 25mins | Ready in:

Ingredients

- 2 pounds asparagus, trimmed
- 1 1/2 tablespoons olive oil
- 3 lasagna noodles, no boil variety, or equivalent
- 1/4 stick unsalted butter
- 2 tablespoons flour
- 3/4 cup chicken broth
- 1/4 cup water
- 4 ounces feta cheese, crumbled
- 1 lemon, zest only
- 3/4 cup parmesan cheese, freshly grated
- 3/4 cup whipping cream

Direction

- Cut tips from asparagus spears and reserve. Cut remaining stalks diagonally into 1/2" pieces and cook until tender-crisp.
- In large bowl of cold water, let sheets of lasagna soak for 15 minutes or until softened.
- In the meantime, melt butter in a saucepan, add flour and cook stirring over low heat for 3 minutes. Add broth and water using whisk. Simmer 5 minutes and whisk in feta, zest and salt to taste, continuing until sauce is smooth.
- Drain pasta well, arrange a layer of noodles in bottom of buttered 9" square pan and spread with 1/4 of the sauce. Top the sauce with 1/4th the reserved asparagus stalks and sprinkle with 1/3 cup parmesan. Continue layering ending with lasagna noodles.
- In bowl, beat whipping cream with a pinch of salt until it holds soft peaks. Arrange the asparagus tips on top of casserole and spoon the savory whipped cream over pasta and asparagus tips. Sprinkle the remaining parmesan on top.
- Bake at 400 for 20-30 minutes or until golden and bubbling. Let stand 10 minutes before serving so that it cuts nicely into squares.
- To double, use 2 pans.
- To make this gluten-free: Use gluten-free lasagna noodles and substitute cornstarch for the flour and you're good to go.

15. Authentic Hungarian Ghoulash Recipe

Serving: 8 | Prep: | Cook: 5mins | Ready in:

Ingredients

- 5 lbs beef (chuck or better yet boneless short ribs) cut into 1" cubes
- 4 T. butter or lite butter
- 4 T. olive oil
- 1 1/2 lbs mushrooms, rinsed and sliced into thick slices
- 3 onions chopped
- 1 15 oz can tomato sauce
- 3 T. tomato paste
- 2 t. Worcester sauce
- 2. t crushed garlic
- ¾ cup sweet Hungarian Tokay, marsala, or cream sherry
- 2-3 T. sweet Hungarian paprika
- 5 bay leaves
- salt and black pepper to taste
- 2 chili peppers, sliced in half lengthwise, seeds, stems and ribs removed (optional)
- 1 pt. sour cream (regular, lite or non-fat as you wish)
- egg noodles

Direction

- In a very large pan, melt butter in oil. Brown beef on all sides. Sprinkle with salt. Remove beef with slotted spoon to large crock pot. Add mushrooms and onions to pay and sauté until soft. Add mushrooms and onions along with juices to the crock pot. Add 2 T. paprika and all other ingredients except sour cream and noodles to crock pot. Include chili peppers if you like it a bit spicy, but depending on the peppers, it could be too spicy for small kids. Cook covered on high for about 5 hours until beef is soft. Adjust salt, pepper and paprika. Remove bay leaves and chili peppers. Add sour cream and mix thoroughly. Serve over noodles. Serves 8-10 as a main dish.

16. BAKED PASTA ZUCCINI And MOZZARELLA Recipe

Serving: 4 | Prep: | Cook: 15mins | Ready in:

Ingredients

- 3/4 lb Pasta; shaped (fusilli, orecchiette or conchiglie)
- 5 sm Zucchini; 1/2-inch slices
- fresh garlic minced to your taste.. I like lots
- salt and pepper to taste
- 1 28 oz can Italian plum tomatoes -- drained/chopped
- 8 Black olives; sliced
- 3 tb Parmesan cheese; freshly grated
- 1 ts Fresh rosemary sprigs
- 1/2 lb Mozzarella cheese; cut in 1/2' cubes or grated.

Direction

- In a large frying pan, heat oil and sauté zucchini until lightly browned, about 5 minutes.
- Add garlic the last minute, do not brown.
- Season with salt and pepper and transfer to an oiled shallow casserole dish.
- Preheat oven to 350 degrees F.
- When pasta is almost cooked, drain and add to zucchini.
- Add tomatoes, olives, Parmesan, rosemary and 1/2 of the mozzarella.
- Sprinkle with a little more salt and pepper if desired and gently mix together.
- Cover with the remaining mozzarella and bake until cheese is melted and the top slightly browned, about 15 minutes.
- I have used fresh tomatoes peeled and sliced thin and it was very good.
- ENJOY

17. BBQ Beef Hamburgers Recipe

Serving: 8 | Prep: | Cook: 15mins | Ready in:

Ingredients

- 500 g beef mince
- ¾ cup self-raising flour
- 1 packet of chicken noodle soup
- Dash curry powder
- Small carrot, finely grated
- ½ zucchini, finely grated
- 1 onion, finely grated
- 2 eggs, lightly beaten
- breadcrumbs (dry, not fresh)

Direction

- 1. Mix all ingredients well.
- 2. Roll small balls of mixture in breadcrumbs.
- 3. Cook on the BBQ, flatten with a spatula.

18. Babas Authentic Polish Haluski Recipe

Serving: 6 | Prep: | Cook: 25mins | Ready in:

Ingredients

- 1 medium to large head of cabbage, chopped
- 3 sticks of butter or more as desired
- 2 large onions ,chopped
- Potatoe dumplings :
- 2 cups mashed potatoes, cooled
- 2 well-beaten eggs
- salt
- flour

Direction

- In large bowl:
- Add mashed potatoes, eggs and blend thoroughly.
- Add enough flour with a little salt in to knead into a soft pliable dough that will not stick.

- Make into rolls and slice in about 1 inch pieces
- Drop into boiling water and boil about 12 min.
- To test for doneness, break one open with fork after you take out of boiling water.
- Drain in small hole colander. (You can rinse if you prefer. I don't)
- While boiling the dumplings, sauté (in large fry pan) butter, cabbage and onions until golden brown.
- Add drained dumplings to fry pan and fry a little longer .Mix it all well while frying but don't overdo so dumplings stay together.

19. Babi Chin Pork Braised In Dark Soy Sauce Recipe

Serving: 8 | Prep: | Cook: 155mins | Ready in:

Ingredients

- 3 tablespoons coriander seeds, toasted and cooled
- 5 cups plus 2 tablespoons water
- 3/4 cup chopped shallots (3 large)
- 8 garlic cloves, chopped
- 1/4 cup vegetable oil
- 1 (3 1/2- to 4-inch) cinnamon stick
- 3 tablespoons yellow soybean sauce, mashed with back of a spoon to a coarse paste (can substitute hoisin sauce or sweet noodle sauce/sweet duck sauce easily)
- 2 tablespoons sugar
- 1/2 teaspoon ground cloves
- 2 1/2 lb boneless pork shoulder (sometimes called pork butt; in 1 or 2 solid pieces), cut into 1 1/2-inch cubes
- 1 tablespoon dark soy sauce
- 1 (1 1/4-lb) can sliced bamboo shoots, drained and rinsed
- ~~~~
- Garnish: 3 (5 1/2-inch) fresh red chiles, halved lengthwise, seeded, and thinly sliced; 1 cup fresh cilantro sprigs

Direction

- Finely grind coriander seeds in grinder. Stir together ground coriander and 2 tablespoons water in a small bowl.
- Coarsely purée shallots and garlic in mini processor, scraping down side occasionally.
- Heat oil in a 6- to 7-quart wide heavy pot over moderately high heat until hot but not smoking, then cook shallot purée with cinnamon stick, stirring occasionally and scraping up any brown bits, until pale golden, 4 to 5 minutes.
- Add coriander mixture, mashed soybean/hoisin sauce, sugar, and cloves and cook, stirring, 2 minutes. Increase heat to high, then add pork and cook, stirring occasionally, until pork is no longer pink on the outside, 2 to 3 minutes.
- Add soy sauce and remaining 5 cups water and bring to a boil, stirring occasionally. Reduce heat and simmer, partially covered, until meat is tender, 1 1/2 to 2 hours.
- Meanwhile, blanch bamboo shoots in a large saucepan of boiling water 1 minute, then drain well in a colander.
- Stir bamboo shoots into braised pork and simmer, uncovered, until tender, about 15 minutes. (Liquid should be reduced to about 2 cups. If necessary, transfer pork and bamboo shoots with a slotted spoon to a bowl and boil liquid to reduce, then stir in pork and bamboo shoots.) Discard cinnamon stick and season with salt.
- ~~~~
- **Pork improves in flavor if braised 1 to 3 days ahead. Cool completely, uncovered, then chill, covered. Reheat over moderate heat, stirring occasionally.

20. Bacon Cheeseburger Pasta Recipe

Serving: 4 | Prep: | Cook: 20mins | Ready in:

Ingredients

- 8 ounces uncooked penne pasta
- 1 pound ground beef
- 6 bacon strips, diced
- 1 can (10-3/4 ounces) condensed tomato soup, undiluted
- 1 cup shredded cheddar cheese
- barbecue sauce and ptepared mustard, optional

Direction

- 1. Cook pasta according to package directions. Meanwhile, in a large skillet, cook beef over medium heat until no longer pink; drain and set aside.
- 2. In the same skillet, cook bacon until crisp; remove with slotted spoon to paper towels. Discard drippings. Drain pasta; add to the skillet. Stir in the soup, beef and bacon; heat through. Sprinkle with cheese; cover and cook until the cheese is melted.
- 3. Serve with barbecue sauce and mustard if desired.

21. Baked Mac And Cheese Recipe

Serving: 12 | Prep: | Cook: 60mins | Ready in:

Ingredients

- 1 16oz box macaroni
- 2 - 8 oz Extra sharp cheddar cheese
- 1 quart milk
- seasoned bread crumbs
- salt, pepper, garlic powder to taste

Direction

- Cook mac according to box...but only for about 8 min, as you want it undercooked.
- While that is cooking cut up cheese in smallish chunks, spray a three quart baking dish with cooking spray. Makes clean up a breeze!!
- Drain macaroni

- Put macaroni in pan, add the quart of milk, add cheese, salt, pepper and garlic powder to taste, and mix well
- Put in oven at 350, cook for about 15 min. Carefully put a thin layer of bread crumbs over mixture cook for about another 45 min. Top should be golden brown and inside should not be runny.

22. Baked Pierogi Rollups Recipe

Serving: 5 | Prep: | Cook: 35mins | Ready in:

Ingredients

- For the dumpling dough:
- 2 1/3 cups flour
- 1 egg
- 1 cup warm (not hot) water
- 1 tsp. salt
- For the filling:
- 1/2 lb ground pork
- 1/2 lb ground beef
- 1 tbsp. steak rub seasoning
- 1 tsp. salt, pepper to taste
- 1/2 cup light cream, OR milk
- 2 onions, chopped
- 1 carrot, shredded
- 2 med. tomatoes, chopped
- oil for sauteeing
- 1 handful fresh parsely leaves, chopped
- 1/2 cup shredded cheese (like cheddar, colby, or mozzarella)

Direction

- For the dumpling dough:
- Combine flour, egg, 1 cup water and salt in a large bowl. Mix well to combine. Transfer dough on a flowered surface and knead until it is smooth and comes together nicely, about 6 minutes. Work in a little more flour if the dough is too sticky.
- Roll out the dough into a thin rectangle.

- For the filling: Sautee the onions and carrot in about 2 tbsp. of oil, until lightly golden. Add chopped tomatoes and sauté until most of the liquid evaporates. Season with salt and pepper. Stir in the chopped parsley and turn off the heat.
- In another medium bowl, combine raw ground beef and pork. Add 1 tsp. salt, 1 tbsp. steak rub seasoning and pepper to taste. Add 1/2 cup of milk or light cream. Mix well.
- Spread the meat mixture over the dumpling dough, leaving about 1 inch from the side that would be sealed.
- Spread 1/2 of the vegetable mixture over the meat, sprinkle with 1/2 of the shredded cheese.
- Roll up tightly, starting from the end with the meat. Seal the roll (no need to seal the side edges).
- Cut in to small rolls. Dip each roll into flour on both sides. Place them on a lightly greased cookie sheet. Top with the rest of the vegetable mixture. Cover with foil and bake in a preheated 375F oven for 30 minutes.
- Uncover, sprinkle with the rest of the cheese and bake 5 min. more, or until the cheese is melted.
- Serve hot with a dollop of sour cream on top, if desired.

23. Baked Rigatoni With Sausage And Broccoli Rabe Recipe

Serving: 6 | Prep: | Cook: 30mins | Ready in:

Ingredients

- 24 garlic cloves, peeled
- 1/3 cup olive oil
- ****
- 1 1/2 lb. italian sausage, halved and cut into 1/2-inch-thick slices
- 1-2 tbsp. olive oil
- ****

- 2 bunches broccoli rabe/rapini or broccolini, cut into 1-inch pieces
- NOTE: I love broccoli rabe/rapini, but it does have a bitter bite. If you don't mind it, then cook according to the recipe. However, if you want to take the "bite" out of the broccoli rabe, parboil it for five minutes. (You could use the water leftover from cooking the rigatoni.) Drain well and continue with recipe as written.
- ****
- 1/2 cup dry white wine
- 8 oz. cipollini onions, peeled and halved (feel free to use regular onions, as cipollini can be hard to find)
- 3 fresh thyme sprigs
- 1/2 lb. rigatoni, cooked until al dente
- salt and freshly ground pepper, to taste
- 1 cup ricotta cheese
- Pinch or two of red chili flakes
- 2 oz. parmigiano-reggiano cheese, grated

Direction

- Preheat an oven to 400°F.
- ****
- In a small pan over medium-low heat, bring 1/3 cup of olive oil and garlic cloves to a simmer. Cook until garlic cloves are soft and just starting to take on color, 10-12 minutes.
- Remove garlic with a slotted spoon and reserve the garlic-flavored oil.
- NOTE: The recipe only uses the garlic cloves to season the oil. You can discard them at this point OR use them in garlic butter or to smear, as is, on tasted bread, etc. The soft simmering of the garlic in olive oil will make the garlic soft, subtle and a bit sweet.
- ****
- In a sauté pan over medium heat, add 1-2 tbsp. of olive oil and brown the sausage for 2 to 3 minutes. Using a slotted spoon, transfer sausage to a large bowl.
- Add the broccoli rabe to the pan and cook until tender, 6 to 8 minutes, adding the wine after 3 minutes. Season with salt, then add the

broccoli rabe and any cooking liquid to the bowl with the sausage.
- In the same pan over medium heat, warm the reserved garlic oil. Add the onions and thyme, and season with salt and pepper. Cook, stirring occasionally, until the onions are very soft and caramelized, about 15 minutes.
- Using a slotted spoon, transfer to the bowl with the sausage and broccoli rabe; reserve the oil. Add the pasta and garlic to the bowl and season with salt and pepper.
- Spoon half of the pasta mixture into a 3-quart baking dish and dot with half of the ricotta. Top with the remaining pasta and ricotta.
- Drizzle with the reserved oil and sprinkle with the chili flakes.
- ***
- NOTE: This is not a saucy recipe as written. It has very little liquid to make it so and as written, makes for browned, slightly crunchy outer edges. The ricotta stays in pats where you place them - it gets hot surely, but doesn't melt. The components stay distinct, yet melded in flavor, in my opinion. This appeals to me and perhaps others, but maybe not for everyone. Please feel free to doctor the recipe to your liking and let us know what you did and how you liked it.....it's all good and I welcome all input!
- ****
- Bake for 20 minutes, then sprinkle with the Parmigiano-Reggiano cheese and bake until hot and golden brown, about 10 minutes more.
- Serves 6.

24. Baked Spaghetti Recipe

Serving: 10 | Prep: | Cook: 90mins | Ready in:

Ingredients

- 2 cups canned diced tomatoes
- 2 cups tomato sauce
- 1 cup water
- 1/2 cup diced onions

- 1/2 cup diced bell pepper
- 1/2 cup chopped fresh parsley
- 1+1/2 italian seasoning
- 1 teaspoon garlic powder
- 2 teaspoons seasoned salt
- 2 teaspoons sugar
- 2 bay leaves (remove after cooking sauce)
- 1+1/2 pounds ground beef
- 8 ounces thin spaghetti
- 1 cup grated sharp cheddar
- 1 cup grated monterey jack cheese

Direction

- In pot, combine tomatoes, tomato sauce, water, onions, peppers, parsley, bay leaves, sugar, and seasonings. Bring to a boil, then reduce heat and simmer, covered 1 hour.
- Crumble ground beef in saucepan; brown and drain. Add to sauce and let sauce cook another 20 minutes.
- While sauce simmers, cook pasta.
- Cover bottom of a baking pan (13x9x2) with sauce.
- Add 1/2 the pasta, then half the cheese. Add the remaining pasta, then sauce.
- Bake at 350 for 30 minutes.
- Top with remaining cheese and continue to cook till cheese is melted and bubbly
- Let sit for 10 minutes
- Cut into squares and serve

25. Baked Spaghetti With Fresh Basil And Smoked Mozzarella Recipe

Serving: 5 | Prep: | Cook: 30mins | Ready in:

Ingredients

- 3/4 pound Dry spaghetti
- 1 tablespoon olive oil
- 1 medium onion diced

- 6 cloves garlic more or less to taste, minced or pressed
- 4 roma tomatoes halved and then sliced
- 1 can (14.5-oz) Fire-roasted crushed tomatoes (regular crushed toms would work too - just adjust seasonings)
- 1 cup heavy cream
- 2 teaspoons Dried oregano
- 1 teaspoon salt
- 1 1/2 teaspoons black pepper
- 20 fresh basil leaves (or more if you have them)
- 2 cups smoked mozzarella cheese grated

Direction

- Preheat oven to 350°F
- Cook spaghetti until almost al dente (be careful not to overcook - it will cook more when it bakes; it should still be a little white in the middle when you put it in the oven).
- In a medium skillet, heat oil, add onions, and sauté until soft. Add garlic, and cook about a minute more. Add tomatoes, and cook about a minute or two. Add crushed tomatoes, and cook until sauce begins to simmer. Add cream, and cook until sauce begins to simmer. Add oregano, salt, and pepper, and simmer 5 minutes. Taste, and adjust seasonings - sauce should have a good, full flavor that won't be overwhelmed by the pasta.
- Lightly oil a 9x9 baking dish, and add spaghetti. Pour sauce over spaghetti. Arrange basil leaves so that they cover the top. Sprinkle smoked mozzarella over the basil leaves.
- Bake for about 10-15 minutes, until cheese is completely melted and a little bubbly.

26. Baked Veggie Spring Rolls Recipe

Serving: 4 | Prep: | Cook: 20mins | Ready in:

Ingredients

- 2 tablespoons reduced-sodium soy sauce
- 1/2 teaspoon grated peeled ginger root
- 1/2 teaspoon packed light brown sugar
- 1/2 teaspoon salt
- 1 minced garlic clove, to taste
- 1/3 cup cooked rice noodles (also known as cellophane noodles, and I sometimes use more and pack 'em in!)
- 1 green onion (scallion), julienned
- 1 carrot, finely grated
- 1 red bell pepper, seeded and julienned
- 1/2 green or yellow bell pepper, seeded and julienned (I prefer the yellow)
- 1/4 cup finely shredded or julienned cabbage
- 1 cup trimmed snow pea pods, julienned
- 1 cup bean sprouts
- 1/4 cup water chestnuts, julienned
- 4 7-inch square egg roll wrappers
- 2 teaspoons olive or vegetable oil
- 1 teaspoon Asian sesame oil or toasted sesame oil
- hot Chinese mustard and/or plum sauce, for garnish

Direction

- Preheat the oven to 375 degrees F. Spray a cooking sheet with non-stick cooking spray, or line with parchment.
- In a large bowl, combine the soy sauce, ginger, brown sugar, salt, and minced garlic. Add the rice noodles, green onion, carrot, bell peppers, cabbage, snow peas, bean sprouts, and water chestnuts; toss to coat. Place the egg roll wrappers on a clean dry work surface. Divide the mixture evenly among the wrappers; fold in the ends and roll up jelly roll fashion.
- Combine the olive or vegetable oil and sesame oil. Lightly brush each spring roll with oil mixture and place on the prepared baking sheet.
- Bake at 375 degrees F until the spring rolls are crisp on the bottoms; about 10 minutes; turn and bake until crisp all over, about 7 to 10 more minutes.

- Serve with mustard or plum sauce if desired. If you can't get egg roll wrappers, you can also use phyllo sheets.

27. Baked Ziti Recipe

Serving: 6 | Prep: | Cook: 30mins | Ready in:

Ingredients

- 1 pkg of Ziti noodles or mostaccioli noodles,
- 1.5 lbs. of ground hamburger (sirloin is less greasy, but more expensive)
- 1 BIG jar of spaghetti sauce
- 1 jar of ricotta cheese
- 1 lb. bag of mozzarella cheese
- 1 green pepper
- 1 onion

Direction

- 1. In a large pot boil water with some salt in it. Add noodles, boil for about 10 to 12 minutes. Then drain. Preheat the oven to 350°.
- 2. Chop up onion and peppers into small pieces.
- 3. Start to brown O & P in a large skillet.
- 4. While they are browning add ground beef. Season and cook.
- 5. Mix the sauce into the skillet and heat. Then add the ricotta cheese and mix it all together. Then add the noodle and make sure that it all gets covered evenly.
- 6. Pour the mixture into a 9 x 13 in. baking dish. Then cover with mozzarella cheese, not too thick.
- 7. Bake uncovered for about 30 min.
- 8. Let cool and serve.

28. Baked Ziti With Spinach And Smoked Gouda Recipe

Serving: 5 | Prep: | Cook: 15mins | Ready in:

Ingredients

- 8 oz uncooked ziti
- 1 T olive oil
- 1 c chopped onion
- 1 c chopped yellow bell pepper (it's still good if you leave this out!)
- 3 garlic cloves, minced
- 1 can diced tomoatoes with basil, garlic, and oregano
- 1 can italian seasoned diced tomatoes
- 4 c baby spinach
- 1 1/4 c shredded, smoked gouda cheese, divided (can substitute smoked cheddar)
- cooking spray

Direction

- Heat the oil in a Dutch oven over medium-high heat.
- Add onion and pepper, sauté 5 minutes.
- Add garlic to pan, sauté 2 minutes or until onion is tender.
- Stir in tomatoes; bring to a boil.
- Reduce heat, and simmer 5 minutes, stirring occasionally.
- Add spinach to pan; cook 30 seconds or until spinach wilts, stirring frequently.
- Remove from heat. Add pasta and 3/4 c cheese to tomato mixture, tossing well to combine.
- Spoon pasta mixture into an 11x7" baking dish lightly coated with cooking spray. Sprinkle evenly with remaining 1/2 c cheese.
- Bake at 375 for 15 minutes or until cheese melts and begins to brown.
- **Note: I usually have plain diced tomatoes on hand so I use those and add my own spices instead of buying the ones with the seasonings already added.

29. Bechamel Lasagne Recipe

Serving: 8 | Prep: | Cook: 30mins | Ready in:

Ingredients

- 1/2 pound lasagne noodles
- 2 tablespoons olive oil or unsalted butter
- 1 cup diced onions
- 6 cloves crushed garlic
- 1 teaspoon dried basil or 2 teaspoons fresh
- 1 teaspoon dried tarragon or 2 teaspoons fresh
- 2 cups sliced mushrooms (chanterelles are nice in this)
- 1 pound ricotta cheese
- 1 pound small curd cottage cheese
- 4 eggs, lightly beaten
- 1 cup (packed) chopped fresh spinach
- 1/4 teaspoon salt
- 1/4 teaspoon fresh ground black pepper
- 1/4 teaspoon freshly ground nutmeg
- 1/2 - 1 cup freshly grated Asiago or parmesan cheese
- 1 1/2 cups grated mozzarella cheese.
- For the sauce:
- 1/4 cup butter
- 1/4 cup flour (unbleached, please!)
- 1 3/4 cups milk
- 1/2 cup finely grated parmesan or asiago cheese
- dash of salt
- black pepper to taste.

Direction

- Cook the noodles in plenty of boiling water until al dente. Drain, fill the pan with cold water and let the noodles sit while you prepare the rest of the dish.
- Heat oil or butter in a large pan over medium heat and sauté the onions, garlic, basil, and tarragon. When onions are translucent, add the mushrooms and continue to cook until the mushroom are done.

- Combine the ricotta and cottage cheese in a large bowl, along with the eggs, cooked vegetables, spinach, salt, pepper, nutmeg, Asiago or Parmesan, and 1/2 cup of the mozzarella.
- For the béchamel, melt the butter in a sauce pan. Add the flour and cook over low heat for a few minutes, stirring constantly. Slowly add the milk, still stirring constantly. Add the Parmesan or Asiago, salt and pepper. Cook, stirring frequently until the sauce is the desired thickness.
- To make the lasagne, first spoon a bit of sauce in the bottom of a 9" x 12" pan. Add a layer of noodles, then the cheese-and-veggie mixture. Repeat with another layer of noodles and cheese-veggie mixture, and then top with the remaining sauce and grated cheese.
- Bake, covered, for about 30 minutes. Let stand for about 10 minutes before serving.
- I like this with a nice Pinot Grigio and a lettuce and tomato salad.

30. Beef Braised In Red Wine Recipe

Serving: 6 | Prep: | Cook: 150mins | Ready in:

Ingredients

- 2 lb boneless beef chuck, cut into 1 1/2-inch pieces
- 1 (750-ml) bottle dry red wine (preferably Burgundy or
- Côtes du Rhône)
- 2 medium onions, halved lengthwise, then thinly sliced lengthwise (2 cups)
- 1 teaspoon finely chopped fresh thyme
- 1 Turkish bay leaf or 1/2 California
- 4 sprigs fresh flat-leaf parsley plus 1/4 cup chopped fresh parsley leaves
- 1 carrot, thinly sliced
- 1 1/2 teaspoons salt
- 1 teaspoon black pepper
- 2 tablespoons vegetable oil
- 2 large shallots, finely chopped
- 2 large garlic cloves, finely chopped
- 2 tablespoons all-purpose flour
- 6 oz thick-sliced bacon (preferably from slab bacon, rind removed if necessary; not smoked)
- 1 (10-oz) package pearl onions (2 1/2 cups)
- 1/4 cup water
- Special equipment: parchment paper
- Accompaniment: buttered egg noodles

Direction

- Put beef, wine, onion, thyme, bay leaf, parsley sprigs, and carrot in a large resealable plastic bag. Seal bag, pressing out excess air, and put in a bowl. Marinate beef, chilled, 16 to 24 hours.
- Drain beef in a colander set over a large bowl, reserving marinade. Wipe off any solids clinging to beef, then pat beef dry. Season with 1 teaspoon salt and 1/2 teaspoon pepper.
- Put oven rack in middle position and preheat oven to 350°F.
- Heat oil in a 3 1/2- to 4-quart heavy ovenproof pot with lid over moderately high heat until hot but not smoking, then brown beef well in 2 batches, without crowding, about 8 minutes per batch, transferring as browned with a slotted spoon to a plate.
- Reduce heat to moderate, then add shallot and garlic and cook, stirring, until shallot begins to soften, about 2 minutes. Add flour and cook, stirring constantly, until shallot and flour are browned, 4 to 5 minutes.
- Add reserved marinade liquid to flour mixture, stirring and scraping up brown bits. Add beef along with any juices accumulated on plate and cover with a round of parchment paper and lid. Simmer mixture while you prepare bacon.
- Cut bacon slices crosswise into 1/4-inch strips and cook in an 8-inch heavy skillet over moderate heat, stirring occasionally, until fat is rendered and bacon is beginning to crisp. Transfer bacon with slotted spoon to beef (reserve fat in skillet). Re-cover beef with

parchment and lid and braise in oven, 1 1/2 hours.

- While meat is braising, blanch pearl onions in a 3- to 4-quart pot of boiling water, 1 minute. Drain onions in a colander, then peel, leaving root ends intact. Cook onions in reserved bacon fat in skillet over moderate heat, stirring occasionally, until golden, 6 to 8 minutes.
- Pour off excess fat, then add 1/4 cup water and scrape up brown bits with a wooden spoon or spatula.
- After meat has braised 1 1/2 hours, add pearl onions (with liquid in skillet), remaining 1/2 teaspoon salt, and 1/2 teaspoon pepper to beef and continue to braise, covered with parchment and lid, until onions are tender and meat is very tender, about 1/2 hour more.
- Skim any fat from surface of beef and serve beef with buttered egg noodles sprinkled with chopped fresh parsley leaves.
- Cooks' note: Boeuf vigneronne can be made and cooled, uncovered, then chilled, covered, up to 4 days. Reheat slowly over moderately low heat, adding water if necessary to thin boeuf vigneronne, until heated through.

31. Beef Pho From Vietnamese Recipe

Serving: 4 | Prep: | Cook: 115mins | Ready in:

Ingredients

- 3 litres (12 cups) water
- 1kg gravy beef
- 1 star anise
- 2.5cm piece (45g) fresh galangal
- 1/4 cup (60ml) soy sauce
- 250g bean thread noodles
- 1 1/4 cups (100g) bean sprouts
- 1/4 cup loosely packed fresh coriander leaves
- 1/3 cup loosely packed fresh Vietnamese mint leaves
- 4 green onions, sliced thinly

- 1 fresh long red chilli, sliced thinly
- 1/3 cup (80ml) lime juice

Direction

- Combine the water, beef, star anise, galangal and sauce in large saucepan; bring to a boil. Reduce heat; simmer, covered, 30 minutes. Uncover; simmer, 30 minutes or until beef is tender.
- Place noodles in medium heatproof bowl, cover with boiling water; stand until just tender, drain.
- Combine remaining ingredients in medium bowl.
- Remove beef from pan; reserve broth. Remove fat and sinew from beef; slice thinly. Return beef to reheat broth just comes to a boil.
- Divide noodles among serving bowls; top with hot beef and broth then sprout mixture.

32. Biltong Potjie Recipe

Serving: 8 | Prep: | Cook: 40mins | Ready in:

Ingredients

- 1kg biltong (Jerky) beef is best and not too dry - carpaccio like
- 500g Shell noodles
- 1 packet pepper sauce
- 400ml boiling water
- 500ml Ultramel cream (Longlife) or similar
- 3 Green/Yellow/Red (Bell) peppers (1 each) - slices
- 2 Large onions - chopped
- 4 Cups Grated cheddar cheese
- olive oil

Direction

- Cook noodles separate until Al Dente
- Fry onions and peppers in oil until transparent in black pot
- Add biltong and noodles to onion/pepper mix

- Mix pepper sauce with boiling water and add to black pot
- Stir mixture well
- Add cream and stir mixture again
- Cover over very low heat (ash coals work very well) for 30minutes
- Enjoy a glass of your favourite wine
- Add cheese 15 minutes before serving
- Cheese must be melted
- Serve with more wine, perhaps with a green salad.

33. Black Olives With Tomatoes And Capers Over Pasta Recipe

Serving: 4 | Prep: | Cook: 30mins | Ready in:

Ingredients

- 1 tablespoon olive oil
- 3 medium garlic cloves chopped fine
- 1 small white onion coarsely chopped
- 16 ounce can whole tomatoes
- 1 cup black olives
- 3 tablespoons capers drained and rinsed
- 1 tablespoon balsamic vinegar
- 1 tablespoon double concentrate tomato paste
- 2 teaspoons granulated sugar
- 1/2 tablespoon dried oregano
- Hot cooked pasta

Direction

- In a large skillet or saucepan, heat the olive oil with the garlic and onion over moderate heat.
- When they sizzle, add the tomatoes, breaking them up with your hands then stir in the remaining ingredients.
- Simmer sauce for 10 minutes then serve over cooked pasta.

34. Bloody Mary Shrimp Pasta Recipe

Serving: 4 | Prep: | Cook: 10mins | Ready in:

Ingredients

- 1 pound large shrimp, peeled and deveined
- 1 1/2 cup tomato juice
- 1/4 cup roughly chopped Italian parsley
- 3 cloves garlic, diced
- 1/2 teaspoon celery seed
- 3 ounce vodka
- 1 1/2 teaspoons worcestershire sauce
- 2 lemons, juiced
- 1 1/2 teaspoons prepared horseradish
- 1/2 teaspoon freshly ground peppers
- 2-3 dashes of your favorite hot sauce
- 3 tbsp. of oil (if you saute instead of broil)
- 1 package of whole wheat linguine

Direction

- Peel and devein the shrimp. Keep cold.
- Mix together tomato juice, parsley, garlic, celery seed, vodka, Worcestershire sauce, lemon juice, horseradish and pepper and hot sauce.
- Marinate shrimp for a minimum of 20 minutes or up to 2 hours.
- Bring water to a boil and start the linguine cooking.
- Preheat oven to broil, 500 degrees.
- Drain shrimp from marinade.
- Broiling shrimp will take about 3-4 minutes per side; oven roasting at 400 degrees will take about 10 - 12 minutes.
- Heat any remaining marinade to a boil and toss with the cooked drained hot linguine.
- Top with Hot Shrimp.
- Serves 4
- I've tried to pan sauté the shrimp, and it doesn't work unless drained and patted dry. Cook in a scant tablespoon or two of oil or combo of butter/oil.
- Then add the sauce back in the pan to coat the shrimp and then pour over the linguine

noodles. You just want to heat the vodka enough to make the flavor palatable.

35. Blue Onion Bistros Macaroni And Blue Cheese With Chives Recipe

Serving: 8 | Prep: | Cook: 45mins | Ready in:

Ingredients

- 1 lb uncooked spiral tube-shaped pasta
- 1 teaspoon olive oil
- 2 tablespoons butter
- 1/4 cup flour
- 2 cups whole milk
- 1 cup whipping cream
- 3 cups grated cheddar cheese
- 1 1/2 cups crumbled blue cheese, divided (Maytag or Danish)
- salt & freshly ground black pepper or tricolor pepper, to taste
- 1 dash cayenne, to taste (optional)
- 1 1/2 tablespoons minced fresh chives

Direction

- Preheat oven to 350 degrees F; butter a 13x9x2-inch glass baking dish.
- Cook the pasta according to package directions until tender but still firm to bite, stirring occasionally; drain and set aside (about 8 minutes).
- While the pasta is cooking, in a large heavy saucepan over medium low heat, melt the olive oil and butter together; add the flour and, stirring constantly, cook for 1 minute (don't let it brown), then gradually whisk in the milk and cream.
- Simmer mixture until it slightly thickens, whisking occasionally, for 3 minutes.
- Reduce the temperature to low, then gradually stir in the grated cheddar and 1 cup of the blue cheese and cook, stirring, until the cheese melts.

- Season to taste with salt, freshly ground pepper, and cayenne (if using).
- Stir in the cooked pasta, making sure it's well-coated with the sauce.
- Pour mixture into the buttered baking dish, sprinkle with the reserved 1/2 cup crumbled blue cheese, and bake at 350 degrees F for 30 minutes.
- Sprinkle with the minced chives and serve.
- Note: also good with a serving of caramelized onions and sautéed mushrooms; also, you can use 2% or skim milk instead of whole, but using whole is how they make it at the restaurant.

36. Bob Barkers Summertime Pasta Salad Recipe

Serving: 4 | Prep: | Cook: 15mins | Ready in:

Ingredients

- 1 pound tri-color fusilli pasta
- 3 bell peppers (yellow, red and green), cut into strips
- 6 ounces grape tomatoes, halved (1 cup)
- 1/2 cup pitted kalamata olives, coarsely chopped
- One 6.5-ounce jar marinated artichokes, drained and chopped
- 1 red onion, sliced
- 2 cloves garlic, finely chopped
- 1/2 cup extra-virgin olive oil
- 1/4 cup red wine vinegar
- 1 cup packed fresh basil leaves, chopped
- 1 teaspoon lemon juice
- Italian seasoning
- salt and pepper

Direction

- In a large pot of boiling, salted water, cook the pasta until al dente. Drain and transfer to a baking sheet to cool to room temperature, about 10 minutes.

- Meanwhile, in a large bowl, toss together the bell peppers, tomatoes, olives, artichokes, onion, garlic, olive oil and vinegar.
- Add the pasta, basil and lemon juice and toss again.
- Season to taste with Italian seasoning, salt and pepper.

37. Braised Chicken With Mushrooms And Sun Dried Tomatoes Recipe

Serving: 4 | Prep: | Cook: 30mins | Ready in:

Ingredients

- 1/3 cup thinly sliced drained sun-dried tomatoes packed in oil, reserving 1 1/2 tablespoons of the oil
- 1 large whole chicken breast with skin and bones (about 1 1/4 pounds), halved
- 1 small onion, chopped fine
- 2 large garlic cloves, minced
- 1/2 teaspoon dried basil, crumbled
- 1/4 teaspoon dried hot red pepper flakes, or to taste
- 1/2 pound mushrooms, sliced
- 1/4 cup dry red wine
- 1/4 cup balsamic vinegar
- 1/2 cup chicken broth
- 2 tablespoons tomato paste
- a beurre manié made by kneading together 1 1/2 teaspoons softened unsalted butter and 1 1/2 teaspoons all-purpose flour
- 3 tablespoons minced fresh parsley leaves (preferably flat-leafed)
- cooked rice or noodles

Direction

- In a heavy skillet heat the reserved tomato oil over moderately high heat until it is hot but not smoking, in it, brown the chicken, patted dry and seasoned with salt and pepper, and transfer it to a plate.
- In the fat remaining in the skillet cook the onion, the garlic, the basil, and the red pepper flakes over moderately low heat, stirring, until the onion is softened.
- Add the mushrooms and salt and pepper to taste and cook the mixture over moderate heat, stirring, until the mushrooms are softened.
- Whisk in the wine, balsamic vinegar, the broth, and the tomato paste, add the chicken to the skillet, and bring the liquid to a boil. Simmer the mixture, covered, for 20 to 25 minutes, or until the chicken is cooked through.
- Transfer the chicken to a platter and keep it warm, covered. Whisk the beurre manié into the sauce, whisking until sauce is smooth, add the sun-dried tomatoes, and simmer the sauce, whisking, for 2 to 3 minutes, or until it is thickened.
- Stir in the parsley. Place chicken on the rice or noodles and pour the sauce over.

38. Braised Short Ribs With Penne Recipe

Serving: 6 | Prep: | Cook: 210mins | Ready in:

Ingredients

- 4 pounds beef short ribs
- salt and pepper, to taste
- ¼ cup olive oil
- 1 large onion, diced
- 5 cloves garlic, chopped
- 1 tbsp fresh rosemary, chopped
- 1 can (14 oz) diced tomatoes, drained
- ½ can tomato paste
- 1 cup red wine
- 3 tbsp Dijon mustard
- 2 cups beef broth
- 1 pound penne

- ¼ cup fresh Parmesan
- ¼ cup parsley, chopped

Direction

- Place an oven rack in the lower 1/3 of the oven. Preheat the oven to 350.
- Season the ribs with salt and pepper. Heat the olive oil in a large heavy bottomed Dutch oven over medium heat. Brown the ribs, in batches, 8-10 minutes. Remove the ribs to a plate. Add the onion and cook for 2 minutes, add the garlic and rosemary and cook for 30 seconds more. Add the tomatoes, wine, and mustard; stir. Bring the mixture to a boil and scrape the bottom to loosen up the browned bits. Return the ribs to the pan, add the beef broth, and cover the pan then place in the oven for 2 ½ hours until the meat is fork tender. The meal can be made up to this point 1 day in advance; just let cool and refrigerate.
- Remove the ribs from the cooking liquid. Using a large spoon remove any excess fat from the surface of the cooking liquid. Using a ladle, transfer the cooking liquid to a food processor or blender (or use an immersion blender). Pour the sauce into a saucepan and keep warm over low heat. Remove the meat from the rib bones; discard the bones. Shred the meat into small pieces. Season, if necessary and add to the saucepan.
- Bring a pot of water to a boil; add the penne and cook to al dente. Place penne in a serving bowl, add the meat and sauce. Sprinkle with Parmesan and parsley just before serving. Serve with crusty bread.

39. Broccoli Bean Pasta Recipe

Serving: 5 | Prep: | Cook: 15mins | Ready in:

Ingredients

- 10 cups water
- 6 ounces uncooked small pasta shells

- 3 cups broccoli florets
- 3 garlic cloves, minced
- 2 tablespoons olive or canola oil
- 1 can (15 ounces) garbanzo beans or chickpeas, rinsed and drained
- 2/3 cup white wine or vegetable broth
- 1/8 teaspoon crushed red pepper flakes
- 2 teaspoons cornstarch
- 1/2 teaspoon salt
- 1/2 cup fat-free evaporated milk
- 1/2 cup shredded parmesan cheese, divided

Direction

- In a large saucepan, bring water to a boil. Add pasta; cook for 7 minutes. Add broccoli; cook 4-5 minutes longer or until pasta and broccoli are tender. Meanwhile, in a large non-stick skillet, sauté garlic in oil for 1 minute. Add the beans, wine or broth and pepper flakes. Bring to a boil. Reduce heat; simmer, uncovered, for 7-8 minutes or until slightly reduced.
- Drain pasta and broccoli; keep warm. Combine cornstarch, salt and milk until smooth; stir into bean mixture. Bring to a boil; cook and stir for 2 minutes or until thickened. Reduce heat; stir in 1/4 cup Parmesan cheese.
- Add pasta mixture; toss to coat. Sprinkle with remaining cheese. Yield: 5 servings.

40. Bucatini Carbonara With Pancetta And Baby Peas Or Zucchini Recipe

Serving: 6 | Prep: | Cook: 40mins | Ready in:

Ingredients

- 8 ounces sliced pancetta or bacon, cut into 1/4-inch-wide strips (I've used both, but prefer the pancetta)
- 1 cup whipping cream
- 2 garlic clove, finely chopped
- 1/2 teaspoon dried crushed red pepper

- ****
- 2 tablespoons olive oil
- 1 1/2 pounds zucchini, thinly sliced (or 1 lb. of frozen baby peas and omit the 2 tbsp. of olive oil above)
- ****
- 1 pound bucatini or spaghetti (bucatini is a ribbed spaghetti with a tiny opening through the middle - it takes the sauce really well and I highly recommend it.)
- 3 large eggs
- 1 cup freshly grated parmesan cheese
- salt and pepper to taste

Direction

- Cook pancetta in medium skillet over medium heat until brown, stirring often, about 8 minutes. Using slotted spoon, transfer pancetta to paper towels; drain.
- Pour off all but 2 tablespoons drippings from skillet. Add cream, garlic, and crushed pepper to drippings in skillet; bring to boil. Set aside.
- ****
- **IF USING ZUCCHINI: (If not, skip this step)
- Heat oil in heavy large skillet over medium-high heat. Add zucchini; sauté until tender, stirring occasionally, about 10 minutes. Transfer to large plate. Season to taste with salt and pepper.
- ****
- NOTE: Pancetta, cream mixture, and zucchini can be made 2 hours ahead. Let stand at room temperature.
- ****
- Cook pasta in large pot of boiling salted water until just tender but still firm to bite. Drain well. Return pasta to pot.
- Meanwhile, place eggs in their shell in small bowl. Add enough hot water to cover. Let stand 5 minutes. Crack eggs into large bowl and whisk to blend.
- Bring cream mixture to boil in skillet. Gradually whisk hot cream mixture into eggs. Mix in 1/2 cup Parmesan cheese.
- **IF USING PEAS: Add baby peas - the heat will thaw them in about 1 minute or so.

- Add sauce to pasta and toss over medium heat until sauce coats pasta (do not boil). Add pancetta (and zucchini) and toss to heat through. Season with salt and pepper. Serve, passing remaining cheese.
- Serves 6 happy people. =)

41. Buffalo Chicken Mac And Cheese Recipe

Serving: 8 | Prep: | Cook: 30mins | Ready in:

Ingredients

- 1 pound small elbow macaroni
- 2 cups chopped green onions (about 8 large),divided
- 8 tablespoons (1 stick) butter, divided
- 1 cup chopped onions
- 2 large garlic cloves, chopped
- 1/2 cup all purpose flour
- 4 cups whole milk
- 4 oz. cream cheese
- 1 pound sharp cheddar cheese, coarsely grated (about 4 cups packed)
- 4 oz. smoked cheddar (extra for topping if desired)
- 4 oz. provolone cheese
- 8 fried chicken tenders, chopped(I use popeyes, KFC's or Caines)
- salt and black pepper
- 1 cup hot pepper sauce (preferably Frank's Red Hot Original)

Direction

- Cook macaroni in large pot of boiling salted water until just tender but still firm to bite, drain, and placed in large bowl.
- Melt 6 tablespoons butter in same large pot over medium heat.
- Add chopped onions and garlic.
- Cover; sauté until onions are soft but not brown, stirring often, about 4 minutes.
- Add flour; stir 2 minutes.

- Gradually whisk in milk.
- Bring to boil, whisking constantly.
- Reduce heat and simmer sauce for about 2 minutes.
- Add all cheeses, cream cheese, 1 1/2 cups of the green onions, salt, and pepper.
- Whisk until cheeses melt and sauce is smooth, about 2 minutes. Remove from heat.
- Mix cheese sauce into macaroni.
- Add chicken.
- Place in 13x9x2-inch glass baking dish.
- Top with additional shredded cheddar cheese or bleu cheese crumbles and 1/2 cup chopped green onions
- Preheat oven to 350°F.
- Melt remaining 2 tablespoons of butter in microwave.
- Stir in hot pepper sauce.
- Spoon 1/3 mixture over mac and cheese (reserve remaining to pass around as extra sauce for individual taste)
- Bake macaroni uncovered until heated through, about 30 minutes.
- Serve with the extra sauce on the side.

42. Buttered Noodles

Serving: 8 | Prep: | Cook: 120mins | Ready in:

Ingredients

- 2-1/4 cups uncooked egg noodles
- 1/4 cup shredded part-skim mozzarella cheese
- 2 tablespoons butter, melted
- 2 tablespoons grated Parmesan cheese
- 2 teaspoons minced fresh parsley
- 1/4 teaspoon salt
- 1/4 teaspoon garlic powder
- 1/8 teaspoon pepper

Direction

- Cook noodles according to package directions; drain. Transfer to a serving bowl. Immediately add the remaining ingredients and toss to coat.

- Nutrition Facts
- 3/4 cup: 162 calories, 8g fat (5g saturated fat), 39mg cholesterol, 264mg sodium, 16g carbohydrate (1g sugars, 1g fiber), 6g protein.

43. Cabbage And Pasta Recipe

Serving: 6 | Prep: | Cook: 25mins | Ready in:

Ingredients

- 1 (12 ounce) package bow tie (farfalle) pasta
- 1 medium head cabbage, chopped
- 3 garlic cloves, finely diced
- 1 medium onion, diced
- 1 cup butter
- 1/2 tsp salt
- 1/4 tsp pepper

Direction

- Boil a large pot of lightly salted water, then add the pasta. Cook for 8-10 minutes or until 'al dente' and drain.
- In a skillet over medium heat, melt the butter then add in the cabbage, garlic, and onion, and season with salt and pepper. Cook for 15 minutes, until both the cabbage and onion are tender.
- Mix together the cooked pasta and cabbage mixture in a large sized bowl. Serve warm.

44. Cajun Chicken Lasagna Recipe

Serving: 4 | Prep: | Cook: 115mins | Ready in:

Ingredients

- 1](16 ounce) package lasagna noodles
- 1 tablespoon finely chopped garlic
- 1 pound andouille sausage, quartered lengthwise and sliced
- 2 (10 ounce) containers alfredo sauce, divided

- 1 pound skinless, boneless chicken breast halves, cut into chunks
- 1 1/2 cups shredded mozzarella cheese
- 2 teaspoons cajun seasoning
- 1/2 cup grated parmesan cheese
- 1 teaspoon dried sage
- 1/2 cup chopped onion
- 1/4 cup chopped red bell pepper

Direction

- Preheat oven to 325 degrees F (165 degrees C).
- Cook pasta in a large kettle of boiling water for 8 to 10 minutes, or until al dente; drain.
- In a large skillet over medium-high heat, combine sausage, chicken, Cajun seasoning and sage.
- Cook until chicken is no longer pink and juices run clear, about 8 minutes.
- Remove meat from skillet with a slotted spoon, and set aside.
- Sauté onion, bell pepper and garlic until tender.
- Remove from heat, and stir in cooked meat and one container Alfredo sauce.
- Lightly grease a 9 x 13-inch baking dish.
- Cover bottom with 4 lasagne noodles.
- Spread with 1/2 of the meat mixture.
- Repeat layers, and cover with a layer of noodles.
- Spread remaining Alfredo sauce over top.
- Top with mozzarella cheese and sprinkle with Parmesan cheese. Bake in preheated oven for 1 hour.
- Let stand 15 minutes before serving.

45. Cajun Chicken Pasta Recipe

Serving: 4 | Prep: | Cook: 20mins | Ready in:

Ingredients

- 12 oz. uncooked linguine
- 2 lb. chicken breast strips
- 1 Tbsp. cajun seasoning

- 1 1/4 tsp salt, divided
- 1/4 cup butter
- 1 small red bell pepper, thinly sliced
- 1 small green bell pepper, thinly sliced
- 1 (8oz) package fresh mushrooms
- 2 green onions (white and light green parts only), sliced
- 1 1/2 cups half-and-half
- 1/4 tsp lemon pepper
- 1/4 tsp dried basil
- 1/4 tsp garlic powder
- Garnish: chopped green onions

Direction

- Prepare pasta according to package directions.
- Sprinkle chicken evenly with Cajun seasoning and 1 tsp. salt. Melt 1/4 cup butter in large non-stick skillet over medium-high heat; add chicken and sauté 5 to 6 minutes or until done. Remove chicken.
- Add bell peppers, mushrooms, and green onions to skillet, and sauté 9 to 10 minutes or until vegetables are tender and liquid evaporates.
- Return chicken to skillet; stir in half-and-half, next 3 ingredients, and remaining 1/4 tsp. salt. Cook, stirring often, over medium-high heat 3 to 4 minutes or until thoroughly heated. Add linguine; toss to coat. Garnish, if desired, and serve immediately.

46. Cajun Macaroni Recipe

Serving: 4 | Prep: | Cook: 20mins | Ready in:

Ingredients

- 1/2 pound ground beef
- 1/3 cup chopped onion
- 1/3 cup chopped green pepper
- 1/3 cup chopped celery
- 1 can (14 1/2 ounces) diced tomatoes, undrained
- 1 1/2 teaspoons cajun seasoning

- 1 package (7 1/2 ounces) macaroni and cheese dinner mix
- 2 tablespoons milk
- 1 tablespoon butter

Direction

- In a large skillet, cook the beef, onion, green pepper and celery over medium heat until meat is no longer pink; drain
- Add the tomatoes and Cajun seasoning
- Cook uncovered for 15-20 minutes, stirring occasionally
- Meanwhile, prepare the macaroni and cheese, using 2 tablespoons milk and 1 tablespoon butter
- Stir in the beef mixture; cook for 2-3 minutes or until heated through

47. Cajun Macaroni Salad Recipe

Serving: 10 | Prep: | Cook: 40mins | Ready in:

Ingredients

- 2 lbs shrimp, unpeeled with heads on
- 1 quart water
- 2 tbs liquid crab boil
- 1 medium onion, quartered
- 3 tbs salt
- 1 1/2 cups uncooked elbow macaroni
- 1 large onion, chopped
- 1 cup chopped celery
- 1/2 lb bacon, cooked, drained and crushed. Reserve bacon fat.
- 1 tbs garlic, minced
- 1 cup fresh parsley chopped
- 5 boiled egges
- 1 tsp cayenne pepper
- 1 tsp salt
- 1 tsp crab boil
- 1 cup mayonnaise
- reserved bacon fat
- 1 tbs paprika

Direction

- Cook shrimp with heads on and unpeeled in 1 quart of water. Add 2 tbsp. of crab boil and medium quartered onion to water and boil for 20 minutes.
- Remove from heat and add 3 tbsp. of salt, stir and let stand for 5 minutes. Drain and peel shrimp. Reserve liquid and cook the elbow macaroni in it until al dente.
- In a large bowl, combine drained macaroni, chopped onion, celery, bacon, garlic, chopped egg whites and parsley.
- In a separate bowl, combine mashed egg yellows with 1 tsp. salt, 1 tsp. cayenne, 1 tsp. crab boil, mayonnaise and bacon fat until well blended.
- Add to macaroni and mix well. Sprinkle paprika on top.

48. Campanelli With Asparagus Basil And Balsamic Glaze Recipe

Serving: 6 | Prep: | Cook: 30mins | Ready in:

Ingredients

- 1 lb campanelli
- 3/4 c balsamic vinegar
- 5 tbs EVOO
- 1 lb asparagus, tough ends snapped off, spears halved length-wise if larger than than 1/2 inch in diameter and diagonally cut into 1 inch lengths
- 1 medium to large red onion, halved and sliced thin
- 1/2 tsp ground black pepper
- 1/4 tsp red pepper flake
- 1 cup chopped fresh basil leaves
- 1 tbs juice from one lemon
- 2 oz pecorino romano cheese, shaved with a vegetable peeler

Direction

- Boil pasta to al dente.
- Drain and return to the pot.
- Meanwhile bring balsamic vinegar to a boil in an 8 inch skillet over a med to high flame; reduce the heat to medium and simmer slowly until syrupy and reduced to a 1/4 cup, 15-20 minutes.
- While the vinegar is reducing, heat 2 tbsp. of the oil in a 12 inch non-stick skillet over high heat until it begins to smoke. Add the asparagus, onion, black pepper, red pepper flake and 1/2 tsp. salt and stir to combine.
- Cook, without stirring, until the asparagus begins to brown, about 1 minute, then stir and continue to cook, stirring occasionally, until the asparagus is tender-crisp, about 4 minutes longer.
- Add the asparagus mixture, basil, lemon juice, 1/2 cup of the cheese, and remaining 3 tbsp. of oil to the pasta and stir to combine.
- Serve immediately, drizzling 1 to 2 teaspoons of the balsamic glaze over each serving and passing the cheese separately.

49. Cappellini Florentine Recipe

Serving: 4 | Prep: | Cook: 15mins |Ready in:

Ingredients

- 16 oz. package angel hair pasta
- 2 Tbsp olive oil
- 4 large cloves garlic, minced
- 1 8-oz package of sliced mushrooms
- 1 10-oz package of fresh spinach
- 2 Tbsp balsamic vinegar
- 1 Tbsp crushed red pepper (or to taste)
- 1/4 lemon
- 2 chicken breasts, cooked and shredded
- 4 oz. mozzarella cheese, cut into cubes
- salt and pepper to taste

Direction

- Put water for pasta to boil on stovetop.
- In a large skillet, sauté garlic in oil over medium heat until the garlic takes on a little color, but do not allow to turn golden.
- Add mushrooms. Sauté 3-4 minutes until cooked through.
- Add spinach, stirring frequently until cooked down and wilted.
- Add red pepper, vinegar, and salt and pepper to taste. Cook 1-2 minutes longer.
- Take the pan off heat and add lemon juice. Toss to distribute evenly.
- Add pasta to the water and cook. When the pasta is ready (2-3 minutes), drain. Return pasta to pot and mix in spinach-mushroom mixture, chicken, and mozzarella cubes. Serve immediately.

50. Caramelized Onion And Asparagus Orzotto Ci Recipe

Serving: 8 | Prep: | Cook: 20mins |Ready in:

Ingredients

- 1lb orzo
- 2 cups chicken stock
- 1/2 stick butter
- 1 medium onion, diced
- 1lb fresh asparagus, trimmed and cut into 1 inch pieces
- 1 cup heavy cream
- 1/2-3/4 cup fresh Parmesan, grated
- 1/2 lemon (for it's zest)
- sea or kosher salt and fresh ground pepper

Direction

- Prepare orzo per box directions, but using chicken stock for 2 cups of the water
- In large skillet (I use cast iron, of course ;), sauté asparagus and onions in butter.
- Cook until asparagus is al dente and onion begins to caramelize.

- Add salt and pepper and cream, and continue to simmer to thicken
- When orzo is done, drain, but reserve the liquid.
- Add orzo and 3/4-1 cup of the pasta liquid to veggies and cream.
- Add lemon zest and Parmesan cheese, stir, and heat through.

- Place half of the noodles in a greased 3 quart casserole dish.
- Spread with cheese mixture over the noodles.
- Place the rest of the noodles over the cheese mixture.
- Cover with all of the beef mixture. Sprinkle with Parmesan cheese if desired. Bake at 350*F for 30-40 minutes, or until heated through.

51. Carry Out Casserole Recipe

Serving: 12 | Prep: | Cook: 40mins | Ready in:

Ingredients

- 8 oz wide egg noodles
- 2 lbs ground beef
- 3 T butter
- 2 c tomato sauce
- 2 T flour
- 2 c Ricotta or cottage cheese
- 1 c sour cream
- 1 t salt
- 1/2 t pepper
- 1/4 c chopped black olives
- 1/3 c grated onion
- 1/2 c chopped green pepper
- 1/3 c grated parmesan cheese (optional)

Direction

- Cook the noodles according to package directions in salted boiling water.
- Drain.
- Brown beef in 2 tablespoons of butter.
- Add the flour to the beef and cook for one minute.
- Add the tomato sauce to the beef mixture and cook for 10 minutes on medium heat.
- Mix Ricotta with sour cream, salt, pepper and the olives.
- Sauté the onion and green pepper in the remaining tablespoon of butter.
- Add the onion pepper mixture to the cream cheese mixture.

52. Cauliflower Spaghetti Recipe

Serving: 2 | Prep: | Cook: 25mins | Ready in:

Ingredients

- spaghetti - 1 Packet
- cauliflower - 1 No , cut into florets
- olive oil - 2 Tbsp (or canola/sunflower oil)
- Red chili/ pepper - To Taste
- garlic clove - 1 No Crushed
- salt - To Taste.
- Grated cheese - optional

Direction

- Cook Pasta according to package directions.
- Heat 2 tsp. oil, add garlic, flakes, florets & salt on high heat.
- Add drained pasta to florets & toss by adding remaining olive oil
- Serve garnished with cheese if desired....

53. Char Koay Teow Recipe

Serving: 5 | Prep: | Cook: 15mins | Ready in:

Ingredients

- 250 gm Koay Teow (flat rice noodles)
- 150 gm prawns - shelled
- 125 gm bean sprouts
- 5 stalks chives - cut into 2cm lengths
- 100 gm vegetable oil

- 4 eggsEggs
- 2 garlic cloves - chopped
- 2 tsp Ground chiliGround Chili (add more if you prefer it spicier)
- 2 tsp light soy sauce
- 2 tsp dark soy sauce
- 10 gm Cooked crab Meat
- pepper to taste

Direction

- 1] Heat oil, add garlic and fry till fragrant in a very hot wok.
- 2] Add prawns and ground chili.
- 3] Stir-fry for about 15 secs.
- 4] Add kway teow, soy sauce and additional oil if necessary.
- 5] Mix in vegetables and beansprouts.
- 6] Push mixture to edge of wok, add a little oil in centre.
- 7] Add and fry the eggs and then mix everything together.
- 8] Garnish with pepper and cooked crab meat.
- 9] Serve immediately when it's hot.

54. Cheese Stuffed Italian Meatloaf Recipe

Serving: 6 | Prep: | Cook: 60mins |Ready in:

Ingredients

- 1 egg
- 1 cup seasoned dry bread crumbs
- 1 teaspoon minced garlic
- 1/2 cup of your favorite pasta sauce, homemade or in the jar
- 1 cup chopped onions
- 1/4 cup chopped fresh basil
- 3/4 lb lean ground beef
- 1/2 lb hot italian sausage
- 1 cup cubed mozzarella cheese, in about 1/4 inch pieces
- additional pasta sauce, for garnish

Direction

- Preheat oven to 350 degrees F.
- In a large bowl, stir together the egg, breadcrumbs (I whir herbed dry stuffing mix in my food processor to make these), garlic, and 1/2 cup pasta sauce until well-mixed.
- Add remaining ingredients (except the garnish), and mix together well (I do the whole thing in my sturdy KitchenAid mixer, which works quite well).
- Put into a large loaf pan, top/garnish with additional pasta sauce (I like a*lot* of sauce and so use about a half-cup, but three or four tablespoons would do, too), and bake at 350 degrees F for 1 hour.
- Serve with rice, spaghetti, or scalloped potatoes.

55. Cheesey Chicken Pasta Florentine Recipe

Serving: 8 | Prep: | Cook: 25mins |Ready in:

Ingredients

- EVOO
- 3 T margarine
- 3 cups thinly sliced mushrooms
- 1 cup chopped onion
- 2 T micnced garlic
- 1 cup chopped roasted red peppers
- 3 cups chopped fresh spinach
- 1 tablespoon chopped fresh oregano
- 1/4 teaspoon freshly ground black pepper
- 1 (15-ounce) carton ricotta
- 4 cups hot cooked penne (about 8 ounces uncooked tube-shaped pasta)
- 2 cups shredded roasted skinless, boneless chicken breast
- 1 cup (4 ounces) shredded reduced-fat sharp cheddar cheese, divided
- 1/2 cup (2 ounces) grated fresh parmesan cheese, divided

- 1/4 cup skim milk
- 1/4 cup fat free half and half
- 1 can cream of mushroom and roasted garlic soup
- ** I have used 1/2 c sour cream instead of milk **

Direction

- Preheat oven to 425°.
- In a large non-stick skillet melt the margarine with a drizzle of EVOO over medium-high heat, add mushrooms, garlic, onion, and pepper; sauté 4 minutes or until tender.
- Add spinach, oregano, and black pepper; sauté 3 minutes or just until spinach wilts.
- Combine spinach mixture, ricotta cheese, pasta, chicken, 3/4 cup cheddar cheese, 1/4 cup Parmesan cheese, milk, and soup in a large bowl.
- Spoon mixture into a 2-quart baking dish coated with cooking spray. Sprinkle with remaining 1/4 cup cheddar cheese and remaining 1/4 cup Parmesan cheese.
- Bake at 425° for 25 minutes or until lightly browned and bubbly.

56. Cheesey Italian Spinach And Chicken Casserole Recipe

Serving: 8 | Prep: | Cook: 45mins | Ready in:

Ingredients

- 8 oz. uncooked rigatoni or rotini
- 1 Tbsp. olive oil
- 1 cup chopped onion
- 1 cup chopped fresh mushrooms, or canned
- 1/2 T chopped garlic
- 1 (16 oz.) bag frozen chopped spinach
- 2-3 cups cubed cooked chicken breasts
- 1 (14.5 oz) can Italian style diced tomatoes
- 1 (8 oz) container chive and onion cream cheese
- ½ tsp. salt

- ½ tsp pepper
- 1 T italian seasoning
- 1/2 c parmesan cheese
- 2 cups shredded mozzarella cheese

Direction

- Prepare pasta according to directions.
- Spread oil on bottom of 11 x 7 (or same volume) baking dish.
- Add onion, garlic and fresh mushrooms in a single layer.
- Bake 375 degrees for 15 min.
- Transfer onion mixture to a large bowl and set aside.
- Drain chopped spinach well, pressing between layers of paper towels.
- ***OR****Butter the baking dish and sauté together in a little EVOO and pad of margarine the onion, garlic, mushrooms and spinach. Drain if needed, the bag spinach is not frozen together in an icy block, and there is rarely anything to drain once it's sautéed. IF you do it this way, just include the spinach in the onion mixture layer ****
- Stir pasta, spinach, chicken, tomatoes, cream cheese, Italian seasoning and salt/pepper into onion in bowl.
- Spoon mixture into baking dish and sprinkle with parmesan and shredded mozzarella.
- Bake, covered at 375 degrees for 30 min. uncover and bake 15 more min. or until bubbly.

57. Cheesy Italian Beef And Noodle Bae Recipe

Serving: 8 | Prep: | Cook: 30mins | Ready in:

Ingredients

- 1-1/2 pounds lean ground beef
- 14 ounce can tomatoes
- 7-1/2 ounce can tomato sauce
- 1/4 cup parmesan cheese

- 2 cloves garlic minced
- 1-1/2 cups medium egg noodles
- 1 cup sour cream
- 8 ounce package cream cheese
- 6 green onions

Direction

- In large frying pan sauté ground beef and garlic then drain off fat.
- Add tomatoes, tomato sauce and Parmesan cheese then simmer 10 minutes.
- Cook egg noodles and toss with sour cream, cream cheese and green onions.
- Spoon half of the noodle cheese mixture into a greased casserole dish and top with half the meat mixture.
- Add remaining noodles and top with remaining sauce.
- Bake covered for 30 minutes.

58. Chicken Broccoli Alfredo Recipe

Serving: 4 | Prep: | Cook: 20mins | Ready in:

Ingredients

- 1/2 pkg. linguine (8 oz.)*
- 1 cup fresh OR frozen broccoli flowerets
- 2 tbsp. butter
- 1 lb. skinless, boneless chicken breasts, cut into cubes
- 1 can (10 3/4 oz.) Campbell's® condensed cream of mushroom soup OR Campbell's® Condensed 98% Fat Free Cream of Mushroom Soup
- 1/2 cup milk
- 1/2 cup grated parmesan cheese
- 1/4 tsp. ground black pepper

Direction

- COOK linguine according to pkg. directions. Add broccoli for last 4 min. of cooking time. Drain.
- HEAT butter in skillet. Cook chicken until browned, stirring often.
- ADD soup, milk, cheese, black pepper and linguine mixture and heat through. Serve with additional Parmesan cheese.
- TIP: *Or substitute spaghetti for linguine.
- Serve with a mixed green salad topped with grape tomatoes and balsamic vinaigrette. For dessert serve pear halves.

59. Chicken Alfredo Recipe

Serving: 2 | Prep: | Cook: 20mins | Ready in:

Ingredients

- 6 ounces dry fettuccine pasta
- 8 ounce package cream cheese
- 6 tablespoons butter
- 1/2 cup milk
- 1/2 teaspoon garlic powder
- 1 teaspoon salt
- 2 teaspoons freshly ground black pepper
- 2 skinless boneless chicken breast halves cooked and cubed
- 2 cups chopped fresh broccoli
- 2 small zucchini julienned
- 1/2 cup chopped red bell pepper

Direction

- Bring a large pot of lightly salted water to a boil.
- Add pasta and cook 10 minutes then drain well.
- While pasta is cooking melt cream cheese and butter in a skillet over low heat.
- Stir until smooth.
- Stir in milk and season with garlic powder, salt and pepper.
- Simmer for 3 minutes stirring constantly.

- Mix in chicken, broccoli, zucchini and red pepper.
- Cook 3 minutes over medium heat then reduce heat and simmer 5 minutes.
- Serve over fettuccine.

60. Chicken Andouille With Creamy Tomato Sauce Pasta Recipe

Serving: 4 | Prep: | Cook: 15mins | Ready in:

Ingredients

- 1 lb. chicken andouille sausage links
- 1 boneless skinless chicken breast
- 1/2 sweet onion, chopped (or less)
- McCormick roasted garlic and red bell pepper seasoning blend (or omit, not necessary)
- 1 28 oz. can crushed tomatoes
- 1 14 oz. can chicken broth
- 1 Tbls. Dijon mustard
- 1 8 oz. block of cream cheese (I used Philly light)
- 1 Tbls. dried basil (if you use fresh, about 1/4 cup chopped, or more)
- 1 tsp. marjoram
- pasta, Any type you like, I used short wide egg noodles approx. 10 oz. dry (I didn't measure, just dumped in what I thought I needed)

Direction

- Chop onion, set aside
- Cut each Andouille link in half lengthwise and slice in 1/4 inch pieces, set aside
- Cube chicken breast, set aside
- Meanwhile bring water to boil for pasta, add when ready
- Sauté onion in a little olive oil till just about clear, remove
- Add chicken and Andouille and cook till just done
- Return onions to pan

- Add crushed tomatoes and chicken broth and bring to simmer
- Add mustard and seasonings
- Turn off heat (or remove if using electric heat)
- Add cream cheese and slowly incorporate (I use the back of my spoon and press on it gradually pulling away till dissolved)
- Return to heat and add pasta, stir till heated through
- Serve immediately

61. Chicken Au Gratin Casserole Recipe

Serving: 6 | Prep: | Cook: 40mins | Ready in:

Ingredients

- 2 tbsp softened butter
- 1 1/2 lb boneless chicken breasts
- 1/3 cup dry white wine
- 1 1/2 cup chicken broth
- 1 tsp dried tarragon
- 2 whole cloves (optional)
- 1 onion, chopped
- 1 garlic clove, minced
- salt and pepper to taste
- 4 cups rigatoni (or any other short pasta)
- 2 cups broccoli florets
- 2 tbsp all-purpose flour
- 1/2 lb havarti cheese, shredded
- 3/4 cup breadcrumbs

Direction

- Melt half the butter in a large pot over medium heat, add chicken and brown on both sides.
- Pour in wine and chicken broth, add tarragon, cloves, onion, garlic, salt and pepper.
- Bring to a boil over high heat.
- Cover and let simmer over low heat for about 20 to 25 minutes, until chicken is tender.

- Cook the rigatoni according to instructions on package, adding broccoli florets to the cooking water together with pasta.
- Drain and set aside.
- Remove the chicken from the pot and cut into dice. Keep warm.
- Mix together the second half of butter and the flour.
- Stir mixture into remaining juices in pot.
- Bring to a boil over medium heat, stirring constantly.
- Remove from heat, gently stir in tortiglioni, broccoli and chicken dices.
- Pour in ovenproof dish, top with shredded Canadian Havarti cheese and breadcrumbs.
- Bake in the oven at 350 for 8 to 10 minutes, until golden brown. Serve hot.

62. Chicken Broccoli Pasta Recipe

Serving: 4 | Prep: | Cook: 23mins | Ready in:

Ingredients

- 1 pound boneless, skinless chicken breast, cut into pieces
- 12 ounces pasta, cooked according to package directions and drained
- 2 cups frozen broccoli cuts
- 10 3/4 ounce can cream of chicken soup
- 3/4 cheddar cheese, grated

Direction

- Sauté chicken pieces in an oiled non-stick frying pan until they are no longer pink in the center. Place noodles in slow cooker; top with chicken, broccoli, and soup. Mix well. Sprinkle cheese on top and cover. Cook on low for 2-3 hours.

63. Chicken Cacciatore Recipe

Serving: 68 | Prep: | Cook: 45mins | Ready in:

Ingredients

- 2 chickens 3 lb each cut into serving size
- 4 Tbl olive oil
- 1/2 cup butter
- 2 cups onions (finely chopped)
- 1 chopped green pepper
- 4 cloves garlic (minced)
- 1/2 Tsp dried basil
- 1 1/2 Tsp salt
- 1/2 Tsp pepper
- 1 cup stewed tomatoes
- 1/2 cup dry red wine
- 1/2 lb noodles

Direction

- Sauté: chicken portions in the olive oil and butter for about 10 minutes, or until golden brown on all sides.
- Add: onion, green pepper, garlic, dried basil, salt and pepper and cook for 5 minutes.
- Add: stewed tomatoes and stir to mix. Bring to a boil, cover and cook over low heat for 20 minutes, stirring occasionally.
- Add: red wine and cook for 10 minutes more.
- While the chicken is cooking: cook the noodles in a pot of rapidly boiling salted water for 8-10 minutes.
- Serve the chicken and sauce over the hot cooked noodles.

64. Chicken Chow Mein Recipe

Serving: 4 | Prep: | Cook: 20mins | Ready in:

Ingredients

- 1 pound mung bean sprouts
- 2 boneless, skinless chicken breasts thinly sliced

- 2 tablespoon oyster sauce
- 2 teaspoon soy sauce
- salt and black pepper, to taste
- 1 cornstarch (mix in water)
- 1/4 low-sodium chicken broth
- 1/2 pound dry wonton noodles
- 2 medium celery medium sliced
- 1/2 white onion medium sliced
- 2 cups cabbage meduim sliced
- 1 green onion (scallion, spring onion) long sliced
- 2 glove garlic chopped
- 4 tbsp of sesame oil
- ** snowpeas and mushroom can be use if desire

Direction

- One or 2 hours before cooking, rinse the mung bean sprouts so that they have time to drain thoroughly.
- Cut the chicken into thin strips and set aside.
- Soften the noodles by placing them in boiling salted water. Plunge into cold water to stop the cooking process and drain thoroughly.
- Heat a wok or frying pan over medium-high to high heat. Add 2 tablespoons oil. When the oil is hot, add noodles. Fry in batches until golden. Remove the noodles from the pan.
- Heat 2 tablespoons oil in a wok. Add garlic and meat. Let the meat brown briefly, then stir-fry until the redness is gone and the meat is nearly cooked through.
- Add the rest of the vegetables (except for the green onion), chicken broth mix well for 2-3 minutes.
- Making a "well" in the middle of the wok for the sauce. Add oyster sauce, soy sauce, salt, pepper, and cornstarch and quickly stir and mix everything together. Stir in noodle and green onions.
- Place on serving plate and it ready to serve. Best serve hot.

65. Chicken Crunch Casserole Recipe

Serving: 0 | Prep: | Cook: 40mins |Ready in:

Ingredients

- 1/4 c. chicken broth
- 2 10 oz. cans mushroom soup
- 3 c. cooked chicken
- 1/4 c. minced onion
- 1 c. celery, minced
- 1 5 oz. can water chestnuts, sliced
- 1 3 oz. can chow mein noodles
- 1/2 c. toasted almonds, sliced

Direction

- Blend broth and soup.
- Mix chicken, onion, celery, chestnuts, and noodles in greased baking dish.
- Pour soup mixture over top.
- Cook at 325 degrees for 40 minutes.
- Sprinkle almonds on top.

66. Chicken Lo Mein Recipe

Serving: 4 | Prep: | Cook: 25mins |Ready in:

Ingredients

- 12 oz asian noodles (the refrigerated ones)
- 8 oz boneless chicken breasts, sliced thinly
- 3 Tbs soy sauce, divided
- 1 Tbs rice vinegar
- 1 Tbs sesame oil
- 4 Tbs olive oil, divided
- 2 cloves garlic, finely chopped
- 2 oz snow peas, trimmed
- 2 oz ham, finely sliced
- 1 1/2-2 Tbs oyster sauce
- 4 green onions, finely chopped
- salt and pepper, to taste

Direction

- Cook the noodles according to directions.
- Rinse under cold water, and set aside.
- Slice the chicken, and add it to a bowl with 2 tsp. of soy sauce, the rice vinegar and sesame oil, toss to coat.
- Heat half the olive oil in a wok or large frying pan over high heat.
- Let the oil get hot and add the chicken.
- Cook for 2 minutes, then transfer the chicken to a plate and keep warm.
- Wipe the pan out and heat the remaining olive oil.
- Add garlic, snow peas, and ham to the pan.
- Cook for 2-3 minutes.
- Add the drained noodles to the pan, and continue to stir fry till the noodles are heated through, about 2 minutes.
- Add the remaining soy and the oyster sauce, taste and adjust seasonings with salt and pepper.
- Add the chicken and any juices back to the pan, then add the green onions.
- Give a final stir and serve immediately.

67. Chicken Long Rice Recipe

Serving: 10 | Prep: | Cook: 75mins |Ready in:

Ingredients

- 3 lb chicken wings or 2 lb boneless skinless chicken thighs
- 3 T oil
- 2 – 3 garlic cloves, minced
- 6 – 7 c water for chicken wings or 1 large can of chicken broth if using chicken thighs or use Knorr bullion granulars to make broth
- 1 ½ t soy sauce
- 1 – 6 oz can whole mushrooms or 1 c fresh button mushrooms
- 1 – 6 oz pk long rice/saifun (bean threads - clear coils of noodles found in the Asian section of the supermarket or Asian stores) or use oriental vermicelli

- 2 T chopped green onions

Direction

- Cover and soak long rice in cold water for 30 minutes; cut into 2" lengths.
- Wash chicken wings or clean, wash and cut chicken thighs into 1" slivers.
- In a large pot add chicken wings, garlic and soy sauce and boil for 1 hour
- Or if using the boneless chicken thighs, heat oil in a large skillet and sauté chicken and garlic until browned and in a large pot bring chicken broth and soy sauce to a boil add chicken mixture.
- Reduce heat and simmer for 1 hour, or until chicken is tender.
- To either method used, add long rice and mushrooms to broth and chicken mixture.
- Simmer for an additional 15 minutes.
- Garnish with green onions and serve. Serves: 10 – 12.

68. Chicken Parmesan Again Recipe

Serving: 4 | Prep: | Cook: 15mins |Ready in:

Ingredients

- 4 each boned and skinned chicken breasts, about 4 ounces each
- 2/3 cup seasoned bread crumbs
- 1/2 cup grated parmesan cheese
- 1/2 teaspoon dried Italian seasoning
- 1/8 teaspoon black pepper
- 1/3 cup flour, all-purpose
- 3 large egg whites, lightly beaten
- 2 teaspoons olive oil
- 4 cups spaghetti, cooked and drained (about 8 oz raw)
- 3 cups pasta sauce (make it yourself or bought)
- 1 cup shredded mozzarella cheese
- 1/2 cup diced tomato (optional)

- 2 tablespoons chopped basil, fresh or dried basil leaves

Direction

- Place each chicken breast between 2 sheets of heavy-duty plastic wrap. Flatten to 1/4 inch thickness using a meat mallet or rolling pin.
- Start bringing pasta water to a boil in a pasta pot or large saucepan.
- Combine breadcrumbs, parmesan cheese, Italian seasoning and pepper in a shallow dish. Dredge each chicken breast in flour. Dip in egg whites, dredge in breadcrumb mixture.
- Heat oil in a large non-stick skillet over medium-high heat. Add chicken and cook 5 minutes on each side or until done.
- Start cooking the spaghetti separately.
- Preheat broiler.
- Place the cooked and drained spaghetti in the bottom of a medium sized glass baking dish. Spoon one cup of the pasta sauce over the spaghetti. Spread the diced tomatoes on top. Arrange cooked chicken breast in a layer on top of that. Spoon the rest of the pasta sauce over the chicken. Sprinkle the shredded mozzarella on top of all.
- Place the baking dish on a cookie sheet and broil for three minutes or until the cheese melts and starts to brown slightly. Garnish with basil and serve.

69. Chicken Picatta Recipe

Serving: 4 | Prep: | Cook: 25mins | Ready in:

Ingredients

- coarse salt and ground pepper
- 1/2 cup all-purpose flour
- 1 1/2 pounds chicken cutlets
- 2 tablespoons olive oil
- 8 ounces linguine
- 3 packed cups loose baby spinach (about 5 ounces), torn into pieces
- 3 tablespoons butter
- 3/4 cup dry white wine
- 2 tablespoons fresh lemon juice
- 2 tablespoons capers, rinsed and drained

Direction

- Bring a large pot of salted water to a boil.
- Place flour in a shallow bowl. Season cutlets with salt and pepper, then dip into flour, turning to coat; shake off excess.
- In a large skillet, heat 1 tablespoon oil over medium-high. Add half the chicken; cook until lightly browned and opaque throughout, 1 to 2 minutes per side. Transfer to a plate; cover with foil to keep warm. Repeat with remaining tablespoon oil and chicken (reserve skillet for sauce).
- Meanwhile, cook linguine in boiling water until al dente, according to package instructions. Reserve 1/2 cup pasta water. Add spinach, and stir until submerged. Drain pasta mixture and return to pot. Toss with 1 tablespoon butter; season generously with salt and pepper. Add some reserved pasta water if necessary. Cover to keep warm.
- Into skillet, pour wine and lemon juice. Cook over medium-high, stirring to loosen browned bits, until liquid has reduced to 1/3 cup, 4 to 5 minutes. Remove from heat; swirl in 2 remaining tablespoons butter until melted. (For a smoother sauce, strain through a fine-mesh sieve, if desired.) Add capers, and season with salt and pepper. Divide chicken and linguine among four serving plates; top chicken with sauce.

70. Chicken Puttanesca Recipe

Serving: 3 | Prep: | Cook: 20mins | Ready in:

Ingredients

- 2 boneless chicken breasts (or could use bone-in, just cook longer)

- fresh ground black pepper
- 2 Tablespoons extra virgin olive oil
- 1/2 large onion, sliced thin
- 4 garlic cloves, chopped
- 1 teaspoon crushed red pepper flakes
- 4 anchovies
- 1 14 1/2 ounce can diced tomatoes
- 1/2 cup dry white wine
- 1/2 cup chicken stock
- 2 Tablespoons tomato paste
- 1 teaspoon Italian herbs
- 1/4 cup olives (I used Kalamata, but any you like would work)
- 2 Tablespoons capers
- 1/2 pound of pasta (cook it while you prepare chicken & sauce)

Direction

- Season chicken with pepper while 1 Tablespoon of oil heats over medium-high.
- Brown chicken on both sides and remove to a plate.
- Add remaining olive oil and turn heat down to medium.
- Cook onions for a couple minutes, until starting to soften.
- Add garlic and red pepper, cook 1 minute.
- Add anchovies and cook stirring until they dissolve.
- Add white wine, tomatoes, chicken stock, herbs and tomato paste.
- Stir to combine.
- Return chicken to pan, reduce heat to medium-low, and simmer until chicken is cooked. For boneless breasts, this could be as short as 5 minutes, or as much as 20-25 minutes for bone-in.
- Serve mixed with pasta of your choice. I used whole wheat rigatoni.

71. Chicken Rice Casserole Recipe

Serving: 4 | Prep: | Cook: 60mins | Ready in:

Ingredients

- 2 lb chicken leftovers
- 1/2 green bell pepper, chopped finely
- 1/2 yellow bell pepper, chopped finely
- 1/2 red bell pepper, finely chopped
- 1 good sized onion, finely chopped
- 3 cups elbow or bow-tie macaroni
- 2 cups uncooked rice
- salt & pepper to taste
- 1 tbsp oregano
- 1 tsp garlic powder (NOT garlic salt!)
- 1 cup chopped celery
- 1/2 chopped carrots
- 1 cup diced tomatoes
- 1 can mushrooms, or 12-16 fresh, chopped
- Old cheddar, grated (AMOUNT TO YOUR PREFERENCE)
- mozzarella cheese, grated (AMOUNT TO YOUR PREFERENCE)
- 2 tbsp balsamic vinegar
- 1 tbsp lemon juice
- 1 tsp hot sauce

Direction

- Cook the rice, preferably to the al dente stage (still some bite left in it)
- In a saucepan (large) combine all of the aforementioned ingredients except the cheeses.
- Simmer over low heat for 40 minutes, or until everything is tender.
- Next, add the rice, and continue simmering until the rice is tender.
- Plate it, and sprinkle with the cheeses.
- Delicious!!

72. Chicken Scarpariella Recipe

Serving: 4 | Prep: | Cook: 40mins | Ready in:

Ingredients

- 3 1/2 lbs. broiler-fryer chickens, cut up (you can use just thighs and legs if you prefer)
- 1 tsp. salt
- 1/2 tsp. pepper
- 1/2 to 3/4 cup extra virgin olive oil or canola oil
- 1 karge clove garlic, minced or pressed
- 1 Tbsp. minced fresh parsley
- 2 tsp. dried rosemary
- 1 cup dry white wine
- 1 cup whipping cream
- 1/2 cup fresh, grated parmesan cheese
- Hot cooked spaghetti or noodles

Direction

- Wash and dry chicken pieces. Sprinkle with salt and pepper. Heat oil in large skillet. Brown chicken over high heat.
- Add garlic. Lower heat and sauté for 10 minutes. Drain of fat.
- Add parsley rosemary and wine. Simmer about 15 minutes or until wine evaporates and chicken is done (juices run clear when pierced with a fork).
- Remove chicken to a platter. Add cream to skillet. Boil until reduced by half and thickened, scraping pan drippings. Return chicken to skillet. Cook 3-4 minutes more or until chicken is reheated.
- Sprinkle with Parmesan cheese. Serve over a bed of hot spaghetti. Sprinkle with fresh chopped parsley. Garnish with a lemon wedge.

73. Chicken Spinach Alfredo Lasagna Recipe

Serving: 8 | Prep: | Cook: 13mins | Ready in:

Ingredients

- 1 (8 ounce) package lasagna noodles
- 3 cups heavy cream

- 2 (10.75 ounce) cans condensed cream of mushroom soup
- 1 cup grated parmesan cheese
- 1/4 cup butter
- 1 tablespoon olive oil
- 1/2 large onion, diced
- 4 cloves garlic, sliced
- 5 mushrooms, diced
- 1 roasted chicken, shredded
- salt and ground black pepper to taste
- 1 cup ricotta cheese
- 1 bunch fresh spinach, rinsed
- 3 cups shredded mozzarella cheese

Direction

- 1.) Preheat oven to 350 degrees F (175 degrees C). Bring a large pot of lightly salted water to a boil. Cook lasagna noodles for 8 to 10 minutes, or until al dente. Drain, and rinse with cold water.
- 2.) In a saucepan over low heat, mix together heavy cream, cream of mushroom soup, Parmesan cheese, and butter. Simmer, stirring frequently, until well blended.
- 3.) Heat the olive oil in a skillet over medium heat. Cook and stir the onion in olive oil until tender, then add garlic and mushrooms. Mix in the chicken, and cook until heated through. Season with salt and pepper.
- 4.) Lightly coat the bottom of a 9x13 inch baking dish with enough of the cream sauce mixture to coat. Layer with 1/3 of the lasagna noodles, 1/2 cup ricotta, 1/2 of the spinach, 1/2 the chicken mixture, and 1 cup mozzarella. Top with 1/2 the cream sauce mixture, and repeat the layers. Place the remaining noodles on top, and spread with remaining sauce.
- 5.) Bake 1 hour in the preheated oven, or until brown and bubbly. Top with the remaining mozzarella, and continue baking until cheese is melted and lightly browned.

74. Chicken Tetrazini Recipe

Serving: 6 | Prep: | Cook: 15mins | Ready in:

Ingredients

- 1 1/2 lbs. chicken breasts
- 1 lb. spaghetti noodles
- 1 lb. mushrooms
- 1 1/2 sticks of butter (salted)
- 6 cups of chicken stock
- 8 Tbsp. Wondra (or flour)
- 1 cup white wine (chardonnay or sauvingnon blanc)
- 6-8 Tbsp. heavy whipping cream
- Italian breadcrumbs
- parmasean cheese
- cracked sea salt & pepper to taste

Direction

- Begin by slicing mushrooms and set aside.
- Wash the chicken breasts well.
- Place chicken breast and stock in large pot and boil for about 20 mins or until cooked thoroughly.
- Start water for spaghetti (approx. 10 mins to boil).
- Set chicken aside to cool.
- Be sure to keep 3 cups of chicken broth for sauce (add later).
- In large sauce pan, melt one Tbsp. of butter and sauté mushrooms for about 5 mins or until tender, do not overcook; drain excess juice and set aside.
- Boil pasta (approx. 10 mins.).
- Preheat oven at 350 degrees.
- On a medium heat, melt remaining butter in sauce pan.
- Add Wondra, stir well, and bring to slight boil.
- Quickly add chicken broth and boil until sauce begins to thicken.
- Add wine and boil for 1-2 mins more.
- Lower heat, add the heaving whipping cream and mushrooms; simmer on low for about 5 mins.
- Check seasoning. Feel free to add a pinch or two of parmesan to your tastes.
- Drain pasta and place in a 13"x9" deep casserole dish; spread evenly.
- Sprinkle parmesan over pasta.
- Chop cooled chicken breast and place over pasta.
- Pour sauce evenly over bed of pasta and chicken.
- Lightly sprinkle breadcrumbs over top.
- Bake, uncovered, at 350 degrees for about 15 mins or until bubbly.
- Cool for 5 mins. before serving
- Makes 4-6 servings

75. Chicken And String Bean Medley Recipe

Serving: 4 | Prep: | Cook: 10mins | Ready in:

Ingredients

- 3 white onions chopped
- 2 small green peppers chopped
- 2 small red peppers chopped
- 2 celery ribs chopped
- 3 tablespoons olive oil
- 1/4 cup cooked string beans
- 1 cup chopped pieces of chicken
- 1 pound macaroni
- 1 teaspoon salt
- 1 teaspoon freshly ground black pepper
- 1 cup buttered bread crumbs

Direction

- Sauté onions, peppers and celery in oil until soft.
- Add peas and meat.
- Cook macaroni until al dente then drain well and place in a baking dish.
- Stir in the vegetable meat sauce and sprinkle with salt and black pepper then stir well.

- Top with buttered bread crumbs then place under broiler for 7 minutes.

76. Chinese Carryout Noodles Recipe

Serving: 4 | Prep: | Cook: 20mins | Ready in:

Ingredients

- 1 ts canola oil
- 1 ts Asian sesame oil
- 1 c Onion; chopped
- 1 clove garlic
- 4 oz Chicken breast; skinless & boneless
- 1 tb Ginger; grated
- 2 lg Stalks bok choy
- 8 oz angel hair pasta
- 1/4 c chicken stock
- 2 tb dry sherry
- 1 tb soy sauce
- 1 1/2 tb hoisin sauce
- 2 scallions
- 1/8 ts salt

Direction

- Bring water to a boil in a covered pot. Cook the pasta according to package directions.
- Heat the canola and sesame oils together in a non-stick skillet or wok until very hot.
- Chop the onion. Stir fry in the oils. Mince the garlic. Add to the wok. Continue cooking.
- Wash and dry the chicken and cut into bite-size pieces. Add to the wok. Stir fry until the chicken browns. Add the grated ginger.
- Wash, trim and cut the bok choy into small pieces. Stir into the wok. Add the chicken stock, sherry, soy sauce and the hoisin. Stir well. Reduce heat. Continue cooking. Wash, trim and slice the scallions. Drain the pasta. Stir into the wok. Season with salt. Sprinkle with scallions. Serve.

77. Chinese Fire Pot With Fish Balls Recipe

Serving: 12 | Prep: | Cook: 5mins | Ready in:

Ingredients

- 2 pounds flank steak, sliced thinly against the grain
- 2 pounds chicken breast, thinly sliced
- 1 pound large shrimp, U-15's peeled and de-veined (15 shrimp per pound)
- 20 fish balls
- 2 pounds bay scallops
- 3 packages soaked mung bean noodles
- 4 Shanghai cabbage, whole leaves
- 4 baby bok choy, whole leaves
- 1 napa cabbage large chopped
- 2 quarts chicken stock
- 1 pound shiitake mushrooms, de-stemmed
- boiling water
- For the table, jars/small bottles of the following to make your own dipping sauce:
- Samba Oelek
- peanut butter
- Chinese sesame paste
- sesame oil
- oyster sauce
- rice wine vinegar
- shaoxing wine
- Thin soy sauce
- 2 cups chopped scallions
- 2 cups chopped cilantro
- eggs (optional)

Direction

- Thread beef, chicken, shrimp, fish balls and scallops on wooden skewers and set aside. Combine water and chicken stock in an electric wok and bring to a boil. Add mung bean noodles, cabbage, bok choy and shiitake mushrooms. Place skewers in pot and cook according to individual taste. Ladle broth into

bowls with skewered meats and seafood and serve with condiments.
- FISH BALLS:
- 2 pounds Chilean sea bass or other fatty white fish
- 4 eggs, separated
- 1 teaspoon white pepper
- 1 teaspoon kosher salt
- 1 teaspoon sesame oil
- 1 tablespoon fish sauce
- 3 minced Thai bird chilies
- 1/3 cup sliced scallions
- In a food processor, puree fish with egg yolks until smooth. Add pepper, salt, sesame oil, fish sauce, and chilies; pulse processor a few times. Transfer mousse to a large, chilled bowl and fold in the scallions. Using a mixer, lift the egg whites to a stiff peak. Gently fold in the egg whites with the mousse. Cook a very small portion either in boiling water or in a microwave oven to verify seasonings. Using wet hands, make small balls (1-inch in diameter). Quickly blanch in salted boiling water for only 2 minutes. Drain and set aside to cool.
- Huge appetite,
- The serving will be round 8 to 12 depending the each person serving.

78. Cincinnati Chili Skyline Style Recipe

Serving: 6 | Prep: | Cook: 60mins | Ready in:

Ingredients

- 1 lb. natural ground beef (85/15 is what I prefer)
- 16 oz. spaghetti noodles
- 8 oz. bag shredded sharp cheddar cheese
- 1 29 oz. can tomato sauce
- 1 cup water
- 1 large diced yellow sweet onion
- 1-2 cloves garlic, minced

- 1 tbsp. Worchestershire sauce
- 1 tbsp. unsweetened powdered cocoa
- 1 cube or tbsp beef boullion
- 1 tsp. cumin
- 1 tsp. cinnamon
- 1 tsp. chili powder
- 1/8 tsp. cloves
- 1/8 tsp. allspice
- oyster crackers and red or sweet yellow onion to top

Direction

- Cook ground beef on stovetop over medium to medium high heat until browned through (about 5 min.) Add about 1/2 to 3/4 cup onion and the 1-2 cloves minced garlic and cook about 2 more minutes or until onion is translucent. The key with the onion is to cut the pieces pretty small, almost minced, so they are not noticeable. This is not your normal chunky chili, should be more of a saucy consistency. Break up the meat while you are cooking also!
- Then, pour into a large (2-3 quart) soup pot. Add other ingredients (except cheese, noodles, crackers, and remainder of onion) and stir well. Bring to rapid boil, stirring frequently.
- Once mixture boils, reduce heat to low, cover, and let simmer for 50-60 minutes. Meanwhile, boil spaghetti to desired tenderness and drain.
- Layer in a bowl as follows: noodles, chili, onion, cheese, oyster crackers. I recommend eating with a knife and fork. Delicious!

79. Clam Linguine Recipe

Serving: 5 | Prep: | Cook: 10mins | Ready in:

Ingredients

- 1 (8 oz) package dry linguine
- 1 (6 and 1/2 oz) can of minced clams
- 2 Tbl olive oil
- 2 Tbl margarine or butter

- 2 cloves garlic, minced
- 1/4 to 1/2 tsp pepper
- 1/4 tsp dried basil, crushed
- 1/4 tsp dried oregano, crushed
- salt to taste
- 2 Tbl fresh parsley, snipped
- Grated parmesan cheese

Direction

- Cook the linguine according to package directions, then drain and set aside.
- Drain the clams, but reserve the liquid and set aside.
- In a 2 qt. saucepan over medium high heat, heat the olive oil and butter until the oil is hot, and butter is melted. Add the garlic, cook and stir for 2-3 minutes. Do not brown the garlic.
- Carefully add the reserved clam liquid, pepper, basil, oregano, and salt to taste. Reduce heat and simmer, uncovered, for 3 minutes. Stir in the clams and simmer until heated through. Stir the parsley into the clam sauce.
- Pour the clam sauce over the hot linguine and toss gently to mix. Sprinkle with Parmesan cheese, and serve immediately.

80. Clam Sauce Recipe

Serving: 4 | Prep: | Cook: 20mins | Ready in:

Ingredients

- 1/4 cup good extra virgin olive oil
- 3-5 cloves of garlic, minced well
- 3 can cans minced clams and their liquid, reserved
- 1/2 cup white wine that you like to drink
- 1 tsp. dried basil
- 1 tsp. dried oregano
- 1 tsp. pepper (or to taste)
- 1/2 freshly chopped flat parsley
- 1 pound of linguine, cooked
- freshly grated parmesan to serve on the side

Direction

- Lightly sauté the garlic in the olive oil. Do not let this brown or it will be too bitter.
- Add the clams, their liquid, the wine, and the herbs and simmer. Cook until the flavors come together and season with pepper to taste.
- In a serving bowl, pour this sauce over the pasta.
- Pass the cheese around.

81. Classic Spaghetti And Meatballs Recipe

Serving: 6 | Prep: | Cook: 30mins | Ready in:

Ingredients

- Meatballs:
- 2 eggs
- 1/2 cup whole milk
- 3 slices fresh French bread made into crumbs in food processor or blender
- 2 pounds ground beef
- 1/2 cup finely chopped onion
- 2 tablespoons chopped parsley
- 1 clove garlic, smashed, minced
- 1 teaspoon kosher salt
- 1/2 teaspoon freshly cracked pepper
- Sauce:
- 3 tablespoons olive oil
- 1/2 cup chopped onion
- 2 cloves garlic, smashed and minced
- 1 tube double concentrated tomato paste
- sugar, to taste
- 2 teaspoons kosher salt
- 2 teaspoon dried leaf oregano
- 2 teaspoon dried leaf basil
- freshly cracked black pepper to taste
- 1 large can (28 to 36 ounces total) crushed Italian tomatoes (I like to use "Glen Muir" organic fire roasted tomatoes)
- 16 ounces thin spaghetti

- parmesan cheese, fresh parsley

Direction

- Make meatballs: In a medium bowl, beat eggs lightly; add milk and bread and let stand for about 5 minutes. Add ground beef, onion, parsley, garlic, salt, and pepper; mix gently until well blended. Shape into about 24 meatballs, about 1 1/2 inches in diameter. Place meatballs in a generously greased large shallow baking pan. Bake meatballs at 450° for 25 minutes.
- In a Dutch oven, in hot oil over medium heat, sauté the onion until tender and just begins to turn golden. Add remaining sauce ingredients; bring to a boil. Reduce heat, cover, and simmer for 30 minutes. Taste and adjust seasoning, adding more salt, if necessary. Add meatballs, along with juices from pan; cover and simmer 50 to 60 minutes longer, stirring from time to time.
- Cook spaghetti according to package directions; drain and toss in a little butter and parmesan cheese for flavor.
- Serve spaghetti topped with meatballs in sauce; sprinkle with freshly grated Parmesan cheese and minced parsley.

82. Country Chicken Spaghetti Recipe

Serving: 8 | Prep: | Cook: 45mins | Ready in:

Ingredients

- 1 fryer chicken
- 2 cans cream of mushroom soup
- 2 cups grated sharp cheddar cheese
- 1/4 cup finely diced green pepper
- 1/2 cup finely diced onion
- 1-4 oz jar diced pimentos, drained
- 3 cups dry spaghetti, broken into two inch pieces
- 2 cups reserved chicken broth from pot

- 1 teaspoon Nature's seasons Season salt
- 1/8 teaspoon cayenne pepper (just a shake or two)
- salt & pepper to taste
- 1 additional cup grated sharp cheddar cheese

Direction

- Rinse chicken well. Place into a large stockpot, cover with water and bring to a rolling boil. Boil for about 20 minutes, then turn down temp and simmer the chicken for about 30 minutes.
- Remove chicken from broth, and reserve 2 cups of cooking broth in a measuring cup or bowl.
- Pick chicken from bones, discarding most fat and skin. You'll need 2 cups of the chicken meat. You should now have a pot with broth in it, 2 cups of broth in a cup and 2 cups of shredded up chicken meat.
- Place your broken up spaghetti pieces into the broth pot and cook until it's just al-dente. You DON'T want to overcook your noodles here.
- Drain the al-dente noodles and place into a large mixing bowl. Add shredded chicken, seasonings, 2 cups shredded cheddar, veggies, pimiento, broth, soups.
- Pour everything into a buttered casserole dish. I like to use a 2 1/2 quart glass Pyrex, but whatever you have that fits will work.
- To make ahead: You can make this dish ahead of time and refrigerate for up to three days, before preparing!
- Top with remaining 1 cup cheese. Cover with foil tightly. Bake at 350 degrees for 45 minutes, or until bubbly. Remove foil and let top brown for a few minutes. Serve and enjoy!!
- To freeze: Cover tightly and freeze for up to 3 months. To reheat: Take out of the freezer and place in fridge for 24 hours before baking. Bake as directed.
- This is one of the most amazing dishes to prepare/freeze ahead of time. I like to make two of these and freeze one. I figure, "Hey-- since I'm boiling a chicken anyway..." Plus---

the flavors meld if you freeze/prepare ahead. Try this one. You'll get rave reviews!!

- --Kn0x--

83. Cowboy Spaghetti Recipe

Serving: 8 | Prep: | Cook: 30mins | Ready in:

Ingredients

- 6 slices bacon,chopped
- 1 lb lean ground sirloin
- 3 tbsp olive oil
- 1 medium onion chopped
- 3 cloves garlic chopped
- 1 tbsp worchestershire sauce
- 1-2 tsp chipotle Tabasco sauce (or to taste)
- 1 28 oz can crushed fire roasted tomatoes (such as Muir Glen)
- 1 8oz can tomato sauce
- Salt and pepper to taste
- 1 lb thin spaghetti

Direction

- Cook spaghetti in boiling salted water, drain
- In large skillet over medium-high heat brown chopped bacon, drain on paper towels and set aside
- Drain bacon grease, saving 1 Tbsp.
- Brown ground sirloin in reserved bacon grease until cooked and crumbled, drain and set aside
- Heat olive oil in skillet, sauté onion and garlic until translucent
- Return sirloin to pan, add Worcestershire and tabasco
- Add crushed tomatoes and tomato sauce bring to a boil, reduce heat and simmer for 10 minutes
- Add drained spaghetti, mix well, turn heat to low and simmer an additional 10 minutes until thickened
- Serve in pasta bowls, topped with shredded cheddar, scallions and chopped bacon

84. Crabmeat And Shrimp Casserole Recipe

Serving: 6 | Prep: | Cook: 25mins | Ready in:

Ingredients

- ½ pound macaroni ,penne or pasta of your choice
- 1 tablespoon salt
- 1 tablespoon vegetable oil
- 4 tablespoons butter or margarine
- ½ pound fresh mushrooms, sliced
- 2 tablespoons butter or margarine
- 1 cup light cream
- 1 10-ounce can cream of mushroom soup
- ¾ cup grated sharp cheddar cheese
- 1 pound cooked shrimp, shelled and deveined
- 1 cup cooked crabmeat
- 1 cup soft bread crumbs
- 1 tablespoon butter or margarine
- Add-ins: peas or Chopped green peppers

Direction

- Add the salt and vegetable oil to 3 quarts boiling water. Add the macaroni and boil rapidly for 10 minutes. Drain and toss with 4 tablespoons butter or margarine.
- Sauté the mushrooms in 2 tablespoons butter or margarine for about 5 minutes, shaking the pan frequently. Mix the cream, mushroom soup and cheddar cheese together and add to the macaroni. Add the mushrooms, shrimp and crabmeat, which has been cut into bite-size pieces.
- Place in a buttered casserole, top with soft bread crumbs which have been tossed with the 1 tablespoon melted butter or margarine. Bake in a 350 degree oven for 25 minutes.

85. Creamy Basil And Roasted Red Pepper Pasta Recipe

Serving: 45 | Prep: | Cook: 17mins | Ready in:

Ingredients

- 2 cups uncooked penne pasta
- 4oz (half an 8 oz brick) cream cheese
- 7 oz roasted red peppers, drained
- 1/4 cup of milk
- 1/2 cup of fresh basil leaves
- 2 tbsp grated parmesan cheese
- 1 lb chicken breasts, cut into bite sized pieces (I omitted the chicken and used peas and broccoli. I added it to the last minutes of the boiling pasta)

Direction

- Cook pasta as directed on package.
- Meanwhile, place peppers, cream cheese, milk, basil and parmesan cheese in a blender and blend until nice and smooth.
- Cook chicken in a large skillet until cooked through.
- Stir in pepper mixture and simmer for 5-10 minutes, stirring frequently.
- Drain pasta and add chicken mixture. Stir gently until pasta is well coated.
- ** When I just use the broccoli and peas instead of the chicken, I add it to the drained pasta, stir until well coated and serve. It is just as nice.

86. Creamy Noodles Recipe

Serving: 6 | Prep: | Cook: 25mins | Ready in:

Ingredients

- 8 ounces uncooked thin spaghetti
- 3 garlic cloves, minced
- 3 Tbsp butter, divided
- 6 ounces cream cheese, cubed

- 3 Tbsp sour cream
- 2 Tbsp milk
- 3/4 tsp salt
- 1/2 tsp onion powder
- 1/4 tsp cajun seasoning
- 1/4 tsp white pepper
- 4 1/2 tsp minced fresh parsley

Direction

- Cook spaghetti according to package directions. Meanwhile, in a saucepan, sauté garlic in 1 Tbsp. butter until tender. Add the cream cheese, sour cream, milk, salt, onion powder, Cajun seasoning, pepper and remaining butter. Cook and stir over low heat just until smooth (do not boil). Remove from heat.
- Drain spaghetti; toss with cream sauce. Sprinkle with parsley. Serve immediately.

87. Creamy Noodles With Poppy Seeds Recipe

Serving: 4 | Prep: | Cook: 30mins | Ready in:

Ingredients

- 6 ounces wide egg noodles
- 1 tablespoon vegetable oil or butter
- 1 small onion, peeled and thinly sliced
- 10 ounces shredded cabbage (about 1/2 of a small head)
- salt and freshly ground black pepper
- 1-1/2 tablespoons poppy seeds
- 1 cup cottage cheese
- 3/4 cup sour cream
- 1 egg, beaten
- 1/4 cup freshly grated parmesan cheese
- paprika

Direction

- Preheat the oven to 375 degrees.

- Bring a large pot of salted water to a boil. Add the egg noodles and cook until al dente (the point just before the pasta is completely cooked through - it will still be slightly chewy.) Drain the pasta and set aside.
- Heat the oil or butter over medium heat in a large pan. Add the onion and cook for 2 to 3 minutes, stirring frequently. Add the cabbage and cook until wilted and slightly browned (about 8 minutes.) Season with salt and pepper while the cabbage is cooking. When cooked, add the poppy seeds and mix thoroughly. Remove from heat.
- In a large bowl, combine the cottage cheese, sour cream and beaten egg.
- Add the cabbage and onions and the drained noodles and mix together.
- Put the noodle mixture into an oiled 9X9-inch baking dish. Sprinkle with the parmesan cheese and a touch of paprika for color and bake in the oven for 20 to 30 minutes, uncovered, until browned and bubbling.
- Let the casserole sit for about 10 minutes and then cut into 4 equal servings.

88. Creamy Pasta With Bacon Recipe

Serving: 6 | Prep: | Cook: 20mins |Ready in:

Ingredients

- 1 pkg (9oz) refrigerated linguine
- 1 med. onion,chopped
- 1 Tb canola oil
- 2 garlic cloves,minced
- 2 Tb flour
- 1-1/2 c heavy cream
- 3 eggs,beaten
- 8 cooked strips of bacon,chopped
- 1/2 c parmesan cheese

Direction

- Cook linguine according to directions. Meanwhile, in large skillet, sauté onion in oil until tender. Add garlic, cook 1 min longer.
- In small bowl, whisk flour and cream until smooth; stir into the pan. Bring to boil, stirring constantly. Reduce heat; cook and stir for 1 min or till thickened. Remove from the heat. Stir a small amount of hot mixture into eggs; return all to pan, stirring constantly. Bring to gentle boil; cook and stir 2 mins longer.
- Drain linguine, add to the pan. Stir in bacon and cheese; heat through.

89. Creamy Spinach And Orzo Recipe

Serving: 5 | Prep: | Cook: 10mins |Ready in:

Ingredients

- 2 cups cooked Orzo
- 1/4 cup fresh grated parmesan cheese
- 1 egg,beaten
- 2 Tblsp.heavy cream
- 1 IB spinach,stemmed
- 2 Tblsp. olive oil
- 3 garlic cloves,sliced
- 1/4 Tsp.red pepper flakes
- salt & pepper to taste
- 1 dash balsamic vinegar

Direction

- Cook Orzo, according to directions, drain
- Mix cheese, egg, cream, add to hot orzo. The heat will cook the egg mixture.
- Heat oil, add garlic, sauté until soft, and add spinach in batches until wilted. Season with red pepper, salt & pepper. Drizzle with vinegar. Top orzo with spinach.

90. Creole Macaroni Salad Recipe

Serving: 6 | Prep: | Cook: 15mins | Ready in:

Ingredients

- 4 cups cooked macaroni (6 or 7 ounces or 2 cups uncooked)
- 2 cups diced tomatoes
- 1 cup grated sharp cheddar cheese, or your favorite!
- 1 cup mayonnaise
- 1/4 cup sliced pimiento stuffed olives
- 1/2 small onion, grated
- 1 - 2 cloves garlic, more or less, depending on your taste
- 1/8 teaspoon cayenne pepper, or more if you like

Direction

- If macaroni is uncooked, prepare according to package directions, boiling until tender, but not mushy, blanch (rinse well in cold water), drain until thoroughly dry.
- Mix all together.
- Refrigerate several hours (at least 4), or overnight.
- Can be served on lettuce leaves or just as it is.
- Enjoy!

91. Crispy Lamb Spare Ribs With Honey Creme Fraiche With Chopped Pea Salad Recipe

Serving: 8 | Prep: | Cook: 30mins | Ready in:

Ingredients

- For sauce
- --------------
- 1 cup crème frîache
- 1/2 cup honey
- 1 tablespoon whole cumin seeds, toasted and finely ground using spice or coffee grinder (about 1 teaspoon ground)
- 1 tablespoon whole coriander seeds, toasted and finely ground using spice or coffee grinder (about 1 teaspoon ground)
- 1/2 teaspoon kosher salt
- 1/4 teaspoon freshly ground black pepper
- --------------------
- For lamb ribs
- --------------------
- 6 pounds Denver lamb ribs (lamb breast spareribs; 6 small racks)
- 3 teaspoons kosher salt
- 3 teaspoons freshly ground black pepper
- 2 tablespoons extra-virgin olive oil
- 4 onions, coarsely chopped
- 8 carrots, coarsely chopped
- 8 stalks celery, coarsely chopped
- 2 heads garlic, cloves peeled and coarsely chopped (about 1/2 cup total)
- 4 tablespoons fresh rosemary, coarsely chopped (from 12 sprigs)
- 4 cups dry red wine
- 1 quart veal or chicken stock or low-sodium chicken broth
- -------------
- For salad
- -------------
- 2 cups frozen peas (from one 10-ounce package), unthawed
- 1 red onion, finely chopped
- 1/4 cup extra-virgin olive oil
- 2 tablespoons fresh lemon juice
- 1/2 teaspoon kosher salt
- 1/4 teaspoon freshly ground black pepper
- To serve
- ----------------------
- 2 cups vegetable oil
- 1 cup all-purpose flour
- 1 cup semolina flour (pasta flour)
- 1/2 cup parmigiano-Reggiano, finely grated
- 1 tablespoon whole cumin seeds, toasted and finely ground using spice or coffee grinder (about 1 teaspoon ground)

- 1 tablespoon whole coriander seeds, toasted and finely ground using spice or coffee grinder (about 1 teaspoon ground)
- 1/2 teaspoon kosher salt

Direction

- Make sauce

92. Crock Pot Beef Stroganoff Casserole Recipe

Serving: 6 | Prep: | Cook: 360mins | Ready in:

Ingredients

- 2 lbs chuck roast, cubed in 2-3 inch cubes
- Approx 6 oz uncooked wide egg noodles
- 16 oz can condensed mushroom soup
- 8 oz can beef broth, fill empty can with warm water and add to crock pot.
- 4 oz sour cream
- 1 tsp salt, pepper to taste

Direction

- In crock pot add meat cubes, salt and pepper, and then uncooked noodles on top of meat. Then add beef broth, water, sour cream, and mushroom soup. Cook on medium heat for at least 6 hours, covered. There is no need to stir or mix ingredients. The soup, broth & water will make a tasty broth with the sour cream, meat and noodles.
- NOTES:
- Make sure you place the meat and noodles in the crock pot first so the noodles absorb the sauce and cook evenly. This recipe can also be made exactly the same way using an 8 oz. bag of frozen meatballs, just as delicious!

93. Crock Pot Chicken Cacciatore Recipe

Serving: 6 | Prep: | Cook: 240mins | Ready in:

Ingredients

- 1/2 cup all-purpose flour
- 1 teaspoon salt
- 1/4 teaspoon red pepper
- 2 pounds boneless, skinless chicken breast halves
- 3 tablespoons olive oil
- 1 can (14-1/2 oz.) chicken broth
- 1 can (14-1/2 oz.) diced Italian tomatoes, undrained
- 1 can (14 oz.) artichokes hearts, drained and cut into quarters
- 1 cup sliced fresh mushrooms
- 1/3 cup chopped onion
- 1 package (3 oz.) thinly sliced prosciutto
- 2 tablespoons chopped pimiento-stuffed green olives
- 2 teaspoons minced fresh garlic
- 1/4 teaspoon dried oregano, crushed
- 1/4 teaspoon dried thyme, crushed
- Hot cooked linguine

Direction

- In a large resealable plastic bag combine the flour, salt, and red pepper. Add chicken, a few pieces at a time, and shake to coat. In a large skillet brown chicken in hot oil in batches. Transfer to a 5-quart slow cooker. Stir in the broth, undrained tomatoes, artichoke hearts, mushrooms, onion, prosciutto, olives, garlic, oregano, and thyme. Cover and cook on low heat for 4 to 4 1/2 hours or until chicken is no longer pink. Serve over rice or pasta.

94. Crock Pot Macaroni Recipe

Serving: 46 | Prep: | Cook: 181mins | Ready in:

Ingredients

- 2 eggs
- 12 oz. can evaporated milk
- 1-1/2 cups milk
- 1/2 lb. elbow macaroni pasta
- 3 cups shredded cheddar cheese
- 1 cup shredded American cheese
- 1/4 cup grated parmesan cheese
- 1/2 tsp. salt
- 1/8 tsp. white pepper
- 1/2 tsp. onion powder (Or finely chopped onions if you prefer)
- 1/8 tsp. garlic powder

Direction

- Spray the inside of the slow cooker with non-stick cooking spray.
- In a large bowl, beat eggs with the fresh and evaporated milks.
- Stir in UNCOOKED macaroni and all of the shredded cheeses, salt and pepper, and onion and garlic powders; mix well.
- Pour into 4 quart crockpot.
- Cover cook on low for 5 to 6 hours.
- Do NOT stir or remove the lid while this dish is cooking. Serves 4-6

95. Crockpot Beef Stroganoff Recipe

Serving: 4 | Prep: | Cook: 420mins | Ready in:

Ingredients

- 2 Tbs all-purpose flour
- 1/2 tsp garlic powder
- 1/2 tsp black pepper
- 1/4 tsp paprika
- 2 lb London Broil (or other beef roast)
- 1 can cream of mushroom soup (I use low-sodium)
- 1/2 cup beef broth
- 1/4 cup onion flakes (dehydrated onion)

- 1 cup sliced mushrooms (I like baby bellas)
- 1 Tbs parsley
- 1/2 cup sour cream
- 4 servings of cooked egg noodles.

Direction

- Slice meat into thin strips.
- In slow cooker, combine flour, garlic powder, pepper, and paprika. Add meat and toss till well coated. Add mushroom soup broth and onion. Stir well. Cover and cook on Low for 6-7 hours or on high for 3-4 hours.
- 1/2 hour before serving stir in mushrooms and parsley. 10 min before serving stir in sour cream and heat through.
- Serve on a bed of egg noodles.

96. Crockpot Lasagna Recipe

Serving: 10 | Prep: | Cook: 360mins | Ready in:

Ingredients

- 1 pound lean ground beef cooked and drained
- 2 jars spaghetti sauce
- 1 onion, chopped and sauteed
- 8-9 mushrooms sliced and sauteed
- 2 teaspoons minced garlic
- 1 bay leave
- 1 (12 ounce) package lasagna noodles
- 15 oz. ricotta cheese
- 1/2 cup grated parmesan cheese
- 16 ounces shredded mozzarella cheese

Direction

- First spray crockpot with pam or whatever!
- Spoon a layer of the meat mixture onto the bottom of the slow cooker.
- Add a double layer of the uncooked lasagna noodles.
- Break to fit noodles into slow cooker.
- Top noodles with a portion of the cheese mixture.

- Repeat the layering of sauce, noodles, and cheese until all the ingredients are used.
- Cover and cook on low heat in slow cooker for 6 to 8 hours.
- When I made this it took 6 hours in an older crockpot.
- Really watch the cooking time with newer crocks it might only take 3 - 4 hours, so keep a close eye on it while cooking.

97. Crockpot Macaroni Recipe

Serving: 6 | Prep: | Cook: 180mins | Ready in:

Ingredients

- 8 oz macaroni noodles, cooked and drained
- 1/2 stick butter (play with this - can be too greasy), melted
- 1 large can evaporated milk
- 1 and 1/2 cups milk
- 2 eggs, beaten
- 3 cups sharp cheddar cheese, grated
- 2 tsp. salt

Direction

- Combine in crockpot, reserving 1/2 cup cheese for top.
- Cook on low for 3 hours.
- Add reserved cheese to top when ready to eat.

98. Crockpot Minestrone Recipe

Serving: 8 | Prep: | Cook: 23mins | Ready in:

Ingredients

- 1 small onion, chopped
- 2 large carrots, peeled and thinly sliced
- 1 medium zucchini, sliced 1" thick
- 2 cloves garlic, minced
- 2 15 oz cans kidney beans, drained and rinsed

- 6 cups beef broth
- 1 28 oz can diced tomatoes, undrained
- 1 cup of V-8 juice
- 1 t dried basil leaves
- 1/8 t. thyme
- 1/2 t. dried oregano leaves
- 1/2 t. salt
- 1/4 t. crushed red pepper flakes
- 1 tbsp of honey (to mellow out the "tart" of the tomato)
- 2 cups cooked small pasta
- 1/4 cup grated parmesan cheese

Direction

- Combine all ingredients except macaroni and Parmesan cheese in the stoneware.
- Cover cook on Low 8 to 9 hours or on High 4 to 5 hours.
- Stir in macaroni.
- Serve sprinkled with cheese.
- We like to serve this hearty soup with an open face sandwich made with thick slices of crusty bread, spread with pesto, topped with mozzarella, slivers of prosciutto, a drizzle of olive oil and broiled until the cheese bubbles.

99. Curried Butternut Squash And Walnut With Angel Hair Recipe

Serving: 4 | Prep: | Cook: 25mins | Ready in:

Ingredients

- 1 pound of butternut squash
- 1 clove of garlic minced
- 1/2 cup of walnut halves
- 1/2 pound of angel hair pasta
- 1/4 cup of onion minced
- 2 tablespoons of olive oil
- 1/2 cup of white wine
- 1 tablespoon of sunflower oil
- 3 tablespoons of sea salt
- a few grinds of black pepper

- 1/2 teaspoon of cinnamon
- 1 tablespoon of curry powder
- 6 quarts of cold water
- 2 tablespoons of nutritional yeast
- 1/4 cup of fresh grated parmesan cheese

Direction

- Peal half of a small butternut squash and chop into half inch cubes
- Smash the garlic clove with the side of your knife separate the skin and mince the garlic.
- Peal and mince enough onion to make for 1/4 cup
- In a small pot place the butternut squash and cover with water
- Heat until it comes to a boil
- Boil the squash for 5 minutes only.
- In the meantime in a separate pot with 6 quarts of water bring to a boil
- Add the sea salt and add the Angel Hair
- Boil pasta for two minutes only, it will be a little on the stiff side.
- In a small pan start the sauce by adding the Olive oil and sunflower oil to the pan add the garlic and the walnuts and the spices cook for 5 minutes add the wine
- Remove the butternut squash with a slotted spoon and reserve the water
- Add the squash and a cup of the reserved water from the squash.
- Add the Angel Hair to the pan with the squash and cook for a few minutes to reduce some of the water.
- Plate the squash and pasta and top with some cheese.

---

100.   Delicious Low Fat Lasagna Recipe

Serving: 12 | Prep: | Cook: 75mins | Ready in:

Ingredients

- 1 cup onion, chopped

- 1 cup green bell pepper, chopped
- 1 1/4 lb. ground turkey
- 2 teaspoons dried Italian seasoning
- One 28 oz. can diced tomatoes
- One 15 oz. can tomato sauce
- 15 oz. cottage cheese or ricotta cheese
- 8 oz. shredded low-fat mozzarella cheese, plus 2 oz. to sprinkle on top
- One 10 oz. package chopped frozen spinach, thawed and drained
- One 24 oz. package of ready-to-bake lasagna noodles (use only 16 noodles)
- salt and pepper, to taste
- Optional: One pinch of nutmeg

Direction

- Preheat oven to 400 degrees F.
- Spray a skillet with non-stick cooking spray and heat until hot over high heat.
- Add the chopped onion and green bell pepper and cook for 3 minutes, stirring occasionally.
- Add the ground turkey and sauté until browned and cooked through, about 5 minutes. Stir frequently.
- Add the Italian seasoning, diced tomatoes (with the juice from the can) and the tomato sauce; stir to combine and bring to a boil while stirring occasionally. Remove from heat and season to taste with salt and pepper.
- In a bowl mix together cottage cheese or ricotta, 8 ounces of shredded mozzarella and chopped spinach. Stir together and season with salt and pepper. Add a pinch of nutmeg (optional).
- Spray pan with non-stick cooking spray and spread 1 cup of the sauce (from Step 5) across the bottom of pan.
- Add 4 lasagna noodles on top of the sauce. Spread 1/2 of the cottage cheese mixture (from Step 6) or ricotta mixture over the noodles
- .
- Top with 4 more lasagna noodles, spread 3 cups of the tomato sauce (from Step 5) over noodle layer.

- Repeat Step 8 and top with the remaining 4 noodles. Top with the remaining sauce and remaining mozzarella cheese.
- Place lasagna pan on a cookie sheet in the oven to prevent it from bubbling over onto the oven floor.
- Bake at 400 degrees F for 45 minutes until hot and bubbly. Let pan cool 5-10 minutes before cutting and serving.
- Storage: The lasagna can be stored in the fridge for 2 days or in the freezer for up to a week.

101.   Dinner Casserole Recipe

Serving: 8 | Prep: | Cook: 110mins |Ready in:

Ingredients

- 2 tablespoons butter
- 1 1/2 lb. ground beef
- 1 teaspoon chili powder
- 1 teaspoon salt
- 1/4 teaspoon pepper
- 1 1/2 cup uncooked elbow macaroni
- 1 16 oz. can pork & beans
- 1 16 oz. can tomatoes
- 1 10 3/4 oz. can tomato soup
- 1 large onion, chopped

Direction

- In large skillet in hot butter sauté beef with onion, chili powder, salt and pepper until beef loses red color.
- Meanwhile, cook macaroni, drain.
- Place beef mixture and macaroni in casserole, stir in beans, tomatoes and soup. Cover, refrigerate.
- Heat oven 400 degrees. Bake covered 1 hr. 10 minutes. Remove, let stand 10 minutes.

102.   Dirty Deed Meatballs Recipe

Serving: 4 | Prep: | Cook: 60mins |Ready in:

Ingredients

- 1 pound lean ground beef
- 1/2 cup quick cooking oats, uncooked
- 1/2 cup grated onions
- 1/4 cup wheat germ flakes
- 2 eggs
- 1 tsp. salt
- 2 Tbs. veg. oil
- 2 Tbs. flour
- 1 cup half and half (or heavy cream for a slight more creaminess)
- 2 Tbs. drained capers
- 2 Tbs. grated bell pepper
- egg noodles

Direction

- Combine the wheat germ, beef, onion, egg, salt, pepper, Worcestershire sauce, 3/4 cup of milk, oats, bell pepper, and shape into 36 meatballs.
- Brown the meatballs in hot oil
- Stir the flour into the drippings
- Add remaining milk and half and half
- Add salt to taste to gravy
- Add capers....and speaking of capers, start planning yours, honey!
- Cook slowly, stirring constantly, until thickened.
- Put meatballs in gravy and simmer
- Serve with or on noodles

103.   Disneys Chicken Asiago Pasta Recipe

Serving: 6 | Prep: | Cook: 20mins |Ready in:

Ingredients

- 2 quarts water
- 1/2 tsp kosher salt
- 12 oz. Dry penne rigate pasta
- 1 cup flour
- 1/4 tsp kosher salt
- 1/8 tsp freshly ground black pepper
- 1 lb. Boneless skinless chicken breast, pounded and cut into 2 inch
- strips
- 2 Tablespoon olive oil
- 3/4 cup sun-dried tomatoes cut into 1/4-inch strips
- 3/4 cup olive oil
- 1 Tablespoon minced garlic, or to taste
- 1 3/4 cup fresh baby spinach, lightly packed
- 2 cups grated asiago cheese
- 1 3/4 cups grated parmesan cheese
- kosher salt and fresh ground black pepper to taste

Direction

- Pour water into 4-quart pot. Bring to boil over medium high heat. Once water is boiling, add 1/2 teaspoon of salt. Add pasta. Stir to prevent sticking. Once water comes back to boil, lower heat until water is simmering. Cook 8-10 minutes, stirring occasionally.
- While pasta cooks, mix flour with 1/4 teaspoon of salt and 1/8 teaspoon of pepper. Dredge chicken in flour mixture.
- Heat sauté pan over medium high heat. Once pan is hot, add 2 tablespoons of olive oil. Once oil is hot (not smoking), carefully place chicken strips into the pan. Cook 2-3 minutes or until chicken is golden on bottom side. Reduce heat to medium, turn chicken strips over and continue to cook for 5 minutes.
- While chicken is cooking, mix together sun-dried tomatoes, ¾ cup olive oil, and the garlic. Add the spinach.
- Once chicken is cooked, place both the chicken and hot pasta into bowl with sun-dried tomatoes, then add cheeses and toss to mix well.

- Season to taste with salt and pepper. The heat from the chicken and pasta will melt the cheeses.

---

104. EASY HOMEMADE MACARONI AND CHEESE Recipe

Serving: 6 | Prep: | Cook: 30mins |Ready in:

Ingredients

- EASY HOMEMADE macaroni AND cheese
- 1 POUND elbow macaroni (DRY)
- 3 CUPS FINELY CHOPPED OR GRATED cheddar cheese
- 1 sm. pkg. mozzarella cheese
- 1 cup milk
- 3 eggs slightly beaten
- 1 -1/2 CUPS of bread crumbs
- salt and pepper to your taste
- cook macaroni until done. (DRAIN very well!)
- Add your cheeses, then add eggs, milk, salt and pepper.
- Mix and then put into baking pan, then put bread crumbs on top (LAST 20 MINUTES ONLY).
- Heat oven to 350 degrees. HEAT AND COOK FOR 35-40 MINUTES UNTIL GOLDEN BROWN.

Direction

- Cook macaroni until done. (DRAIN very well!)
- Add your cheeses, then add eggs, milk, salt and pepper.
- Mix and then put into baking pan, then put bread crumbs on top (LAST 20 MINUTES ONLY).
- Heat oven to 350 degrees. HEAT AND COOK FOR 30-40 MINUTES UNTIL GOLDEN BROWN.

105. Easy Cheesey Spaghetti Squares Recipe

Serving: 8 | Prep: | Cook: 40mins | Ready in:

Ingredients

- 8 ounces vermicelli
- 1 egg, lightly beaten
- 1/2 cup milk
- 1 (14-ounce) jar spaghetti sauce
- 4 ounces sliced pepperoni
- 2 cups grated mozzarella cheese
- 2 tablespoons grated parmesan cheese
- ***Kicked-Up Version***
- Saute chopped onion, mushrooms and garlic in butter and olive oil, drain and stir into sauce, along with 2 T Italian Seasoning; and add sauce as below

Direction

- Cook pasta according to package directions, drain and place in a large mixing bowl.
- In a small bowl, combine egg and milk.
- Pour over pasta and mix well.
- Coat a 9-by-13-inch pan with non-stick vegetable spray.
- Pour pasta mixture into pan.
- Cover pasta with spaghetti sauce.
- Layer pepperoni over sauce and top with mozzarella and Parmesan cheeses.
- Bake in a preheated 350-degree oven for 25-30 minutes or until golden brown.
- Remove from oven and cool on wire rack for 10 minutes.
- Cut into squares to serve.

106. Easy Chicken And Noodles Recipe

Serving: 8 | Prep: | Cook: 30mins | Ready in:

Ingredients

- 1 large can (49-1/2oz) chicken broth, (if I've poached some chicken I use the reserved broth from that.)
- 2-3 cups water(enough liquid to boil noodles in.)
- 1 (16oz) bag Mrs. Reams Homestyle egg noodles (found in the freezer section)
- 1 to 1-1/2 Cups cooked chicken, shredded or chunked. Use any left over chicken you have poached or canned.
- salt/pepper
- 3 Tbsp. butter

Direction

- In a large pot with the broth & additional water, cook the noodles according to package directions.
- While noodles are cooking, shred or cube the chicken.
- When noodles are done add the chicken, salt, pepper and butter.
- Heat through and serve over mashed potatoes or biscuits.
- The first night it will be more soup like, but kept in the fridge overnight, it thickens up a lot. If my husband wants it thicker the first night, he'll add some cornstarch to make it thicker.

107. Easy Chicken Chow Mein Recipe

Serving: 4 | Prep: | Cook: 20mins | Ready in:

Ingredients

- 1 package fresh celery , sliced
- 1 tablespoon olive oil or vegetable oil
- 1 cup bean sprouts (optional)
- 1 (4 ounce) can mushroom pieces, drained
- 1 (7 ounce) can sliced water chestnuts, drained
- 2 cups cut up cooked chicken
- 3 tablespoons cornstarch

- 1/4 cup water
- 1 (10 ounce) can condensed chicken broth
- 1/4 cup soy sauce
- hot cooked rice
- chow mein noodles

Direction

- In a large pot, sauté celery in oil for approx. 5 minutes or until crisp-tender.
- Add bean sprouts (if using), mushrooms, water chestnuts, and chicken.
- In a large bowl, blend cornstarch with water.
- When smooth, add chicken broth and soy sauce to bowl.
- Mix well and pour over meat and vegetables.
- Bring to a boil, stirring until sauce thickens.
- Reduce heat to low.
- Cover and simmer 10 to 15 minutes.
- Serve over hot, cooked rice and chow mein noodles.

108. Easy Country Ground Beef And Corn Casserole Recipe

Serving: 6 | Prep: | Cook: 30mins | Ready in:

Ingredients

- Easy Country ground beef And corn Casserole
- 1 1/2 pounds of lean ground beef
- 1 cup of chopped onion
- 1 - 12 ounce can of whole kernel corn, drained
- 1 can of cream of chicken soup
- 1 can of cream of mushroom soup
- 1 cup of sour cream
- 1 small can tomato sauce
- 1/4 cup of chopped pimiento
- 3/4 teaspoon of salt
- 1/4 teaspoon of black pepper
- 3 cups of noodles, cooked and drained
- 3 tablespoons of butter, melted
- 1 cup of soft breadcrumbs

Direction

- _____
- Brown the ground beef; add the onion and cook until tender, but not brown. Add the corn, soup, tomato sauce, sour cream, pimiento, salt, and pepper. Mix well; then stir in the cooked noodles. Taste and add more seasoning if needed. Pour into a 2-1/2 quart casserole dish. Add the melted butter to the breadcrumbs and sprinkle over top of the casserole. Bake at 350 degrees for 30 minutes or until hot & bubbly.
- _____

109. Easy Homemade Ravioli Recipe

Serving: 4 | Prep: | Cook: 15mins | Ready in:

Ingredients

- 9 oz. ground round
- 3/4 lb. soft-style cream cheese
- 30 wonton wrappers
- 2-1/4 cups prepared spaghetti sauce
- 1 egg

Direction

- In a bowl stir together ground round and cream cheese.
- Place a spoonful of filling in the center of each wrapper.
- Brush wrapper edges with water or a beaten egg.
- Fold corner to corner to form triangle shape and press edges together firmly.
- Let lay for about 5 minutes to make sure they seal.
- Drop into boiling water and cook for 3-5 minutes or until meat is done.
- Heat sauce in a separate saucepan.
- Top ravioli with sauce.

- Try stuffing with minced pepperoni and cheeses... Yummy
- Enjoy!

110. Easy Mexican Casserole Recipe

Serving: 6 | Prep: | Cook: 30mins | Ready in:

Ingredients

- 1 1/2 lbs lean ground beef
- 1 lg onion,chopped
- 1 pkg taco seasoning *
- 4-8 oz water
- 1 tin (any size) kidney beans,drained and rinsed with cold water
- 1 cup frozen corn kernels
- 1 sweet red pepper, chopped (optnl)
- 1 4oz tin chopped green chillies (optnl)
- 1 box mac 'n cheese (white cheddar or regular)
- (or cook about 2c of your own macaroni and add cheese sauce)
- 1 cup (or more) salsa(or 1 tin rotel tomato and chillies)
- 1-2 cups Tex-Mex cheese blend
- sliced jalapeno peppers (optnl)
- sliced olives (optnl)

Direction

- Prepare Mac' n Cheese according to package directions
- Meanwhile in large frying pan, over medium high heat, brown ground beef with onion, draining fat as you go.
- Add taco seasoning and incorporate well before adding enough water to just make it saucy.
- Turn heat down to medium and add kidney beans, corn, and pepper and chillies if using. Stir well to combine, and simmer for a few minutes.
- Preheat oven to 350F

- Place beef mixture in large casserole dish and top with mac 'n cheese.
- Spoon salsa over noodles and top with grated cheese blend.
- Top with sliced jalapenos and olives, if desired
- Bake at 350F for 30 min until heated through and cheese is bubbly and golden.
- *I buy taco seasoning in a large tub at Costco and just use 2-3 heaping spoonfuls instead of a package of seasoning

111. Easy Pasta Salad Recipe

Serving: 4 | Prep: | Cook: 20mins | Ready in:

Ingredients

- 1 pound pasta - shape of your choice
- 1 or 2 carrots, peeled and diced
- 1 small cucumber, cut into bite-sized pieces
- 1 red pepper, cut into dice
- 1 - 2 cups cut up meat, poultry, or fish (salmon has body and works well)
- 1 large tomato, cut up OR a cup of split cherry tomatoes
- Any additional vegetables you like
- 1 cup frozen peas
- 1 envelope Good Seasons Italian dressing, mixed with vinegar and good olive oil
- Grated parmesan cheese to add on top

Direction

- Bring water to a boil and toss in the pasta to cook for the directed time. While you're boiling the water and the pasta cut up all of your vegetables and the protein and mix the dressing. When the pasta is done cooking pour the frozen peas into your colander and then pour the pasta and its water over the peas. The boiling water will defrost them but leave the peas with body. Mix this in with the other vegetables and cut up protein. Pour the prepared dressing over this to taste, some like it wetter than others. Pass the parmesan to top.

112.   Easy Seafood Pasta Fra Diavolo Recipe

Serving: 6 | Prep: | Cook: 15mins | Ready in:

Ingredients

- 1 (26 ounce) jar marinara sauce
- 1 (8 ounce) bottle clam juice
- 1/3 cup Frank's red hot sauce (or Frank's Xtra Red Hot)
- 1/4 cup tomato paste
- 1 pound large shrimp, shelled and deveined
- 1 pound scallops, halved if large
- Hot, cooked pasta

Direction

- Combine marinara sauce, clam juice, hot sauce and tomato paste in large saucepan.
- Heat to boiling and simmer 5 minutes until slightly thickened.
- Stir in shrimp and scallops. Cook about 5 minutes until seafood is cooked through.
- Serve over cooked pasta.

113.   Easy Sour Cream Paprika Chicken Recipe

Serving: 4 | Prep: | Cook: 30mins | Ready in:

Ingredients

- 4 skinless, boneless chicken breast halves
- Splash of fresh lemon juice
- 1 1/2 tablespoons vegetable oil
- 1/2 cup white onion, chopped
- 1/2 cup shallots, chopped
- 1 Tbs minced garlic
- 1 1/2 tablespoons butter
- 1 heaping Tbs Hungarian sweet paprika (must!)
- 1/2 teaspoon salt
- 1/2 tsp black pepper
- 1 cup chicken stock
- 1/4 Cup white wine
- 1 teaspoon all-purpose flour
- 1 (8 ounce) container sour cream (use Good Stuff)
- fresh parsley, chopped
- egg noodles or white rice

Direction

- You can leave breasts whole or cut them up, whatever your preference. In a large skillet, heat oil over medium-high heat. Add chicken and pan-fry until cooked through and juices run clear, about 10 minutes. Remove chicken from skillet and set aside.
- Using the same skillet, cook onion, shallots and garlic in butter until translucent but not brown, about 5 to 8 minutes. Season with paprika pepper and salt. Pour chicken stock, lemon juice and wine into the pan, and bring all to a boil. Reduce heat to simmer; mix flour with sour cream until smooth, then whisk into chicken stock. Place chicken in skillet; simmer until chicken is heated through and sauce has thickened.
- Serve over noodles or rice and garnish with fresh parsley

114.   Easy Tomato Garlic Pasta Recipe

Serving: 3 | Prep: | Cook: 10mins | Ready in:

Ingredients

- 3 tablespoons olive oil plus more for boiling pasta
- 6 cloves garlic more or less to taste; minced or pressed

- 1 can (14.5 oz) diced tomatoes with italian seasoning
- 6 ounces Dry spaghetti
- salt and pepper to taste
- asiago cheese or parmesan cheese (optional)

Direction

- Boil salted water for pasta (add a little oil to the water).
- Heat 3 tbsp. olive oil over medium heat, and add the garlic. Heat for about 1 minute, and then add the tomatoes. Heat over medium-low heat while the pasta cooks.
- Once the pasta is done, drain, and toss with tomato mixture.
- Garnish with Asiago or Parmesan cheese, and serve with a crusty bread and a salad.

115. Egg Noodles Recipe

Serving: 4 | Prep: | Cook: 60mins | Ready in:

Ingredients

- 2 - 2 1/2 c. flour
- 3/4 t. salt
- 3 eggs plus 1 egg yolk

Direction

- Mix 2 c. of the flour and salt and make a well in the center. Add eggs and yolk to the well, and mix in with your fingers or a wooden spoon from the inside out, until the dough holds together and cleans the bowl; add additional flour as needed.
- Knead the dough at least 10 minutes, until smooth and resilient. Cover with a towel and let rest for 30 minutes. Cut dough into fourths, then with each fourth at a time, flatten it, and then roll it out 1/8-inch thick. Cut into noodles (for kluski, cut into 1/8-inch strips), toss to separate, and spread out on the counter to dry about 30 minutes.

116. Eggplant Parmesan Recipe

Serving: 4 | Prep: | Cook: 30mins | Ready in:

Ingredients

- 1 large eggplant
- olive oil
- asiago cheese
- parmesan cheese
- mozzarella cheese
- bread crumbs
- 2 eggs
- pasta sauce
- garlic powder

Direction

- Wash, peel and slice eggplant into 1/2 to 3/4 inch thick round slices.
- Beat an egg in a small bowl.
- Baste eggplant slice in beaten egg. Make sure both sides are coated.
- In a bowl (I usually use a cereal bowl...otherwise you'll end up with leftover bread and cheese mix), mix 2 parts bread crumbs to 1 part parmesan cheese. Add a pinch of garlic powder (to taste). Blend together with a fork.
- Dip egg basted eggplant slice into bread crumb mix bowl. Again, make sure both sides get coated.
- Brown basted slices in olive oil, in a skillet over medium heat on your stove.
- This might take a few rotations through the skillet depending on how many slices you prepared.
- Bake browned eggplant at 350 degrees for 30 min in a pan layered as follows:
- Sauce (to cover bottom of pan)
- Eggplant
- Asiago cheese
- Mozzarella cheese
- REPEAT (until you run out of eggplant!)

- I always end with a layer of mozzarella. Cover pan with tinfoil for first 20 min of cooking. Remove foil for last 10 min to slightly brown and crisp up the top layer of cheese.
- Enjoy!

117. Emerils Lasagna Recipe

Serving: 12 | Prep: | Cook: 165mins | Ready in:

Ingredients

- 2 cups fresh ricotta
- 8 ounces grated Provolone
- 8 ounces grated Mozzarella
- 8 ounces grated Romano
- 1 egg
- 1/4 cup milk
- 1 tablespoon chiffonade of fresh basil
- 1 tablespoon chopped garlic
- salt
- Freshly ground black pepper
- 1 recipe of Emeril's Meat Sauce, recipe follows
- 1/2 pound grated parmigiano-reggiano cheese
- 1 package of dried lasagna noodles
- ****
- Emerils Meat Sauce:
- 2 tablespoons olive oil
- 1/3 pound ground beef
- 1/3 pound ground veal
- 1/3 pound ground pork
- salt
- Freshly ground black pepper
- 2 cups finely chopped onions
- 1/2 cup finely chopped celery
- 1/2 cup finely chopped carrot
- 2 tablespoons chopped garlic
- 2 (28-ounce) can of peeled, seeded and chopped tomatoes
- 1 small can tomato paste
- 4 cups beef stock or water
- 2 sprigs of fresh thyme
- 2 bay leaves
- 2 teaspoons dried oregano
- 2 teaspoons dried basil
- Pinch of crushed red pepper
- 2 ounces parmigiano-Reggiano

Direction

- Preheat the oven to 350 degrees F.
- In a mixing bowl, combine the ricotta, Provolone, Mozzarella, Romano, egg, milk, basil and garlic. Mix well.
- Season with salt and pepper.
- To assemble, spread 2 1/2 cups of the meat sauce on the bottom of a deep dish lasagna pan.
- Sprinkle 1/4 of the grated cheese over the sauce. Cover the cheese with 1/4 of the dried noodles. Spread a 1/4 of the cheese filling evenly over the noodles.
- Repeat the above process with the remaining ingredients, topping the lasagna with the remaining sauce.
- Place in the oven and bake until bubbly and golden, about 45 minutes to 1 hour.
- Remove from the oven and cool for 10 minutes before serving. Slice and serve. Sprinkle with some fresh basil chiffonade, if desire.
- Makes 12-16 servings.
- ****
- Instructions for Meat Sauce:
- In a large nonreactive saucepan, over medium heat, add the oil.
- In a mixing bowl, combine the meat. Season with salt and pepper and mix well.
- When the oil is hot, add the meat and brown for 4 to 6 minutes.
- Add the onions, celery, and carrots. Season with salt and pepper. Cook for 4 to 5 minutes or until the vegetables are soft.
- Add the garlic and tomatoes. Season with salt and pepper. Continue to cook for 2 to 3 minutes.
- Whisk the tomato paste with the stock and add to the tomatoes. Add the thyme, bay leaves, oregano, basil and red pepper. Mix well.

- Bring the liquid to a boil, reduce the heat to medium and simmer for about 2 hours. Stir occasionally and add more liquid if needed.
- During the last 30 minutes or cooking, reseason with salt and pepper and stir in the cheese.
- Remove from the heat and let sit for 15 minutes before serving.
- Yield: 1 1/2 to 2 quarts

118. Enchilada Lasagna Recipe

Serving: 9 | Prep: | Cook: 75mins | Ready in:

Ingredients

- 3 1/2 lbs ground beef
- 2 small to medium onions, chopped
- 3 (.75-1.5oz)pkg taco seasonings
- 1 1/2 cup water
- 1 (16oz) can fat-free refried beans
- 1 cup dairy sour cream
- 24 corn tortillas
- 1 (28oz) can enchilada sauce, divided
- 3-4oz sliced black olives, divided
- 5 cups mexican blend shredded cheese, divided(3-1 1/3 cups for layers & 1 cup for top of dish)

Direction

- In a large pan, brown ground beef & onions; drain. Return to pan, add taco seasonings & water, bring to a boil and then simmer for 8-10 minutes. Stirring occasionally.
- Pre-heat oven to 375 degrees. In the meantime, mix refried beans and sour cream, set aside.
- In a large deep 11x13 lasagna pan, spray with a non-stick cooking spray. Spread 1/2 cup of enchilada sauce on to bottom of pan.
- In a shallow medium size bowl, pour 1/2 a can of enchilada sauce. This will be used to dip and coat both sides of corn tortillas, using 6 tortillas per layer.

- Assemble & coat 6 corn tortillas, line on the bottom of pan, they will overlap. On top of 1st layer of tortillas, using a slotted spoon, spoon 1/2 of meat mixture evenly, sprinkle with 1 1/3 cups of cheese. Repeat a layer of 6 enchilada coated tortillas. 2nd layer, spread out refried bean mixture evenly, top with 1/2 of black olives, sprinkle 1 1/3 cup of cheese. Repeat with a layer of 6 enchilada coated tortillas. 3rd layer, top with 2nd 1/2 of meat mixture, discard taco sauce used for meat mixture, it's not needed. Sprinkle with 1 1/3 cups of cheese. Repeat with the last 6 enchilada coated tortillas. Spread 2nd 1/2 of canned enchilada sauce over dish and top with remaining cheese and black olives.
- Cover loosely with foil & baked in pre-heated 375 degree oven for 40 minutes. Remove foil and continue baking for 10 minutes or until cheese is melted & lightly golden brown.

119. Family Egg Noodles Recipe

Serving: 6 | Prep: | Cook: 10mins | Ready in:

Ingredients

- 1 egg + 3 egg yolks
- 3 Tbsp. Cold water
- 2 cups flour
- 1/2 Teaspoon salt
- fresh parsley
- chicken broth

Direction

- In a mixing bowl, beat egg and yolks until light and fluffy. Add water and salt; mix well. Stir in flour. Turn onto a floured surface; knead until smooth. (It will get a tad sticky.)
- Then roll out with rolling pin, then roll into 3 cylinder shapes and slice with sharp knife to desired thickness.

- Pick up noodles and shake, so they won't be stuck together.
- Cook for 7-10 minutes over medium heat.
- Cook in quite a bit of chicken broth. Try to drop noodles in while shaking them apart.
- Drain; sprinkle with parsley if desired.
- Serve with butter, garlic & herbs or favorite sauce.

120. Farfalle With Smoked Salmon And Lemon Sauce Recipe

Serving: 6 | Prep: | Cook: 15mins | Ready in:

Ingredients

- 1/2 c. canola oil
- 6 cloves garlic, finely chopped
- 1/2 c. chopped onion
- 1 lb. farfalle pasta (bow tie)
- 3 TB fresh lemon juice
- 1/2 c. chopped scallions
- 1/4 c. chopped Italian parsley
- 1/2 lb. sliced smoked salmon
- salt and pepper
- Thin sliced lemons

Direction

- Heat canola oil in a skillet over low heat.
- Add the garlic and onion; cook until soft; set aside.
- Cook farfalle according to package directions and drain well.
- Put the pasta back into the pot it was cooked in.
- Add the garlic and onion mixture and mix well.
- Add lemon juice, scallions, parsley and salmon and mix well again.
- Season to taste with salt and pepper.
- Garnish with a sprig of parsley and thin lemon slices.

121. Farmhouse Macaroni And Cheese In The Crock Pot Recipe

Serving: 8 | Prep: | Cook: 480mins | Ready in:

Ingredients

- 3 cups cooked elbow macaroni rinsed and drained
- 2 tablespoons bacon bits
- 1/4 cup chopped red onion
- 1 can stewed tomatoes undrained
- 1-1/2 cups shredded sharp cheddar cheese
- 1 can cream of mushroom soup

Direction

- In a slow cooker combine macaroni, bacon bits, onion, undrained stewed tomatoes and Cheddar cheese.
- Pour mushroom soup over top.
- Mix well to combine.
- Cover and cook on low 8 hours.
- Mix well before serving.

122. Fennel And Kale Pasta Recipe

Serving: 2 | Prep: | Cook: 20mins | Ready in:

Ingredients

- fennel bulb sliced thinly-stalks saved for stock, fronds chopped and reserved
- ---------------------------
- one onion. in thin half moons
- bunch of kale, parboiled, stems removed
- olive oil
- salt
- pepper

- wee bit red pepper flakes
- cup of water or chicken broth
- balsamic vinegar
- 1/4 cup parmesan, finely grated
- 1 pound spaghetti, boiled al dente while making sauce, so it is all done at the same time

Direction

- Cook fennel and onion in the olive oil slowly, until tender and beginning to brown.
- Add kale and cook about 5 minutes, sprinkling with salt, pepper and pepper flakes.
- Add cup of the hot pasta water or chicken broth, the balsamic vinegar to taste, and stir in the cheese.
- Drain pasta, add to sauce and mix.
- Sprinkle with fennel fronds, and serve, with additional cheese if you wish, and extra grind pepper.

123. Fettuccine Lasagna Recipe

Serving: 10 | Prep: | Cook: 60mins | Ready in:

Ingredients

- 1 lb. of ground beef
- 3 tbsp. of sliced black olives
- 1/4 cup of beef broth
- 1 can of cream of mushroom soup
- 12 oz. of uncooked fettuccine pasta
- 2 tspn. of oregano
- 1-4 oz. can of sliced mushrooms
- 1 cup of diced red bell pepper
- 1 cup of mozzarella cheese shredded
- 1 tbspn. of butter
- 1/4 cup of parmesan cheese shredded
- 1 cup onion diced
- 1 large can of diced tomatoes
- 1 cup of cheddar cheese shredded

Direction

- In a large pot of boiling water cook pasta for 8 to 10 minutes, or until done; then drain.
- Brown the beef in a large skillet on medium heat. When done, drain the fat from the pan. Place the meat into a bowl. In the skillet, cook the bell pepper and onion in butter until it is tender. Add the mushrooms, beef, tomatoes, olives, and the oregano. Cook on low for approximately 10 minutes.
- Preheat oven to 350. Grease a 9x13 inch baking dish.
- Place half of the fettuccine in the baking dish and top with half of the veggie and beef mixture. Then sprinkle with 1/2 of the cheddar and 1/2 of the mozzarella on top of that. Repeat in layers. Mix the beef broth and soup until it is smooth, then pour it over the casserole. Sprinkle the top with the parmesan cheese.
- Bake in the oven for approximately 30 to 35 minutes, or until it is heated throughout.

124. Fideo Authentic Mexican Pasta Recipe

Serving: 4 | Prep: | Cook: 45mins | Ready in:

Ingredients

- 2 6 oz.bags of Coil Fideo pasta (broken up)
- 4 tbsp. olive oil
- 1 coarsely chopped medium size onion
- 2 bay leaves
- 1 can (15 oz.) Mexican spiced sliced stewed tomatos
- 1 can (15 oz.) low sodium chicken broth
- 1 pinch dried oregano
- 2 pinches chili flakes
- salt and pepper to taste
- (this pasta is good topped with parmesan or grated cheddar cheese)

Direction

- Heat a large sauté pan on high heat adding the olive oil
- Add the chopped onion
- Grab a coil of fideo pasta while holding over sauté pan squeeze to break up and let fall in to the pan do the same to the rest
- Sauté pasta-stirring on high till nice and toasty and begins to change color like you would toast a nice rice pilaf.
- Carefully add canned tomatoes, chicken broth, then the bay leafs, oregano, chili flakes,
- Turn heat down to a simmer stirring occasionally cook pasta till Al dente (do not overcook the pasta) add salt and pepper ....enjoy

---

125.   Filipino Pancit Bihon Recipe

Serving: 4 | Prep: | Cook: 20mins |Ready in:

Ingredients

- 1 boneless skinless chicken breast, cut into thin strips
- 1/2 lb. cooked shrimp (optional)
- 1 lb. Bihon noodles or thin rice noodles, soak in water for 10 minutes.
- 2 cups of chicken broth
- 4 garlic cloves, minced
- 3 shallots, minced
- 1/2 med. Napa or Chinese cabbage, sliced fine
- 1 small pkg of matchstick carrots
- 1 c. green beans, cut diagonally Like French cut green beans
- 1/4 c. vegetable oil
- 4 tbsp. soy sauce
- salt and pepper to taste

Direction

- Heat oil in a large skillet. Sauté garlic and shallots until soft.

- Add the chicken breast, salt, pepper & soy sauce. Sauté for a few minutes to lightly brown chicken.
- Add carrots, green beans & shrimp if using. Cover and cook for a few minutes then add Napa cabbage and chicken broth until it comes to a boil.
- Once the vegetables are all done, add the bihon noodles mixing well to distribute the flavors.
- Cook for about 5 more minutes or until the noodles are soft. Taste and adjust seasonings to desired taste.

---

126.   Finally A Sauce Recipe

Serving: 8 | Prep: | Cook: 60mins |Ready in:

Ingredients

- 3 Large garlic cloves-chopped as fine as possible
- olive oil
- 1 1/2 pounds of lean ground beef
- fresh mushrooms (optional)
- 1 Large onion
- oregano
- basil
- salt
- pepper
- 2 6 oz cans of tomato paste
- 16 oz can of diced tomatoes-I like double the tomatoes so use 32 oz can
- fresh parsley
- cajun seasoning
- garlic powder
- 2 28 oz cans of crushed tomatoes
- 1/3 cup of red wine (optional)
- 1 Teaspoon of sugar
- 1 Bay leaf
- spaghetti-cooked as directed by package (be sure to salt the water when boiling your noodles)

Direction

- Brown ground beef till beef is crumbly-drain and set aside.
- In large saucepan just cover bottom with olive oil.
- Place your garlic in your oil-let soak while you dice up your onion-do not heat yet!
- Place diced onion aside-heat the oil and garlic over medium heat-heat until you see bubbles around the garlic!
- When you see the bubbles around the garlic add your diced onion-lower heat to med-low.
- Simmer all of this for about 5 minutes-at this time add 1 tsp. of Oregano, 1/2 tsp. of basil-dash of salt and pepper.
- Add you two cans of tomato paste-fill up cans with water and to clean outside of can add to your onion and garlic in pot...mix up well-simmer for about 4 minutes, add now 1/2 tsp. of oregano (you will be adding this all the way through) touch of salt and pepper again.
- After 4 minutes add your beef into your roux for your spaghetti sauce.
- Add your diced tomatoes-simmer for about 10 minutes-add 1 tsp. of oregano, 1/2 tsp. of basil, 1 1/2 tsp. of fresh chopped parsley, a dash of Cajun seasoning and 1/2 tsp. of garlic pepper and throw in some black pepper.
- Keep stirring sauce-occasionally.
- Now add your 2 28 oz. can of crushed tomatoes along with 1 tsp. of parsley, 3 dashes of basil, 3 dashes of garlic powder-stir together well-keep at medium heat.
- Add your teaspoon of sugar and bay leaf at this point-mix well again.
- Cover and simmer for about 30 minutes-if you wish you may add your 1/3 cup of red wine at this point.
- I have found the longer this sauce simmers the better it tastes! Before serving remove your bay leaf. Serve over hot spaghetti!

127. Four Cheese Macaroni Recipe

Serving: 6 | Prep: | Cook: 35mins | Ready in:

Ingredients

- 1 (16 ounce) package elbow macaroni
- 9 tablespoons butter (The original recipe calls for 9 tbsp. - I like to use 8 tablespoons of unsalted butter - or one stick. You probably could get by with even less if you are so inclined...)
- 1/2 cup shredded muenster cheese
- 1/2 cup shredded cheddar cheese
- 1/2 cup shredded sharp cheddar cheese
- 1/2 cup shredded monterey jack cheese
- (Feel free to up the cheese quotient. And invite me for dinner!)
- 1 1/2 cups half-and-half
- 8 ounces cubed processed cheese food (Don't be a Velveeta snob like I was - this makes the sauce so darn cheesy/creamy. If you want to remain a V-snob, then go for cream cheese, but it won't be the same. But hey, it's your thang - do what you wanna do. Heh.)
- 2 eggs, beaten
- 1/4 teaspoon salt
- 1/2 tsp. of dry mustard
- 1/8 teaspoon ground black pepper
- ****
- Optional Additions: (any combination)
- ground meat, browned (turkey, chicken, beef, pork)
- breakfast sausage such as Jimmy Dean regular or hot (browned and drained - 1 lb.)
- Keilbasa or Andouille (cut into chunks and browned in a wee bit of olive oil)
- Fresh chorizo, casing removed, browned and broken up
- 1 small onion, diced and sauteed until translucent
- jalapeno peppers, seeded and chopped (for a milder taste, use Poblano, or go crazy and use serranos or a habanero)
- Crushed red pepper flake to taste
- 3/4 c. of roasted red pepper, chopped

- I have even added:
- 1 can of artichoke hearts, drained and loosely chopped
- ~~~~
- CHEESY NOTE: Another great cheese combo and one of my favorite spins is using shredded Asiago, Provolone, Mozzarella and a Sharp Cheddar. Delish!
- Or use a pepper jack cheese in the mix. Or a smoked cheddar. I adore cheese and it all works for me and makes this recipe wonderful, comforting and lusciously decadent.

Direction

- Bring a large pot of lightly salted water to a boil. Add pasta and cook for 8 to 10 minutes or until al dente; drain well and return to cooking pot.
- In a small saucepan over medium heat, melt 8 tablespoons butter; stir into the macaroni.
- In a large bowl, combine the Muenster cheese, mild and sharp Cheddar cheeses, and Monterey Jack cheese; mix well.
- Preheat oven to 350 degrees F (175 degrees C).
- Add the half and half, 1 1/2 cups of cheese mixture, cubed processed cheese food, dry mustard and eggs to macaroni; mix together and season with salt and pepper.
- Transfer to a lightly greased deep 2 1/2 quart casserole dish. Sprinkle with the remaining 1/2 cup of cheese mixture and 1 tablespoon of butter.
- Bake in preheated oven for 35 minutes or until hot and bubbling around the edges.
- Serve and enjoy!

128. Frittata With Chard And Whole Wheat Spaghetti Recipe

Serving: 5 | Prep: | Cook: 13mins | Ready in:

Ingredients

- 1 lb. swiss chard, trimmed ans coarsely chopped
- 5 eggs
- 1/3 cup milk
- 3 Tbsp. grated parmesan cheese
- 1/8 tsp. ground nutmeg
- 1/4 tsp. salt
- 1/4 tsp. black pepper
- 2 cups cooked whole wheat spaghetti
- 1 Tbsp. butter
- 1 cup shredded provolone or mozzarella cheese

Direction

- Wash chard really well and place in a large pot with water clinging to leaves.
- Cover and cook until tender about 10 minutes. Drain thoroughly.
- When cool enough to handle, squeeze out excess water.
- Combine eggs, milk, Parmesan, nutmeg, salt and pepper. Stir in spaghetti and chard.
- Melt butter in a large ovenproof skillet. Add egg mixture, cover and cook over low heat until top is almost set 10 to 13 minutes.
- Preheat the broiler. Sprinkle frittata with provolone cheese and broil 3 minutes or until golden brown.

129. GROUND BEEF CHEESY NOODLE CASSEROLE Recipe

Serving: 6 | Prep: | Cook: 20mins | Ready in:

Ingredients

- 1 pound ground beef
- 2 cloves garlic, minced
- 1 teaspoon salt
- Dash of pepper
- ½ teaspoon sugar
- 2 (8 ounce) can tomato sauce *

- 6 ounces of egg noodles
- 1 (4 ounce) cream cheese, softened
- 6 green onions, chopped
- 1 cup sour cream
- cheddar cheese, shredded

Direction

- Preheat oven to 350 degrees. Brown beef; drain fat. Add next 5 ingredients and simmer. Cook noodles; drain. Mix cream cheese with green onions and sour cream in a small bowl. Add cheese mixture to hot, drained noodles and mix well. In a 9 inch pan, alternate layers of sauce and noodles. Top with shredded cheese. Bake uncovered for 20 minutes.
- *I use the tomato sauce that has basil, oregano & garlic

130.   Garlic Salmon Linguine

Serving: 4 | Prep: | Cook: 20mins | Ready in:

Ingredients

- 1 package (16 ounces) linguine
- 1/3 cup olive oil
- 3 garlic cloves, minced
- 1 can (14-3/4 ounces) salmon, drained, bones and skin removed
- 3/4 cup chicken broth
- 1/4 cup minced fresh parsley
- 1/2 teaspoon salt
- 1/8 teaspoon cayenne pepper

Direction

- Cook linguine according to package directions; drain.
- Meanwhile, in a large skillet, heat oil over medium heat. Add garlic; cook and stir 1 minute. Stir in remaining ingredients; heat through. Add linguine; toss gently to combine.
- Nutrition Facts

- 1 serving: 489 calories, 19g fat (3g saturated fat), 31mg cholesterol, 693mg sodium, 56g carbohydrate (3g sugars, 3g fiber), 25g protein.

131.   Garlic Shrimp Pasta Recipe

Serving: 4 | Prep: | Cook: 10mins | Ready in:

Ingredients

- 1 Pound spaghetti (or linguine)
- 1 Pound medium shrimp, Cleaned And Deveined, And Coarsely Chopped
- 1/4 Cup olive oil
- 1/2 Cup butter
- 1 Cup white wine
- 3 cloves garlic, Finely Chopped
- 1/4 Cup parsley
- salt & pepper
- red pepper flakes

Direction

- Put the pasta on to cook.
- While the pasta is cooking, heat the oil in a large skillet.
- Add the shrimp, garlic, salt and pepper and red pepper flakes to taste.
- After a minute or two, as soon as the shrimp are pink and opaque, remove them from the pan.
- Add butter and wine in the skillet and turn the heat up to medium high.
- Cook until it has reduced by half.
- Drain the pasta, reserving a small cup of pasta water.
- Return the shrimp to the skillet and cook until heated through.
- Add the parsley and mix.
- Add the pasta, and cook another minute or two over high heat.
- If it seems dry, add a little of the reserved pasta water.

- Serve piping hot, garnishing with additional fresh parsley if desired.

132.   Georges Grilled Chicken Macaroni Salad Recipe

Serving: 20 | Prep: | Cook: | Ready in:

Ingredients

- 6 LARGE GRILLED chicken breast fillets OR 10 SMALL (CUT INTO BITE SIZE PIECES)
- 3 BOXES OF elbow macaroni
- 1 PURPLE OR yellow onion(DICED FINELY)
- 1 BUNCH green onions (CHOPPED)
- 1 YELLOW OR red bell pepper(FINELY DICED)
- 1 green bell pepper FINELY DICED
- 5-6 LARGE eggs (BOILED) EACH EGG NEEDS TO BE CUT INTO FOURTHS OR YOU CAN DICE THE EGG INTO SMALLER PIECES
- 2 CUPS OF SHREDDED cheese (YOUR CHOICE) WE USE VELEVETTA
- 2 tomatoes (CHOPPED)
- 2 CUPS celery (FINELY CHOPPED)
- 1 JAR OF HELLMAN'S OR KRAFT MAYONAISE
- seasoning (I USE NATURES seasoning, YOU CAN USE TONY'S, SLAP YA MAMA, ETC.. YOUR CHOICE)
- parsley
- black pepper (TO TASTE)

Direction

- CHOP AND DICE ALL YOUR VEGETABLES
- GRILL THE CHICKEN BREAST
- BOIL THE ELBOW MACARONI
- COMBINE ALL INGREDIENTS TOGETHER
- SERVE
- REFRIGERATE LEFTOVERS

133.   Goulash I Grew Up With Recipe

Serving: 6 | Prep: | Cook: 60mins | Ready in:

Ingredients

- 1 pound cooked ground beef
- 1/2 onion - chopped
- 1/2 green bell pepper - chopped
- 1 T canola oil (or butter)
- 3 cups water
- 3 beef boullion cubes
- 2 14.5 oz cans diced tomatoes
- 2 4 oz. cans tomato sauce
- 1 teas garlic powder
- 1 teas chili powder
- 1 1/2 teas cumin
- 1/4 teas salt (more to taste)
- 1/4 teas pepper
- 2 cups large elbow macaroni

Direction

- Brown ground beef - then drain and rinse
- In a large pot cook onion and green pepper in oil till softened
- Add all ingredients to the pot except macaroni and bring to a boil over medium heat
- Stir in the macaroni and reduce the heat to simmer. Let simmer until the macaroni is done, stirring occasionally to make sure macaroni doesn't stick.
- Great with crusty bread.
- Feel free to adjust the spices as you like, of course!

134.   Gourmet White Cheddar Macaroni And Cheese Recipe

Serving: 6 | Prep: | Cook: 30mins | Ready in:

Ingredients

- 3/4 box elbow macaroni noodles

- 2 T butter
- 2 T flour
- 1/2 cup fresh cut chives
- chili powder (dash)
- salt
- pepper
- either dried mustard or a little Dijon mustard
- 1 1/2 cup whole milk
- 1 cup of shredded white cheddar cheese (use the best stuff you can find, like Tillamook, to make this really decadent)
- 1/2 cup sour cream
- 1/4 cup plain bread crumbs

Direction

- Preheat oven to 375 and butter a 9x9 glass dish.
- Boil the elbow pasta and drain.
- In a large saucepan, melt the butter. When it is just hot (NOT BROWN!) add the chives and sauté for 2 minutes.
- Add the flour/chili powder/mustard/salt/pepper and mix well, getting out all the lumps and stir for 3 minutes. (Just a dash of all of those seasonings.)
- SLOWLY add the first 1/2 cup milk, mixing like crazy until it's smooth and NO lumps. When it's a nice glossy uniform sauce, add another 1/2 cup milk, repeat. Add the rest of the milk and mix well so it's not lumpy.
- Stir constantly for 10 minutes or so, until the mixture is smooth and reduced. Remove from heat, add most of the cheese, and mix well.
- Add the sour cream, mix well.
- Pour into dish, cover with remaining cheese and bread crumbs.
- Cook for 30 minutes until it's brown and bubbling and looks like the yummiest thing you've ever laid eyes on. Let it sit 5 minutes before serving...if you can stand it!
- This recipe can easily be doubled.

135.   Grand Macaroni And Cheese Recipe

Serving: 4 | Prep: | Cook: 25mins |Ready in:

Ingredients

- 1 lb. fettuccine pasta
- 2 cups asiago cheese (plus 1/4 cup), grated
- 2 (8 oz.) containers creme fraiche (or combine 1/2 of sour cream and heavy cream together)
- 1 cup parmesan cheese, grated
- 1 1/2 tablespoons fresh thyme, chopped
- 1/2 teaspoon salt
- 1/2 teaspoon fresh ground pepper

Direction

- Preheat oven to 375F.
- Cook pasta until firm to the bite.
- Drain, and reserve 1 cup pasta water. In a large bowl, combine pasta, water, cheese and seasonings.
- Gently toss until all ingredients are mixed and pasta is coated.
- Turn out into a buttered baking dish and cover
- Top with 1/4 cup Asiago cheese.
- Bake until golden on top, about 25 minutes. Let stand 5 minutes before serving.

136.   Greek Style Pasta Skillet Recipe

Serving: 4 | Prep: | Cook: 15mins |Ready in:

Ingredients

- 1 POUND OF ground beef.......OR ground lamb
- 1 MEDIUM onion, CHOPPED
- 1 (14 OUNCE) CAN OF diced tomatoes
- 5-1/2 OUNCES OF tomato juice
- 1/2 CUP water
- 1/2 TEASPOON INSTANT   beef bouillon granules

- 1/2 TEASPOON ground cinnamon
- 1/8 TEASPOON garlic powder
- 1 CUP macaroni   SMALL TO MEDIUM - SHELLS------OR ELBOW macaroni.
- 1 CUP FROZEN - LOOSE PACK CUT green beans
- 1/2 CUP CRUMBLED feta cheese

Direction

- IN A LARGE SKILLET COOK GROUND BEEF OR LAMB WITH THE ONION UNTIL MEAT IS BROWNED, DRAIN OFF FAT. STIR IN UNDRAINED TOMATOES, TOMATO JUICE, WATER, BOUILLON GRANULES, CINNAMON, GARLIC POWDER; BRING TO A BOIL.
- STIR IN UNCOOKED MACARONI AND GREEN BEANS INTO THE MEAT MIXTURE....RETURN TO BOILING; SIMMER ABOUT 15 TO 18 MINUTES, UNTIL THE MACARONI AND GREEN BEANS ARE TENDER.
- SPRINKLE WITH FETA CHEESE
- MAKES 4 SERVINGS..................

137.   Greek Chicken Recipe

Serving: 8 | Prep: | Cook: 30mins |Ready in:

Ingredients

- 1 pound uncooked angel hair pasta
- 1 tablespoon olive oil
- 4 (6-ounce) skinless, boneless chicken breasts, halved
- 2 cups chopped red onion
- 1 cup chopped yellow bell pepper
- 6 tablespoons fresh lemon juice
- 1 teaspoon dried basil
- 1/2 teaspoon dried oregano
- 2 (14.5-ounce) cans diced tomatoes with basil, garlic, and oregano
- 3/4 cup (3 ounces) feta cheese, crumbled

Direction

- Cook pasta according to package directions, omitting salt and fat.
- Heat oil in a large non-stick skillet over medium-high heat. Add chicken to pan; sauté 3 minutes on each side.
- Add onion and next 5 ingredients (through tomatoes) to pan; stir well.
- Cover, reduce heat, and simmer 25 minutes or until chicken is done.
- Remove from heat; sprinkle with cheese.
- Serve with pasta. Yield:

138.   Greek Goulash Recipe

Serving: 8 | Prep: | Cook: 30mins |Ready in:

Ingredients

- 1 lb. ground beef
- 1/2 cup onion, chopped
- 1 large garlic clove, finely chopped
- 2 tbls. chili powder
- 2 tsp. oregano
- 1 tsp. cinnamon
- 1/2 tsp. mint leaves, dried
- 1 tbls. cocoa powder, unsweetened
- 1 lg. can diced tomatoes, undrained (28 oz.) I used 2 15 oz. cans
- 1 15 oz. can chickpeas
- 1 15 oz. can dark-red kidney beans, I used light red
- 2 tsp. honey
- I box macaroni, cooked
- scallions, chopped
- feta cheese, crumbled
- Greek olives, chopped

Direction

- Brown ground beef, onion and garlic in saucepan until beef is browned
- Add chili powder, oregano, cinnamon, and cocoa and cook 1 to 2 minutes longer

- Stir in tomatoes, beans and honey
- Heat to boil
- Reduce heat and simmer, covered, 15 minutes
- Uncover and simmer another 15 minutes or so
- Serve in bowls over warm macaroni
- Garnish with scallions, cheese and olives

139. Greek Orzo Salad Recipe

Serving: 10 | Prep: | Cook: 15mins | Ready in:

Ingredients

- 3/4 of a 1-pound package of orzo pasta
- 4 green onions, chopped up
- 1 1/2 c. feta cheese
- 1/3 c. fresh dill. . .fresh is sooo much better in flavor then dried
- 4 T. fresh lemon juice
- 3 T. olive oil (I use extra-virgin)
- 2 pounds of medium shrimp, cooked, peeled and deveined (I cooked mine simply in salted water)
- 1 cucumber (My cucumber was about 1 foot long and not overly fat.) Quarter the cucumber lengthwise so that you have 4 long strips and then cut into 1/4-inch thick pieces
- 1/2 cucumber (Used for full, thin slices on top of salad)
- 1 (12-ounce) basket cherry tomatoes, cut in half and divided
- Salt and freshly ground pepper to taste
- fresh dill sprigs for Decorating the top of the salad

Direction

- Cook orzo in a large pot of water. Bring salted water to boiling and cook until tender, about 9 minutes. Stir orzo occasionally. Drain and rinse with cold water to stop the cooking process. Drain well, this is important for later.
- Transfer to a large bowl and add green onions, feta cheese, chopped dill, lemon juice, and olive oil. Mix well.

- Make sure there is no excess water on the cooked medium sized shrimp. Add to salad and mix well. Season to taste with salt and freshly ground pepper. '
- Mix in cucumber pieces, 3/4 of the cherry tomatoes that have been cut in halves. Arrange whole cucumber rounds and cherry tomato halves around edge of bowl and garnish with the pretty little dill sprigs.
- Chill salad until ready to serve. This makes a big bowl of salad but mine only made it 2 days.

140. Grilled Veggie Pasta Recipe

Serving: 8 | Prep: | Cook: 20mins | Ready in:

Ingredients

- 1 lb. dry pasta-such as penne
- 2 lbs. fresh garden vegetables-your choice from the following
- 1 small green zucchini
- 1 small yellow zucchini
- 1 large red onion
- 1 red bell pepper
- 1 yellow bell pepper
- 1 small eggplant
- 1 6-oz. package whole button mushrooms (optional, but they add great flavor)
- 1/4 Cup + 2 TB. olive oil, divided
- 1 1/2 tsp. dried basil leaves, crumbled
- 1 1/2 tsp. oregano leaves, crumbled
- 1 tsp. french thyme
- 1/2 tsp. granulated dried garlic, divided
- 1/2-1 tsp. freshly ground pepper , divided
- 1/4-1/2 tsp. salt (optional)
- 1-2 TB. balsamic or red wine vinegar

Direction

- Bring a large pot of water to a boil for the pasta, and get the grill going for the veggies.

- Mix together the basil, oregano, and thyme, and set aside.
- Wash and dry the veggies, then cut in pieces large enough that they won't fall through the grill top into the coals, but small enough to cook quickly and be two bites at most.
- Place the veggies in a single layer on a pan and coat with 1/4 cup of the olive oil, 1/4 tsp. of the granulated garlic and 1/2 tsp. of the freshly ground pepper.
- Toss to coat both sides well.
- When the water is boiling, cook the pasta according to package directions (penne is 11-12 minutes).
- Do not overcook. Drain and rinse very briefly-the pasta should stay warm.
- Shake all the water off, and then place the pasta in a large bowl.
- Toss with the remaining olive oil, along with half of the herb mixture and remaining garlic granule.
- Cover and set aside while grilling the veggies.
- Grill the veggies in a single layer. It's better to cook them in two batches than to crowd them onto the grill touching each other or bunched up. Lay them out over medium high heat, cover, cook about 4 minutes, then turn and cook until done. Some veggies, like larger cut onion and bell pepper and whole mushrooms will need another 4 minutes, but soft squash will only need about 1 more minute.
- Remove to a clean bowl or platter, sprinkle with 1 tsp. herb mixture.
- When the veggies are all cooked, combine them in the bowl with the cooked pasta. Add extra herbs, pepper and garlic granules if desired.
- Just before serving, sprinkle balsamic or red wine vinegar over the top, and gently toss. Taste and add salt as desired. Serve with a fresh garden salad.

Serving: 6 | Prep: | Cook: 135mins | Ready in:

Ingredients

- 1 lb ground beef
- 1 (15 ounce) can tomatoes
- 1/4 cup chopped onions
- 1/4 cup chopped bell peppers
- 1/4 cup chopped celery
- 1 (8 ounce) can mushrooms
- 2 tablespoons brown sugar or sweet pickle juice
- 2 tablespoons worcestershire sauce
- 1 (10 3/4 ounce) can cream of mushroom soup
- 1/4 lb sharp cheddar cheese
- 1 (6 ounce) package angel hair pasta, cooked, this is an estimated size bag- the original recipe called for 1 small bag
- 1 (8 ounce) can tomato sauce
- salt and pepper

Direction

- Brown meat in large skillet or Dutch oven.
- Add onions, pepper and celery and simmer for 15 minutes.
- Add tomatoes and tomato sauce, mushrooms, brown sugar and Worcestershire sauce.
- Add salt and pepper to taste.
- Cook in skillet for 1 hour.
- Place cooked pasta in bottom of large casserole dish.
- Spoon mushroom soup over pasta.
- Pour sauce over the soup and top with cheese.
- Bake in 350°F oven for 30-45 minutes.
- Can sizes do not have to be exact, just as long as they are within a close range, everything will work out.

142. Ground Beef Stroganoff Recipe

Serving: 6 | Prep: | Cook: 50mins | Ready in:

Ingredients

- 1 Tablespoon extra virgin olive oil
- 1-1/2 cups mushrooms, chopped
- 1-1/2 cups celery, peeled and sliced
- 1 green pepper, chopped (bell peppers work well but you can use any type of pepper you like)
- 1-1/2 to 2 pounds lean ground beef or ground turkey
- 2 cloves garlic, minced or finely chopped
- 1 recipe for spice mix below
- 1-1/2 cups dry egg noodles or any type of pasta will do
- 1 cup organic milk
- 1-1/2 cups low sodium beef or vegetable broth
- 1/2 cup sour cream, organic
- 3/4 to 1 cup grated Provolone. cheddar or Tex Mex cheese
- spice Mix
- 1 package (about 1-ounce) natural onion soup and dip mix
- 1/2 teaspoon black pepper
- 1/2 teaspoon granulated or powdered garlic
- 1 teaspoon granulated or powdered onion
- 1-1/2 teaspoon dried parsley
- 1 teaspoon cornstarch

Direction

- Sauté mushrooms, celery and green pepper in olive oil over medium heat stirring constantly, until most of the moisture has evaporated. About 15 minutes.
- Add ground beef or turkey, and brown until completely cooked.
- Drain any fat.
- Add noodles, spice mix, milk and beef broth. Bring to a boil.
- Reduce heat and simmer, stirring occasionally, for about 20 minutes, or until liquid is absorbed.

- If you find it is a little too dry, you can always add more broth as you go along.
- Stir in sour cream.
- Always check seasonings, adding more if you wish.
- Top with grated Provolone, cheddar or Tex Mex cheese.
- Note: I like to place it under the broiler for a couple of minutes just to lightly brown the top.

143. Ham And Corn Macaroni Medley Recipe

Serving: 4 | Prep: | Cook: 10mins | Ready in:

Ingredients

- 3 white onions chopped
- 2 small green peppers chopped
- 2 small red peppers chopped
- 2 celery ribs chopped
- 3 tablespoons olive oil
- 1/4 cup cooked whole kernel corn
- 1 cup chopped pieces of ham
- 1 pound macaroni
- 1 teaspoon salt
- 1 teaspoon freshly ground black pepper
- 1 cup buttered bread crumbs

Direction

- Sauté onions, peppers and celery in oil until soft.
- Add peas and meat.
- Cook macaroni until al dente then drain well and place in a baking dish.
- Stir in the vegetable meat sauce and sprinkle with salt and black pepper then stir well.
- Top with bread crumbs then place under broiler for 7 minutes.

144. Hamburger Spinach Casserole Recipe

Serving: 4 | Prep: | Cook: 45mins | Ready in:

Ingredients

- 10 ounces spinach (chopped, frozen)
- 8 ounces cream cheese
- 1/2 cup sour cream
- 3 tablespoons milk
- 3 tablespoons onion (minced)
- 4 ounces wide noodles
- 1 pound ground beef
- 15 ounces tomato sauce
- 2 teaspoons sugar
- garlic powder to taste
- salt and black pepper to taste
- cheddar cheese enough to cover top of casserole

Direction

- Cook and drain spinach.
- Mix cream cheese, sour cream, milk and onion in separate bowl and let set to soften.
- Cook noodles in boiling water for 10 minutes.
- Drain.
- Brown beef and drain well.
- Add tomato sauce, sugar, garlic powder, salt, pepper and noodles.
- Heat through.
- In 2 quart casserole, place a layer of the meat-noodle mixture (use 1/2).
- Top with 1/2 of the cream cheese mixture.
- Top with all of spinach and finish with remainder of meat-noodles.
- Cover and bake at 350 for 40 minutes.
- Remove from oven and top with remaining cream cheese mixture.
- Cover completely with cheddar.
- Return to oven uncovered until cheese melts completely (about 5-10 min.)

145. Hard Times Hamburger Casserole Recipe

Serving: 6 | Prep: | Cook: 20mins | Ready in:

Ingredients

- 1 lb ground chuck or sirloin
- 3 cups cooked fusilli, or bow-tie pasta (you can use more or less)
- 1 onion, chopped
- 1 bell pepper, chopped
- 3 celery stalks, chopped
- 1 28 oz can diced tomatoes
- 7 oz can tomato sauce or 1 cup V-8 (preferred)
- 3 cups shredded cheddar cheese, divided
- 1 tsp oregano
- 1 tsp basil
- louisiana hot sauce
- salt and pepper

Direction

- Lightly brown meat and drain. Add veggies and continue cooking until wilted and meat is cooked through. Add tomatoes and sauce or V-8.
- Add oregano and basil.
- Remove from heat and stir in 2 cups cheese and add pasta and adjust seasonings and add three or four dashes Louisiana hot sauce.
- Place in casserole and bake with additional cheese sprinkled on top until cheese is melted and casserole is bubbly.

146. Hearty Ravioli Recipe

Serving: 4 | Prep: | Cook: 30mins | Ready in:

Ingredients

- 450 grams of spinach, large stems removed and chopped
- 1 tbs. grainy mustard
- 1 teaspoon sesame oil

- 1/2 teaspoon nutmeg
- 2 tbs. bread crumbs
- 1 c. semolina four
- 2 tsp. olive oil
- 1/2 cup water
- 1 can crushed tomatoes
- 1 onion, minced
- 1 tbs. olive oil
- 1 clove garlic, minced
- various Italian herbs (fresh would be best)
- salt and pepper to taste
- dash of lemon
- pinch of cayenne pepper

Direction

- In a bowl, combine the semolina flour, 2 tsp. olive oil, 1/2 cup water and a pinch salt to make a dough.
- Wrap in a towel and let sit for 30 minutes.
- Wash the spinach and remove the large tough stems.
- Chop the spinach and steam or sauté in water. (Sweat)
- Place in a large mixing bowl.
- Add the mustard, a pinch of salt and bread-crumbs and mix well.
- Season further with salt, cayenne and pepper.
- Set filling aside
- Sauté the minced onion in the olive oil until the onion is glassy.
- Add the minced garlic and sauté.
- Add the tomatoes and reduce heat to simmer.
- Add the herbs, lemon juice, salt and pepper and continue to simmer on a low heat.
- Season to taste with additional salt, pepper and cayenne.
- Set the sauce aside.
- Divide the dough in fourths and roll out each portion on a floured work space, allowing the first sheet of pasta to sit while rolling out the second. One of the tricks to the pasta is, to make sure you've rolled the dough out very thin (but not too thin!).
- Cut out your ravioli shapes and fill with the filling. Place the top part of the ravioli over the filling and close with a fork. If you have a form

or press, then of course that saves time you merely place 1 sheet of dough on one side, put the filling on the dough and then lay the 2nd sheet of dough on top. Close the form to seal and cut off the extra using a knife.

- Meanwhile, bring a large pot of salty water to boil.
- Put your ravioli into the salty water and cook a few at a time. They are ready when they come floating to the top.
- Place the first cooked raviolis in the oven to keep warm until they are all ready.
- When ready to serve, put a layer of sauce on the plate and lay the raviolis on top.
- You can garnish with some fresh cut herbs or if you have soy cheese, you can dust some on top.

---

147. Homemade Restaurant Pasta Recipe

Serving: 4 | Prep: | Cook: 3mins | Ready in:

Ingredients

- 10 ounces of All-Purpose (or semolina if you have it) flour. (About 2 cups).
- 1 tsp of salt
- 3 eggs

Direction

- Mound the flour on your countertop.
- Make a well in the center add the salt.
- Break in the first egg and gently beat it with a fork until it thickens with some of the surrounding flour.
- Repeat this process with the other two eggs.
- Gather the mixture in a ball.
- Lightly flour a work surface and knead until the dough is smooth, only about two minutes. (Don't overwork the dough!).
- Wrap the dough tightly in saran wrap to keep moist when not using.
- To make pasta -

- Cut dough into 6 pieces working each individually.
- If you have a pasta machine - follow the directions to make the dough as thin as needed and cut into shape preferred.
- If you don't have a pasta machine - you have to roll the dough out with a pin until it is as thin as you can possibly make it. (This takes some elbow grease!). Cut the dough with a pizza or pastry cutter to the shape you want.
- Boil in salted water for about 3 minutes OR allow it to dry completely and store for later.

dough into a zip lock, cut off a tiny corner and squeeze the noodles into the boiling water. They will in that case come out bigger and will need to be chopped when pulled out. My noodles were made using a colander with large holes.
- Toss the cooked noodles with butter and toast lightly in a non-stick skillet.
- Garnish with chopped parsley and serve with sausages, potato pancakes and sweet and sour red cabbage, or with any other meats and veggies.

148. Homemade Spaetzel Recipe

Serving: 5 | Prep: | Cook: 10mins | Ready in:

Ingredients

- 2 cups all-purpose flour
- 4 eggs, lightly beaten
- 1/3 cup milk
- 2 tsp. salt
- 1 tbsp butter
- 2 tbsp. fresh parsely, chopped (optional)
- water for boiling

Direction

- Stir the flour, eggs, milk and salt in a bowl until smooth (dough will be sticky).
- In a lg. saucepan bring water to a boil. Making these is really a lot easier with a spaetzle maker (can be purchased for $15 online). If you don't have one, use a colander with large holes. Pour dough into a colander or spaetzle maker coated with non-stick cooking spray; place over boiling water.
- With a wooden spoon press dough until pieces drop into boiling water. Take care, as the steam will be hot.
- Cook for 2 min, or until dumplings float to the top. Remove with a slotted spoon. You can do this in batches. A really easy way is to put the

149. Homestyle Greek Spaghetti Recipe

Serving: 4 | Prep: | Cook: 15mins | Ready in:

Ingredients

- 1 lb. spaghetti, 100% durum wheat semolina (I use an Italian import called Garofalo, #9 size)
- 1 onion, medium size sweet yellow
- 1 garlic clove, large
- Fresh Greek oregano leaves to taste, stripped from stem
- I Tablespoon capers
- 1/2 cup feta, coarsely crumbled
- 1/4 cup sliced kalamata olives
- 1 lemon
- light olive oil (for saute')
- High quality extra virgin olive oil (to finish the dish)
- Coarse kosher salt
- Coarsely ground black pepper

Direction

- Put at least 3 quarts of salted fresh water on to boil.
- Heat a sauté' pan which is large enough for the cooked pasta and liberally coat pan with cooking grade olive oil.
- Fine dice onion and add to oiled hot sauté pan.

- Season onion dice with salt and pepper and begin clarifying, take care not to brown onions.
- When water is rapidly boiling add spaghetti, stir once after pasta sinks below the surface. Pasta should cook for about 11 minutes. *
- Crush the garlic clove with the flat of a knife and add to almost clarified onions, toss frequently.
- When pasta is cooked, remove garlic clove from sauté pan and add drained but still dripping wet pasta.
- Quickly add oregano leaves, olives and capers (plus any other accent) to sauté' pan.
- Toss ingredients over medium high heat to evaporate remaining moisture and coat pasta. (The steam warms the accents)
- Turn pasta into individual pasta bowls.
- Top with feta cheese, drizzle with extra virgin olive oil to taste.
- Season with coarse black pepper, and 1/4 lemon squeezed over top.

---

150. Honey Chili Shrimp Over Noodles Recipe

Serving: 2 | Prep: | Cook: 10mins | Ready in:

Ingredients

- 2 T vegetable oil
- 2 cloves garlic, chopped
- 1 inch fresh ginger,, grated
- 1-2 red or green chillies, deseeded and chopped
- 1 pound shelled raw shrimp
- 1 medium onion, chopped fine
- 2 T honey
- juice of 1 lemon
- 1 T soy sauce
- 8 ounces Chinese egg noodles
- chopped fresh coriander (optional)

Direction

- Heat the oil in a wok and stir-fry the garlic, ginger and chilli over a high heat for about 1 minutes.
- Add the 8 ounces of egg noodles and stir-fry with the spices.
- Make sure you keep stirring well for about 2-3 minutes.
- Add the shrimp and onions and stir-fry for 1-2 minutes until the shrimp turn pink.
- Don't overcook or the shrimp will become rubbery.
- Add the honey, lemon juice and soy sauce.
- Allow to bubble up.
- Serve immediately.
- Sprinkled with fresh coriander if you have some handy.

---

151. Hot Paprika Cream Sauce W Scallops Recipe

Serving: 4 | Prep: | Cook: 40mins | Ready in:

Ingredients

- 1 pound scallops
- 2 cloves garlic, minced
- 3 tablespoons green onion, thinly sliced
- 1/3 cup dry white wine
- 2 teaspoons virgin olive oil
- 1 tablespoon chopped fresh basil
- 1 cup sliced mushrooms
- 1/3 cup clam broth
- 3/4 cup nonfat cottage cheese
- 1/4 cup nonfat sour cream
- 1/4 cup skim milk
- 1 tablespoon sweet Hungarian paprika
- 1/8 teaspoon hot Hungarian paprika or more if desired.
- salt and pepper to taste
- 8 ounces linguine
- 1 tablespoon chopped fresh parsley
- grated Parmigianno Reggiaonno cheese. if desired.

Direction

- Sauté scallops, garlic, and green onion in wine and 1 teaspoon of the olive oil.
- Cook on high heat until liquid evaporates, stirring a few times to cook scallops through.
- Sprinkle with basil and remove to a plate.
- In same pan, add remaining teaspoon of the olive oil and mushrooms and cook for 2 minutes.
- Stir in clam juice and simmer 2 more minutes.
- Put cottage cheese in a blender and blend until smooth.
- Add sour cream and blend again.
- Add the milk and paprika and blend once more.
- Pour mixture into the pan with mushrooms.
- Add scallops and warm over very low heat until mixture is warmed through.
- You can add Parmigiano Reggiano cheese to sauce if desired, I do this.
- Season with salt and pepper to taste.
- Meanwhile, bring water to a boil, add pasta, and cook until al dente.
- Drain and place in a large serving bowl.
- Pour sauce over pasta, sprinkle with parsley and serve.

---

152.   Hungarian Beef Stew Recipe

Serving: 6 | Prep: | Cook: 3mins | Ready in:

Ingredients

- 1 1/4pounds beef chuck in 3/4" pieces
- 1 pound carrots, sliced
- 2 medium onions, thinly sliced
- 3 cups thinly sliced cabbage
- 2 cups water OR 1 1/2 cups water and 1/2 cup red wine
- 6 ounce can tomato paste
- 1 envelope onion-mushroom soup mix
- 1 tablespoon paprika

- 1 teaspoon caraway seeds
- 8 ounces reduced-fat sour cream
- egg noodles

Direction

- Mix all ingredients EXCEPT sour cream in slow cooker.
- Cover and cook for 8 to10 hours on low until meat is tender.
- Turn off cooker.
- Stir in sour cream until well blended.
- Makes 8 cups stew.

---

153.   Hungarian Noodles And Cheese Recipe

Serving: 8 | Prep: | Cook: 25mins | Ready in:

Ingredients

- 1/2 recipe noodles (noodles.html">Egg noodles) or 1/2 lb. good Amish noodles from the store
- 6 oz. cottage cheese, drained
- 1 t. dill, chopped
- 1/4 lb. bacon
- 6 oz. sour cream

Direction

- Fry the bacon until crisp. Drain, crumble, and reserve.
- Boil the noodles for 15 minutes or so until done in salted water, and drain.
- Mix the noodles with the bacon drippings in the pan. Add the sour cream, cottage cheese, and dill. Mix in the bacon, and serve.
- We ate at a Hungarian restaurant in Chicago, and this was listed on the menu as an appetizer, so we ordered it. She brought a huge salad bowl heaped full of these noodles. How they thought we were supposed to eat all these, plus the goulash and the porkolt AND

dessert, I have no idea. Decadent doesn't even begin to describe these noodles.

---

154. Hungarian Paprika Stew Recipe

Serving: 12 | Prep: | Cook: 480mins | Ready in:

Ingredients

- 4 pounds of boneless beef chuck roast, cut into 1/2-3/4" pieces (I cut off the fat from the sides and put that in the pot for flavor)
- 1 small package of baby carrots, cut in half
- 2-3 large red peppers, slices
- 2 large onions sliced thin
- 2 (8 oz) pkgs sliced mushrooms (I used portabello)
- 2/3 cup flour
- 3 tbsp sweet paprika
- 3 tbsp (hot) or smoked paprika (used smoked)
- 1 tsp salt
- 1 tsp thyme
- 1 tsp pepper
- 1 cup chili or seafood Sauce (yes, seafood sauce) Heinze I used
- 1 (32 oz) container of beef broth
- 1/2 cup red wine
- 1 pkg dry onion soup mix
- 1 (8 oz) sour cream
- 1 (16 oz) wide noodles

Direction

- In a 6-8 quart slow cooker, put beef, carrots, onion & red pepper
- Add flour, paprika, salt, thyme and pepper, toss over beef and vegetables till coated
- Add chili sauce, broth & wine and mix well, pour over meat/veggies
- Cover and cook on high setting for the first 4 hours till hot and bubbly
- Lower temp to "low" and continue cooking for another 4 hours till meat is tender and veggies are cooked to your likings

- Add mushrooms in the 7th hours and continue cooking with them in the pot
- Add sour cream 1/2 hour before serving on low and mix thoroughly
- Cook noodles and serve with stew
- Nice warm buttered rolls or bread for dipping is recommended

---

155. Husbands Delight Casserole Recipe

Serving: 6 | Prep: | Cook: 30mins | Ready in:

Ingredients

- 1 pound ground beef
- 1 medium onion, diced
- 1 can condensed tomato soup
- 1 can condensed cream of mushroom soup
- 1/2 teaspoon ground cumin
- chili powder to taste
- 1 8 oz package egg noodles
- salt
- 8 ounces shredder mozzarella cheese
- Grated parmesan cheese

Direction

- Spray a 9x13 inch baking dish with non-stick cooking spray
- Cook ground beef and onion until no longer pink
- Stir in undiluted soups, cumin and chili powder; remove from heat
- Meanwhile, cook noodles in salted water
- Drain noodles well; stir into beef mixture
- Spoon into prepared baking dish
- Top evenly with mozzarella and sprinkle with parmesan
- Bake 25-30 minutes until golden brown
- VARIATIONS: Use sliced processed cheese or American cheese instead of the mozzarella and parmesan

156. Husbands Delight Recipe

Serving: 6 | Prep: | Cook: 25mins | Ready in:

Ingredients

- 10 ounces egg or macaroni noodles
- 1 1/2 pounds ground beef
- 1 (14 1/2 ounce) can diced tomatoes in juice
- 1 teaspoon salt
- 1 tablespoon sugar
- 1 1/2 cups sour cream
- 1 (3 ounce) package cream cheese, softened
- 1/2 onion, chopped
- 1 cup shredded cheddar cheese

Direction

- Preheat oven to 350. Bring large pot of slightly salted water to a boil. Add pasta. Cook for 8 to 10 minutes or until al dente.
- Meanwhile, in large skillet over medium heat, brown ground beef.
- Add tomatoes and juice, salt and sugar. Simmer for 15 minutes.
- In separate medium bowl, combine sour cream, cream cheese and onion.
- Mix well. In 9 x 13" baking dish, layer half of noodles, all meat mixture and then all sour cream mixture. Top with remaining noodles.
- Sprinkle with cheddar cheese. Bake for 25 minutes. Makes 6 servings.

157. Italian Lemon Butter Chicken Recipe

Serving: 5 | Prep: | Cook: 20mins | Ready in:

Ingredients

- lemon butter Sauce:
- 1/4 cup white wine
- 5 tablespoons fresh lemon juice
- 5 tablespoons heavy cream
- 1 cup butter, chilled
- salt and pepper to taste
- chicken and Pasta:
- 1/2 pound dry farfalle (bow tie) pasta
- 4 skinless, boneless chicken breast halves - pounded to 1/4 inch thickness
- 2 tablespoons olive oil
- 2 tablespoons butter
- 1/4 cup all-purpose flour
- salt and pepper to taste
- 4 ounces bacon
- 6 ounces mushrooms, sliced
- 6 ounces artichoke hearts, drained and halved
- 2 teaspoons capers, drained
- chopped fresh parsley for garnish

Direction

- To make the sauce, pour the wine and lemon juice into a saucepan over medium heat.
- Cook at a low boil until the liquid is reduced by 1/3.
- Stir in cream, and simmer until it thickens.
- Gradually add the butter 1 tablespoon at a time to the sauce, stirring until completely incorporated.
- Season with salt and pepper.
- Remove from heat, and keep warm.
- Bring a large pot of lightly salted water to boil.
- Add pasta, and cook until al dente, about 8 to 10 minutes.
- Drain, and set aside.
- To make the chicken, heat oil and 2 tablespoons butter in a large skillet over medium heat.
- In a bowl, stir together flour, salt, and pepper.
- Lightly coat chicken with flour mixture.
- Without crowding, carefully place chicken in hot oil. (If necessary, cook in batches.)
- Fry until cooked through and golden brown on both sides.
- Remove the chicken to paper towels.
- Stir the bacon, mushrooms, artichokes, and capers into the oil; cook until the mushrooms are soft.

- Cut the chicken breasts into bite-size strips, and return them to the skillet.
- Stir half of the lemon butter sauce into the chicken mixture.
- To serve, place pasta in a large bowl.
- Stir the chicken mixture into the pasta.
- Taste, and adjust seasonings.
- Stir in additional lemon butter sauce as desired.
- Toss well, and garnish with parsley.

158.   Italian Market Pasta Salad Recipe

Serving: 4 | Prep: | Cook: 15mins | Ready in:

Ingredients

- 4 ounces packaged dry mafalda, large bow tie, or campanelle pasta
- 6 cups mesclun or other spring greens
- 1 cup grape tomatoes or cherry tomatoes, halved lengthwise
- 1/2 cup crumbled gorgonzola, blue, or feta cheese (2 ounces)
- 3 tablespoons olive oil
- 3 tablespoons white wine vinegar or balsamic vinegar
- salt and freshly ground black pepper
- 1/4 cup pine nuts, toasted

Direction

- If using mafalda, break into irregular pieces, 2 to 3 inches long. Cook pasta according to package directions. Drain, rinse with cold water, and drain again.
- In a large salad bowl, combine cooked pasta, mesclun or other spring greens, tomatoes, and cheese. Drizzle with olive oil and vinegar, tossing to coat. Season to taste with salt and freshly ground pepper.
- Divide salad evenly among four dinner plates. Sprinkle with pine nuts. Makes 4 LARGE main course servings.

159.   Italian Meatball Sandwich Casserole Recipe

Serving: 6 | Prep: | Cook: 30mins | Ready in:

Ingredients

- 1/3 cup chopped green onions
- 1/4 cup Italian seasoned bread crumbs
- 3 tablespoons grated parmesan cheese
- 1 pound ground beef
- 1 (1 pound) loaf Italian bread, cut into 1 inch cubes
- 1 (8 ounce) package cream cheese, softened
- 1/2 cup mayonnaise
- 1 teaspoon italian seasoning
- 1/4 teaspoon freshly ground black pepper
- 2 cups shredded mozzarella cheese
- 3 cups spaghetti sauce
- 1 cup water
- 2 cloves garlic, minced

Direction

- Preheat oven to 400 degrees F (205 degrees C).
- Mix together onions, bread crumbs, Parmesan cheese and ground beef. Roll into 1 inch diameter balls, and place in a baking pan. Bake for 15 to 20 minutes, or until beef is no longer pink. Reduce the oven temperature to 350 degrees F (175 degrees C).
- Arrange the bread cubes in a single layer in an ungreased 9x13 inch baking dish. Mix together the cream cheese, mayonnaise, Italian seasoning and black pepper until smooth. Spread this mixture over each bread cube. Sprinkle with 1/2 cup of the grated mozzarella cheese.
- In a large bowl, mix together spaghetti sauce, water, and garlic. Gently stir in meatballs. Pour over the bread and cheese mixture in the baking pan. Sprinkle the remaining mozzarella cheese evenly over the top.

- Bake at 350 degrees F (175 degrees C) for 30 minutes, or until heated through.

---

160. Italian Skillet Chicken Recipe

Serving: 4 | Prep: | Cook: 20mins | Ready in:

Ingredients

- 4 boneless skinless chicken breast halves
- 1 medium onion, chopped
- 1 (14 ounce) can diced Italian tomatoes, undrained. If you don't have Italian tomatoes just toss in some italian seasoning along with the tomatoes.
- 2 cups chicken broth
- 1 teaspoon dried basil
- garlic powder or fresh minced garlic, to taste
- 1/4 teaspoon black pepper
- 8 ounces uncooked spaghetti, broken into 2 inch pieces
- 1/4 cup grated parmesan cheese

Direction

- In a large skillet, cook chicken and onion until onion is tender. You may cook as whole pieces but I cut the meat up into pieces.
- Add tomatoes, broth, basil, garlic and pepper to skillet.
- Bring to a boil; stir in spaghetti.
- Reduce heat; cover and simmer for 15 to 20 minutes.
- Sprinkle with Parmesan and serve. I have left off the parmesan cheese at times and didn't feel that it was any less delicious.

---

161. Italian Style Ground Beef Recipe

Serving: 4 | Prep: | Cook: 35mins | Ready in:

Ingredients

- 1 lb. lean ground beef
- 1/4 cup cold water
- 3/4 tsp. seasoned salt
- 1/8 tsp. black pepper
- 1 Tbsp. minced parsley
- all-purpose flour
- 1 egg, slightly beaten
- 1/4 cup fine dry bread crumbs
- 1 Tbsp. oil
- 4 slices Mozzarella or monterey jack cheese
- 1 cup spaghetti sauce
- 2 Tbsp. grated parmesan cheese parsley for garnish

Direction

- Preheat oven to 400.F
- With hands mix lightly together beef, water, seasoned salt, black pepper and parsley. Shape into 4 patties, about 3/4-inch thick.
- Coat both sides of patties with flour. Dip into egg, then into crumbs.
- Brown quickly in hot oil on both sides in skillet.
- Arrange in a shallow 1 1/2-quart baking dish. Put a slice of cheese on each patty.
- Pour spaghetti sauce over patties. Sprinkle with Parmesan cheese.
- Bake for about 25 min.
- Garnish with parsley.

---

162. Jamaican Style Beef Stew Recipe

Serving: 5 | Prep: | Cook: 90mins | Ready in:

Ingredients

- 1 Tbsp. canola oil
- 1 Tbsp. sugar
- 1-1/2 lb. boneless sirloin steak, cut into 3/4" cubes
- 5 grape tomatoes, finely chopped

- 3 large carrots cut into 1/2" slices
- 3 celery ribs, cut into 1/2" slices
- 4 green onions, chopped
- 3/4 cup beef broth
- 1/4 cup barbecue sauce (your choice)
- 1/4 cup soy sauce
- 2 Tbsp. steak sauce (your choice)
- 1 Tbsp. garlic powder
- 1 tsp. dried thyme, crushed
- 1/4 tsp. allspice
- 1/4 tsp. black pepper
- 1/8 tsp. hot sauce
- 1 Tbsp. cornstarch
- 2 Tbsp. cold water
- Hot cooked rice, noodles or mashed potatoes if desired

Direction

- In a Dutch oven heat oil over medium-high heat.
- Add sugar, cook and stir for 1 minute or until lightly browned.
- Add beef and brown on all sides.
- Stir in vegetables, broth, barbecue sauce, soy sauce, steak sauce and seasonings.
- Bring to a boil.
- Reduce heat.
- Cover and simmer for 1 to 1-1/4 hours or until vegetables and meat are tender.
- Combine cornstarch and water until smooth, stir into stew.
- Bring to a boil, cook and stir for 2 minutes or until thickened.

163. Jambalaya Pasta Recipe

Serving: 6 | Prep: | Cook: 45mins | Ready in:

Ingredients

- salt and pepper
- Donman's cajun seasoning mix
- 1 # penne pasta
- 3 tbsp evoo

- 1 # peeled, deveined large shrimp, tails removed
- 1 # boneless, skinless chicken, cut into 1-inch chunks
- 3/4 # andouille sausage, cut into 1/2-inch chunks
- 1 medium yellow onion, chopped
- 1 bell pepper, chopped (red or green)
- 1 jalapeño, chopped (I took the seeds out, but leave them in for more heat)
- 2 garlic cloves, minced
- 1/2 cup chicken stock
- 1 (14.5 ounce) can diced tomatoes
- 1 tbsp fresh thyme, chopped
- 1/2 cup heavy cream (this really makes the recipe great)
- 3 tbsp fresh basil, chopped
- 2/3 cup fresh grated parmesan cheese
- * check out DonMan's profile for his seasoning recipe, and while your there, check out all of his other great recipes!!

Direction

- Boil pasta like normal (duh!)
- Reserve 1 cup of the cooking water
- Season the shrimp and chicken with 2 tsp. each of DonMan's seasoning and 1/8 tsp. salt
- Set a deep sauté pan over medium heat, add 1 tbsp. evoo. Swirl to evenly coat the pan.
- Place the shrimp in the pan and cook for 1 minute on each side, remove and set aside.
- Add another tbsp. of evoo to the skillet and add the chicken, cook for 2-3 minutes per side, remove and set aside with the shrimp.
- Add the remaining tbsp. of evoo and add to the skillet the sausage, onion, bell pepper, and jalapeño. Cook for about 3 minutes. Add the garlic and cook for another 30 seconds.
- Add the chicken stock and scrape the bottom of the pan to pick up the brown bits on the bottom.
- Add the diced tomatoes, thyme, 1 tbsp. of DonMan's seasoning, a pinch of salt, and cook for 2 minutes.
- Add the heavy cream to the pan and cook for 2 minutes.

- Return the shrimp and chicken to the pan, as well as the cooked pasta and reserved pasta cooking liquid.
- Continue cooking for about another 3 minutes till the shrimp and chicken are cooked and heated through.
- Remove from heat and top with basil and parmesan cheese, toss to coat while hot.

164. Jimmys Mexican Lasagna Recipe

Serving: 5 | Prep: | Cook: 20mins | Ready in:

Ingredients

- 1lb. ground turkey (you can use beef)
- 1 red onion Chopped
- 2-3 cloves garlic chopped
- 1 can Rotel tomatoes
- 4 oz. Velveeta
- 1 small can chopped black olives (optional)
- 2-3 tablespoons cilantro chopped
- l can Old El Paso refried beans, warmed
- 1 pkg. Old El Paso Burrito size tortillas
- 1 Pkg. Shredded cheddar cheese

Direction

- Preheat oven to 350 degrees:
- Brown ground Turkey with onion and Garlic; add Rotel tomatoes, Velveeta, black olives and cilantro to ground turkey and stir to let Velveeta melt, remove from heat. Heat refried Beans.
- In a round baking dish, starting with a tortilla; layer tortilla, refried beans, meat mixture and cheese, repeat 4-5 layers ending with meat and cheese.
- Bake in oven for 20 min. or until warmed thru and cheese melts.
- Serve with Old El Paso Thick and Chunky Salsa and chips.
- You can add 1-2 chopped jalapenos for a little kick.

165. Kaposztas Taszta Cabbage Noodles Recipe

Serving: 6 | Prep: | Cook: 40mins | Ready in:

Ingredients

- 2 large head cabbage, grated into small pieces
- 2 heaping tbsp.salt
- 1 cup vegetable oil
- 2 tbsp. pepper
- *Square or bowtie egg noodles
- smoked sausage or keilbasi
- fresh garlic can be added if desired.
- 1 small onion can be grated into cabbage while cooking if desired.

Direction

- In a large bowl put grated cabbage.
- Sprinkle salt over top. Let stand about 45 minutes until juice forms
- In a large pot, add vegetable oil. Squeeze juice out of cabbage and place in pot.
- Add pepper.
- Add onion and garlic if desired.
- Add sausage when cabbage becomes transparent.
- Sautee until golden brown, stirring frequently.
- In Large pot, boil noodles. Drain.
- Add noodles to cabbage mixture. Mix well.
- Enjoy!!
- *Egg noodles can be purchased at most European delis

166. Kellys Triple Bypass Casserole Recipe

Serving: 12 | Prep: | Cook: 37mins | Ready in:

Ingredients

- 1 package lasagne noodles, cooked
- 2 packages sour cream and chive mashed potatoes (or you can make your own
- 1 pound bacon, cooked crispy
- 1/2 pound butter or margarine
- 5 large onions, sliced thin
- 1 pound shredded cheddar cheese

Direction

- Mix potatoes with half a pound of cheese, and half the bacon.
- Sauté' onions in butter until brown and sweet, or caramelized.
- Layer noodles, potatoes, onions with butter, bacon, and cheese (like a lasagne)
- Cover with more onions in butter, cheese, and top with bacon. Bake covered at 350 until hot, then remove cover, and allow cheese to get bubbly and a little browned. Cool for 10 minutes before cutting, or it will fall apart.
- Top with green onions and sour cream, if desired. Enjoy!
- Do NOT eat this if you're having blood tests the next day. You're sure to have a HUGE cholesterol count after a plate of this!

167.   Kentucky Fried Chicken Secret Macaroni Salad Recipe

Serving: 8 | Prep: | Cook: 12mins | Ready in:

Ingredients

- 8 Oz of elbow macaroni
- 2 Ribs celery minced fine
- 1/4 cup thinly diced carrots (very thin!)
- 1 tablespoon Dry minced onion
- 1/3 cup Diced sweet pickles
- 1 1/2 cups Miracle Whip
- 1/2 cup Hellmans Mayonaise
- 1/4 teaspoon black pepper
- 1/4 teaspoon dry mustard
- 1 teaspoon sugar
- salt to taste

Direction

- Cook elbow macaroni to package directions, drain well and let cool.
- Combine remaining ingredients in a mixing bowl and mix well.
- Fold mixture into macaroni and toss to combine. Cover and let chill for several hours.

168.   Kicked Up Chicken Casserole Recipe

Serving: 10 | Prep: | Cook: 45mins | Ready in:

Ingredients

- 3 lbs boneless, skinless chicken
- 2 T garlic
- white wine Worcestershire (Or Lea and Perrins chicken marinade - same thing)
- seasoned Salt
- garlic pepper
- EVOO
- 2 T margarine
- 1/2 white onion, chopped small
- 1 ribs celery, chopped small
- 1/2 red pepper, chopped small
- 1/2 tub fresh mushrooms, sliced (or canned)
- 10 Oz Chopped spinach, OR broccoli florets, OR asparagus Tips (optional - sometimes I use, sometimes I don't)
- Dash red pepper flakes
- 1 c Shredded swiss cheese
- 1 c Shredded Monterrey Jack cheese
- 4 oz cream cheese, softened
- Dash hot sauce
- 1 can creamy chicken and mushroom soup
- 1 can cream of mushroom or cream of celery
- 1 small carton sour cream
- 1/4 c Kraft Real Mayo
- 2 c. wide egg noodles, cooked and drained (optional, sometimes I use and sometimes I don't) (Or use Minute Rice, white or brown, the 4 servings option on box)

- 1/2 c pepperidge Farm herb stuffing mix
- 1/4 c parmesan cheese

Direction

- Preheat oven to 350
- Season both sides of chicken with seasoned salt and garlic pepper
- Cube chicken
- Drizzle large non-stick skillet with EVOO, add margarine (I like my electric skillet)
- Throw in chicken and all ingredients down to red pepper flakes
- Cook until chicken is done and veggies are soft
- (If using noodles or rice, cook according to package directions while the chicken is cooking. Be sure to cook noodles only to al dente stage so that they don't become mushy and fall apart in casserole).
- Turn into large mixing bowl
- Add drained and rinsed pasta, or rice (drained if needed)
- Stir in cheeses while warm
- Stir in remaining ingredients up to Stuffing Mix
- Spread in large casserole dish
- Mix together stuffing mix and parmesan cheese
- Spread over top
- Cook about 35-45 minutes, until bubbly

169. LEMON SHRIMP PASTA Recipe

Serving: 4 | Prep: | Cook: 20mins | Ready in:

Ingredients

- 1 lb large uncooked shrimp, peeled, deveined, and butterflied
- 8 oz angel hair pasta
- 1 tbl extra virgin olive oil
- 1 clove Garlic
- 1/2 cup chicken broth

- 2 tbl lemon juice
- 1/2 cup Imported parmesan cheese, grated
- 1/4 cup whipping cream
- 1 tbl lemon zest
- 1/2 tsp salt
- 3 tbl Fresh cilantro, chopped

Direction

- Prepare pasta according to package directions; drain.
- Meanwhile, heat a large skillet over medium-high heat.
- Add oil and sauté garlic for 1 minute, or until just golden; do not brown.
- Add chicken broth and lemon juice; bring to a boil.
- Add shrimp and cook until pink, about 3 minutes.
- Reduce heat to low, add Parmesan cheese, cream and lemon peel; cook about 3 minutes to thoroughly heat, but do not boil.
- Season with salt.
- Combine shrimp mixture and chopped cilantro with the angel hair pasta; toss to mix.
- Serve immediately.

170. Lamb Alla Puttanesca Recipe

Serving: 8 | Prep: | Cook: 2hours30mins | Ready in:

Ingredients

- 2 tablespoons olive oil
- 4 lamb shanks
- salt & pepper to taste
- 2 cups diced onion
- 2 tablespoons chopped garlic
- 1/2 teaspoon red pepper flakes
- 1 cup dry white wine
- 1 tablespoon anchovy paste
- 4 tablespoons whole capers in brine, drained
- 3/4 cup black olives, quartered

- 2 cups beef stock
- 2 cups canned crushed tomatoes
- 1 pound rigatoni pasta, cooked
- 2 tablespoons chopped parsley, for garnish
- 1/4 cup feta cheese, for garnish

Direction

- Preheat oven to 325 degrees.
- Season lamb shanks with salt and pepper.
- Heat oil in ovenproof pot over high heat.
- Brown shanks on all sides, then remove from pot and set aside.
- Drain off all but 2 tablespoons of fat from pot and add onion, garlic and red pepper flakes. Sauté on medium heat until vegetables are tender, about 6 minutes.
- Add wine, anchovy paste, capers and olives and simmer until liquid has almost evaporated.
- Add stock and tomatoes, stirring to combine all ingredients. Add shanks back to pot. Bring to boil on stovetop before covering tightly and placing in oven.
- Turn lamb shanks after 1 hour, cover and place back in oven for 1 more hour, or until meat is tender enough to fall off the bone. Remove shanks from braising liquid and set aside to cool.
- When shanks are cool enough to handle, shred meat, discarding excess fat and bone.
- Add meat back to braising liquid, stirring to combine. Warm gently over low heat.
- Serve with rigatoni pasta. Garnish with chopped parsley and feta cheese.

171.   Lasagna Recipe

Serving: 12 | Prep: | Cook: 100mins | Ready in:

Ingredients

- 1-1/2 to 2 lbs. lean ground beef
- 1 large onion, finely chopped
- Note: I like to add 1 green bell pepper that has been finely chopped but it's up to you.
- 1/2 tsp. oregano
- 2-1/2 to 3 cups mozzarella cheese, shredded and divided
- 2 cups ricotta cheese
- 1 cup Parmesan/romano cheese, grated and divided
- 1/4 cup chopped fresh parsley
- 1 egg, lightly beaten
- 1 jar (700 mL) spaghetti sauce (your favourite)
- 3-4 garlic cloves, minced
- 1-1/2 cups water
- 12 lasagna noodles, uncooked
- Note: I sometimes add a layer of spinach. I use 1 package of frozen spinach that has been thawed and very well drained. Simple as that.

Direction

- Preheat oven to 350°F.
- Cook meat, onion and oregano in a large skillet on medium heat.
- Meanwhile, mix 1-1/4 cups of the mozzarella cheese, ricotta cheese, 1/4 cup of Parmesan or Romano cheese, parsley and egg until well blended and set aside.
- Drain meat and return to skillet.
- Stir in pasta sauce and minced garlic.
- Pour water into empty sauce jar.
- Replace lid and shake well.
- Add to skillet and stir until well blended.
- Spread approximately 1 cup of the meat sauce onto the bottom of a 13 x 9 inch baking dish.
- Top with layers of 3 lasagna noodles, 1/3 of the ricotta cheese mixture and 1 cup of the meat sauce.
- Repeat layers two more times.
- Top with remaining 3 noodles and remaining meat sauce.
- Sprinkle with remaining 1-1/4 cups or more of mozzarella cheese and 1/4 cup Parmesan/Romano cheese.
- Cover tightly with PAM sprayed foil.
- Bake for 1 hour.
- Remove foil and continue baking for 15-20 minutes or until heated completely through.

- Let stand 15 minutes before cutting to serve.
- Substitute:
- Substitute 2 pkg. (1 cup each) frozen, thawed simulated ground beef for the browned ground beef.
- Shortcut:
- Adding water to the sauce helps cook traditional noodles during baking, so you don't have to cook them beforehand. This saves you 15 to 20 min. of prep time.

172. Lasagna Roll Ups Recipe

Serving: 8 | Prep: | Cook: 60mins | Ready in:

Ingredients

- 6 uncooked plain lasagna noodles (6 ounces)
- 6 uncooked whole wheat lasagna noodles (6 ounces)
- 1 pound lean ground beef
- 1 large onion, chopped (1 cup)
- 1 jar (14 ounces) tomato pasta sauce (any variety)
- 1 can (8 ounces) mushroom pieces and stems, undrained
- 1 container (15 ounces) ricotta cheese
- 1 package (10 ounces) frozen chopped spinach, thawed and squeezed to drain
- 1 cup shredded mozzarella cheese (4 ounces)
- 1/4 cup grated parmesan cheese
- 1 teaspoon salt
- 1/4 teaspoon pepper
- 2 garlic cloves, finely chopped
- Additional grated parmesan cheese, if desired

Direction

- Heat oven to 350°F. Cook and drain noodles as directed on package.
- Cook beef and onion in 10-inch skillet over medium-high heat about 6 minutes, stirring occasionally, until beef is brown; drain. Stir in pasta sauce and mushrooms. Heat to boiling,

stirring constantly. Pour into ungreased rectangular baking dish, 11x7x1 1/2 inches.
- Mix ricotta cheese, spinach, mozzarella cheese, 1/4 cup Parmesan cheese, the salt, pepper and garlic. Spread 3 tablespoons of the cheese mixture over each noodle. Roll up each noodle; cut roll crosswise in half. Place cut sides down in beef mixture.
- Cover and bake about 30 minutes or until hot. Serve with additional Parmesan cheese.

173. Layered Macaroni Casserole Recipe

Serving: 8 | Prep: | Cook: 40mins | Ready in:

Ingredients

- 1 pound lean ground beef
- 1/2 cup chopped onion
- 1 garlic clove, minced
- 1 (28 ounce) can crushed tomatoes
- 1 (6 ounce) can tomato paste
- 2 teaspoons sugar
- 1 teaspoon salt
- 1 teaspoon chili powder
- 1/2 teaspoon dried basil
- 1/2 teaspoon dried oregano
- 1/8 teaspoon pepper
- 8 ounces uncooked elbow macaroni
- 2 cups fat-free cottage cheese
- 1 1/2 cups shredded reduced-fat cheddar cheese
- TOPPING:
- 1/4 cup dry bread crumbs
- 1/4 cup grated parmesan cheese
- 1 tablespoon butter or stick margarine, melted

Direction

- In a non-stick skillet, cook ground beef, onion and garlic over medium heat until meat is no longer pink; drain. Add the tomatoes, tomato paste and seasonings. Bring to a boil. Reduce heat; cover and simmer for 1 hour. Meanwhile, cook macaroni according to package directions; drain. Add cottage cheese.

- In a 13-in. x 9-in. x 2-in. baking dish coated with non-stick cooking spray, layer 1 cup meat sauce, a third of the macaroni mixture and a third of the cheddar cheese. Repeat layers twice. Top with remaining meat sauce. Combine topping ingredients; sprinkle over sauce. Bake, uncovered, at 325 degrees F for 40-45 minutes. Let stand for 10 minutes before serving.

174. Lemon Chicken Pasta Recipe

Serving: 4 | Prep: | Cook: 25mins |Ready in:

Ingredients

- 8 oz Bowtie pasta
- 1 1/2 lbs chicken tenderloins
- large zip top bag
- 1/4 cup flour
- 1 tsp seasoned salt
- 1/4 cup garlic butter
- 2 tbsp capers
- 2 tsp chicken bouillon granules
- 1/2 cup white wine
- 1 lemon
- 1/4 cup heavy whipping cream

Direction

- Prepare bowtie pasta according to package directions
- While pasta cooks, preheat large sauté pan on medium high 2-3 minutes.
- Cut chicken into bite size pieces
- Place flour and seasoned salt in zip top bag, shake to mix
- Add chicken and shake to coat
- Add garlic butter to sauté pan and swirl to coat

- Add chicken, reduce heat to medium and cook 2-4 minutes, stirring occasionally until chicken is no longer pink.
- Stir capers and chicken bouillon into chicken, cook 2 minutes
- Stir in wine, juice from lemon and cream
- Reduce heat to low and simmer 3-4 minutes.
- Stir bowtie pasta into chicken mixture

175. Lemon Chicken And Pasta Recipe

Serving: 4 | Prep: | Cook: 15mins |Ready in:

Ingredients

- 4 boneless, skinless chicken cutlets
- 1 cup Italian bread crumbs
- fresh parsley
- 8-10 artichoke hearts
- 2 tsp capers
- 1 tbsp olive oil
- Spoonful garlic
- 1 box angel hair pasta
- 1 fresh lemon, cut into decorative slices

Direction

- Bread chicken breasts with bread crumbs. Cook on low heat in sauce pan until cooked thoroughly. Add one lemon slice for each chicken breast. Simmer on low heat. Add a spoonful of garlic, or more to taste, a few artichoke hearts and a few spoonfuls of capers. Keep on low heat while you cook pasta. Once pasta is cooked, drain and mix butter and garlic with pasta. Add pasta to plate, and top it off with some chicken mixed with artichoke hearts, lemon, garlic and capers. Top with fresh parsley.

176. Lemon Linguine Recipe

Serving: 4 | Prep: | Cook: 15mins |Ready in:

Ingredients

- 8 oz. linguine
- 1 tbls. olive oil
- 2 tbls. parsley, chopped
- 1 tsp. grated lemon peel
- 1/2 tsp pepper
- 3/4 cup chicken stock or broth
- 2 tbls. lemon juice
- 2 tsp. cornstarch
- 2 tbls. parmesan cheese, grated

Direction

- Cook linguine according to package directions
- Drain well and put in large bowl
- Add oil, parsley, lemon peel and pepper
- Toss to coat
- In a saucepan, combine chicken stock, lemon juice, and cornstarch and whisk to dissolve cornstarch
- Bring to a boil, whisking constantly
- Reduce heat and simmer until thick, about 2 minutes
- Add pasta to sauce and toss to heat through
- Transfer back to bowl
- Sprinkle with parmesan

177. Lemongrass Pork With Vietnamese Table Salad Recipe

Serving: 4 | Prep: | Cook: 20mins |Ready in:

Ingredients

- Dipping Sauce:
- 3/4 cup hot water
- 5 tablespoons fish sauce*
- 3 1/2 tablespoons sugar
- 1 1/2 tablespoons fresh lime juice
- 2 Thai bird chiles with seeds or 1/2 jalapeño chile with seeds, minced
- 1 garlic clove, minced
- ~~~~
- Pork:
- 6 green onions (white and pale green parts only), chopped (about 1/2 cup)
- 3 tablespoons chopped lemongrass
- 2 tablespoons soy sauce
- 1 tablespoon golden brown sugar
- 2 teaspoons fish sauce
- 1/4 teaspoon ground white pepper
- 3 tablespoons vegetable oil, divided
- 1 1/2 to 1 3/4 pounds boneless pork loin chops (each 1/3 to 1/2 inch thick)
- ~~~~
- Salad and Noodles:
- 1 small English hothouse cucumber, halved lengthwise, thinly sliced crosswise
- 1 baby pineapple, peeled, halved, thinly sliced or 1/2 small pineapple, peeled, cut into 2 wedges, cored, thinly sliced
- 2 cups bean sprouts
- 1 cup fresh Thai basil leaves
- 1 cup fresh cilantro leaves
- 1 cup fresh mint leaves
- 20 fresh green shiso leaves
- 1/2 cup finely shredded carrot
- 1 8- to 9-ounce package dried rice vermicelli noodles
- 3 heads of butter lettuce, cored, leaves separated

Direction

- For Dipping Sauce:
- Mix all ingredients in small bowl. Season sauce to taste with salt.
- ** Can be made 1 day ahead. Cover and chill.
- ~~~~
- For Pork:
- Mix first 6 ingredients and 2 tablespoons oil in 11x7-inch glass dish.
- Add pork chops to marinade, turn several times to coat evenly, and then crowd together in single layer. Cover and refrigerate at least 30 minutes and up to 2 hours.

- ~~~~
- For Salad and Noodles:
- Arrange cucumber, pineapple, bean sprouts, all herbs, and carrot around edge of large platter.
- **Can be prepared 2 hours ahead. Cover; chill.
- Cook noodles in large pot of boiling salted water until just tender and turning white, separating often with tongs, about 4 minutes. Drain.
- Arrange in center of platter. Mound lettuce leaves in large shallow bowl.
- Prepare grill (medium-high heat). Brush grill rack with remaining 1 tablespoon oil.
- Grill pork with marinade still clinging to meat until slightly charred and cooked through, 4 to 5 minutes per side, depending on thickness.
- Transfer pork to cutting board. Let rest 10 minutes.
- Cut pork crosswise into 1/3-inch-wide strips. Place pork and any juices from board atop noodles.
- To serve, fill lettuce leaves with pork, noodles, herbs, and vegetables.
- Serve with sauce for dipping.

178.　　Linguine With Clam Sauce Recipe

Serving: 4 | Prep: | Cook: 20mins | Ready in:

Ingredients

- 2 tablespoons olive oil
- 1 white onion chopped
- 2 garlic cloves chopped
- 2 cans minced clams
- 1 tablespoon parsley
- 1/2 teaspoon basil
- 1/2 teaspoon oregano
- 1/4 teaspoon red pepper flakes
- 1/8 teaspoon salt
- 1/8 teaspoon freshly-ground black pepper
- Hot cooked linguine

Direction

- Sauté onion and garlic for 5 minutes.
- Drain in liquid from clams to onion and garlic mix reserving clams.
- Add parsley, oregano, basil, red pepper flakes, salt, and pepper then simmer for 5 minutes and stir in clams.
- Add cooked linguine then stir well and serve.

179.　　Louisiana Crawfish Fettuccine Recipe

Serving: 20 | Prep: | Cook: 25mins | Ready in:

Ingredients

- 2 sticks of butter
- 2 large onion, finely chopped
- 2 cup green onions, finely chopped
- 2 green bell pepper, finely chopped
- 6 stalks celery, finely chopped
- 1 clove garlic, minced
- parsley
- 3 teaspoons of finely chopped jalepenos (less or more, depending on your taste, or you dont have to add at all)
- 1 tablespoon all-purpose flour
- 1 pound peeled crawfish tails (can use frozen crawfish)
- 1 large box of velvetta cheese
- 1 16 oz. half-and-half cream
- 2 teaspoons cajun seasoning
- 2 teaspoons cayenne pepper
- 2 to 2 1/2 boxes fettuccine pasta
- 1/2 cup grated parmesan cheese
- THIS MAKES A LARGE ALUMINUM PAN FULL. THIS RECIPE IS FOR A LARGE CROWD. YOU CAN CUT THE RECIPE IN HALF TO SERVE AT HOME FOR YOUR FAMILY.
- THIS IS NOT THE PICTURE OF MINE, BUT SOMETHING SIMILAR TO MINE!

Direction

- Melt the butter in a large skillet over medium heat. Cook onion, bell pepper, celery, and garlic in butter until onions are tender.
- Stir in flour, and cook for 5 to 10 minutes, stirring frequently.
- Stir in crawfish. Cover, and simmer for 15 to 20 minutes, stirring often.
- Stir in the Velveeta cheese, half-and-half, Cajun seasonings, jalapeno peppers and cayenne pepper. Cover, and simmer for about 20 minutes, stirring occasionally.
- Meanwhile, bring a large pot of lightly salted water to a boil. Cook pasta in boiling water for 8 to 10 minutes, or until done; drain.
- Preheat oven to 350 degrees. Stir noodles into crawfish mixture; pour into prepared dish, and sprinkle with Parmesan cheese.
- Bake in a preheated oven for 20 minutes, or until hot and bubbly.

180. Lovely LEFTOVERS Ala Elaine Recipe

Serving: 2 | Prep: | Cook: 30mins | Ready in:

Ingredients

- leftover pork ribs, whatever amount you have on hand
- fresh green tomatoes, banana peppers, onion, parsley coarsely chopped
- 1 cup orzo
- salt and pepper to taste
- dash powdered cinnamon stick
- 3 tbsp olive oil

Direction

- Combine the oil with a little salt in the pan
- Heat over medium-low flame (I cook with propane gas in the house)
- If you use an electric stove, keep the heat at medium to low as cooking progresses

- Place the leftover ribs in the oven at LOW setting
- Add the onions to the pan, and caramelize slightly.
- In the meantime, cook the orzo in boiling water for only about 5 minutes. Orzo does not take long to cook.
- When the onions are lightly caramelized, add all the remaining ingredients and simmer until soft and tender, about another 20 minutes.
- This dish is both delicious, and economical.

181. Low Fat Southwestern Style Lasagna Recipe

Serving: 10 | Prep: | Cook: 35mins | Ready in:

Ingredients

- 1 tsp canola oil
- 1 pound extra-lean ground turkey
- 1 medium onion, chopped
- 1 medium carrot, diced
- 1 16-ounce jar salsa (spiciness is up to you)
- 1 15-ounce can reduced-sodium black beans, drained
- 1 10-ounce pack frozen sweetcorn
- 1 tsp chili powder
- 1 tsp cumin
- 8 ounces cooked lasagna noodles
- 1 16-ounce tub fat-free ricotta cheese
- 3/4 cup shredded reduced-fat cheddar cheese

Direction

- Preheat oven to 350 degrees.
- Heat oil in a large skillet or Dutch oven. Add onions and carrots; cook until onions are translucent. Crumble in ground beef and cook until no longer pink.
- Drain excess fat. Add salsa, black beans, corn, chili powder and cumin, stirring well.
- Spread one-third of beef mixture in a 9 x 13-inch baking dish. Layer half the noodles on top; spoon half the ricotta cheese over the

noodles. Add another third of the meat mixture, followed by remaining noodles and ricotta cheese. Spread rest of beef on top and sprinkle with shredded cheese. Bake for 35 minutes.
- Serves 10
- Per Serving: Calories 364, Calories from Fat 46, Fat 5.3g (sat 2.3g), Cholesterol 62mg, Sodium 706mg, Carbohydrate 54g, Fiber 6.6g, Protein 25.4g

182.   Low Fat Rosemary Chicken Pasta Recipe

Serving: 4 | Prep: | Cook: 20mins | Ready in:

Ingredients

- • 8 ounces uncooked penne, ziti or other pasta
- • 1 clove garlic, minced
- • 1/2 teaspoon dried rosemary
- • 4 boneless, skinless chicken breasts, cut into thin strips
- • 16 - 18 asparagus spears, sliced thin (fresh or frozen but I think fresh is best)
- • 3/4 cup fat free chicken broth
- • 2 tablespoons fresh parsley, chopped
- • 2 tablespoons reduced fat parmesan cheese
- • salt and pepper to taste

Direction

- Prepare pasta according to package direction; drain.
- Heat 1/4 cup broth in a deep non-stick skillet over medium heat. Add garlic and rosemary and cook 15 seconds. Add chicken and cook, tossing well, until lightly browned, about 3 minutes.
- Add asparagus*, remaining chicken broth, parsley and pasta to skillet. Increase heat to high and bring to a boil, stirring occasionally, until liquid has reduced enough to lightly cover pasta.

- Sprinkle with reduced fat Parmesan, salt and pepper and toss. Serve immediately.

183.   Lydias Lasagna Recipe

Serving: 8 | Prep: | Cook: 165mins | Ready in:

Ingredients

- 1 lb box of wide lasagna noodles - fresh if you prefer
- 1 lb italian sausage - hot is preferred - if you can get the loose type it's easier - otherwise you have to take the skins off...
- 1 lb lean ground beef
- 1 1/2 medium onion, chopped
- 2 - 4 large cloves garlic, minced
- 1 x 2 1/2 lb can tomato puree
- 1 small can tomato paste
- 2 x 14 oz cans tomato sauce
- 1 tsp sugar
- 2 cups Ricotta - or more!
- 1/2 - 1 cup parmesan cheese
- 1 tblsp salt
- 1/2 tsp pepper
- 2 tsp crushed chile
- 1 - 2 bay leaves
- 2 tblsp olive oil
- 1 - 2 tsp Italian mixed spices
- 1/2 cup red wine - if you wouldn't drink it...don't use it!
- 1 lb mozzarella cheese, grated - or more!
- water

Direction

- Sauce: Brown sausage, ground beef in olive oil until almost done, add onions and garlic and finish browning.
- Add puree, paste, sauce, salt, pepper, crushed chili, bay leaves, Italian spices, sugar (to blend flavors) and wine.
- Let simmer for approx. 2 hrs. - add a little water to keep from thickening too much while simmering.

- Cook noodles according to package instructions. When cooked place in a pan with cool water so they don't stick together.
- Preheat oven to 375F
- Spray 13 x 9 x 2 baking pan and start layering: first layer sauce, then noodles, then sauce again, then spoon dollops of ricotta evenly, then sprinkle with shredded mozzarella and parmesan cheese. Continue layers (usually 2 - 3) in this way and end with sauce and parmesan on top.
- Cover with foil and bake for 1/2 hour. Uncover and continue baking for 15 minutes.
- Serve with green salad and vinaigrette dressing and crusty garlic bread. Delicioso!

184. MACHO CASSEROLE Recipe

Serving: 8 | Prep: | Cook: 35mins | Ready in:

Ingredients

- 1 lb. ground beef
- 2 cloves garlic, crushed
- 2 tsp. salt
- 2 tsp. sugar
- 2 -8oz Cans tomato sauce
- 1 C. sour cream
- 1-8 oz. Pkg cream cheese, softened
- 6 green onions, chopped finely
- 1-8 oz. Pkg egg noodles, cooked and drained
- 1 C. cheddar cheese, grated

Direction

- Preheat oven to 350°F.
- Brown beef with garlic.
- Add salt, sugar and tomato sauce and simmer.
- Combine Sour Cream, Cream Cheese, and Onion.
- Spray 2-3 qt. casserole with cooking spray.
- Put 1/2 of the noodles and 1/2 of the tomato sauce mixture in bottom.
- Layer with Sour Cream mixture.

- Top with remaining noodles and tomato sauce mixture.
- Bake for 35 minutes.

185. Macaroni Cheese Southern Way Recipe

Serving: 10 | Prep: | Cook: 1mins | Ready in:

Ingredients

- 1 lb. of macaroni (cooked according to package directions)
- 2 cups of heavy cream and 1 cup of milk (mixed)
- 1 cup of Velveeta cheese Block (cut into 1/4 inch cubes)
- 1/4 lb of melted butter
- 2 cups of sharp cheddar cheese (grated)
- 2 cups of Extra-sharp cheddar cheese (grated)
- 1 cup of mozzarella cheese (grated)
- 1 cup of asiago cheese (grated)
- 6 eggs (beaten)
- 1 pinch of salt
- 1 tps of ground black pepper
- 1/2 tsp of cayenne pepper

Direction

- (Preheat oven to 325F.)
- Drain the pasta after cooked, put in a large mixing bowl and quickly add the Velveeta while pasta is hot, stir in 1/2 of the milk mixture and the melted butter.
- Stir ingredients and mix all together for the pasta to start melting the Velveeta cubes.
- (It will be a little soupy but when we add the eggs and it bakes, it'll bring all tight and together)
- Add the 6 beaten eggs and the rest of the cheeses, the pinch of salt, the black pepper and the cayenne, turn and toss until well combined.

- After all is combined, add the rest of the remaining milk mixture and stir all that right in.
- After all is nicely combined, pour the pasta mixture into a greased or sprayed baking dish and spread it into a nice even layer.
- Bake for about 45 minutes to 1 hour, depending on how quickly it starts to brown.
- The last 5 minutes turn the broiler for a nice brown on top.
- After 45 minutes in the oven, keep an eye on it.

186.   Macaroni PIe Memas Favorite Recipe

Serving: 8 | Prep: | Cook: 65mins | Ready in:

Ingredients

- 1 ten ounce package of elbow macaroni
- 1 quart of water
- 1 pound of medium sharp cheddar cheese, grated
- 3 eggs beaten
- 2 cups of milk
- 4 tablespoons of unsalted butter
- 1 tsp of salt
- 1/2 tsp of black pepper
- 1 tsp of dry mustard
- 1/4 tsp of cayenne pepper
- 6-8 grates of fresh nutmeg on microplane

Direction

- Preheat oven to 450 degrees
- Bring one quart of cold water to a boil and cook the macaroni to the al dente stage, you want them firm because you are baking it longer, stir it occasionally to keep from sticking.
- DO NOT DRAIN.
- You will need the residual water in the pan, most of it will be absorbed at this point anyway.

- Add all the remaining ingredients and mix well.
- Place mixture in a buttered casserole and bake in the very hot oven for 35 to 40 minutes until the top is lightly browned.
- Allow to rest at least 10 minutes before attempting to eat, it will be very hot.

187.   Macaroni With Gruyere Cheese Serrano Ham And Leeks Recipe

Serving: 4 | Prep: | Cook: 20mins | Ready in:

Ingredients

- 1 1/2 cups elbow macaroni
- 1 Tablespoon vegetable oil
- 1 cup 1/8-inch diced Serrano ham
- 1 large leek, white part only thinly sliced
- 2 cups cream
- 1 cup grated parmigiano Reggiano cheese
- salt and pepper
- 1 cup grated gruyere cheese
- 1/3 cup bread crumbs
- 4 Tablespoons chopped chives

Direction

- Preheat oven to 450°F.
- Cook pasta in a large pot of salted boiling water until al dente, about 8 to 10 minutes, then drain and set aside.
- Heat oil in a medium-sized skillet over medium heat.
- Add the ham and cook until brown.
- Add the leek.
- Then add the cream.
- When the cream begins to simmer, add the Parmigiano Reggiano cheese and pasta, and season with salt and prepare.
- Divide the pasta into 4 oven-proof dishes.
- Top with Gruyere cheese and bread crumbs.

- Bake for about 8 to 10 minutes or until golden brown.
- Remove from oven and sprinkle with chopped chives.
- Macaroni will be very hot so it is best to let it sit just a few minutes before serving.

---

188. Making Tomato Sauce On Bbq Recipe

Serving: 8 | Prep: | Cook: 180mins | Ready in:

Ingredients

- Regular tomatoes
- Roma
- Cherry
- and any other tomatoe
- Chopped bell pepper
- Chopped onion
- Fresh crushed garlic
- italian seasoning
- salt
- pepper

Direction

- Blanch all the tomatoes to remove skins, even the cherry.
- Chop bell pepper to about 1/2 inch. I use the largest Zyliss chopper.
- Chop Onion
- The pan in the pics is the largest I could get at the local restaurant supply store. The bigger the better.
- After blanching I slip off the skins, put the tomatoes, pepper, onions, and seasonings in the pan and let it cook on the BBQ for about 3 hours on low heat. Stirring frequently and carefully.
- I usually cook over an open flame but for this I insert a heavy large metal plate under the grill to spread the heat and not burn the bottom. It has a tendency to boil pretty well, sometimes over the edges. At first it seems like not much happening, but given time it cooks down.
- Once it has cooked about 3 hours, it has reduced itself and I bring it in, transfer to a large the pot for the final reduction and the option of adding meat. Reduce it until it is the consistency (thickness) you want.
- I have made it two ways.
- I have cooked hamburger and added it to the sauce and let it simmer on the stove for about 20-30 minutes. Let cool, spoon into freezer zip lock bags to have all winter.
- Second is to just freeze the sauce.
- There are no rules for the amount of onion, pepper, garlic etc. It's just put stuff in until it looks right, and cook. BBQ-ing the tomatoes for sauce is the best. You get a unique smoky flavor.
- I have defrosted a bag with the hamburger, nuked it and ate the sauce by itself. Of course with fresh grated Parmesan cheese on top. HMMMMMMMM!
- Not much you can't do on a BBQ. I use mine year round. I am brutal to my BBQ but it keeps on ticking. The front lower part is now bowed out about 1/2 inch, I love it.
- You are also seeing a stack of plastic bowls. I am always looking for large nesting bowls. They are great for mixing or stirring up stuff.
- One year the cherry tomatoes grew to about 12 feet. I kept them growing up a wall of string. It was very cool looking. The regular tomatoes, roma's, ace, etc. always huge plants and tons of tomatoes.
- 30 years of adding to the garden, I have raised the soil over 12 inches, it is some of the richest soil (I don't have dirt) you could every want to grow your vegies in. It is so rich even the weeds get big if I don't spot them and yank them out.
- Gardens are good for the soul. JJ

189. Mammas Baked Mac N Cheese Recipe

Serving: 6 | Prep: | Cook: 45mins | Ready in:

Ingredients

- 1 (8 ounce) package elbow macaroni
- 1 (8 ounce) package shredded sharp cheddar cheese
- 1 (12 ounce) container small curd cottage cheese
- 1 (8 ounce) container sour cream
- 1/4 cup grated parmesan cheese
- salt and pepper to taste
- 1 cup dry bread crumbs
- 1/4 cup butter, melted

Direction

- Preheat oven to 350 degrees F (175 degrees C).
- Bring a large pot of lightly salted water to a boil, add pasta, and cook until done; drain.
- In 9x13 inch baking dish, stir together macaroni, shredded Cheddar cheese, cottage cheese, sour cream, Parmesan cheese, salt and pepper.
- In a small bowl, mix together bread crumbs and melted butter. Sprinkle topping over macaroni mixture.
- Bake 30 to 35 minutes, or until top is golden.

190. Marinated Scallops Wrapped In Bacon Recipe

Serving: 2 | Prep: | Cook: 15mins | Ready in:

Ingredients

- 3/4 cup maple syrup
- 1/4 cup low sodium soy sauce
- 1 tablespoon Dijon mustard
- 12 large sea scallops, halved
- 12 slices smoked bacon, halved
- 24 toothpicks
- 2 tablespoons brown sugar
- 1/2 package garlic and herb spegetti noodles

Direction

- Stir together maple syrup, soy sauce, brown sugar and Dijon mustard in a bowl until smooth.
- Add the scallops, and toss to coat.
- Cover bowl with plastic wrap, and marinate at least one hour.
- Preheat oven to 375 degrees F (190 degrees C). Line a rimmed baking sheet with a sheet of aluminum foil.
- Arrange bacon pieces on baking sheet so they do not overlap.
- Bake in preheated oven until some of the grease has rendered out of the bacon; the bacon should still be very soft and pliable, about 8 minutes. Remove bacon from the baking sheet and pat with paper towels to remove excess grease.
- Wrap each scallop piece with a piece of bacon, and secure with a toothpick.
- Cook spaghetti as package directs.
- Place in a baking dish.
- Pour marinate over the scallops
- Broil on low until the scallops are opaque and the bacon is crisp, 10 to 15 minutes, turning once.
- Yield 24 pieces
- NOTE:
- I used the largest scallops I could find and bought 1 pound of them. This was heaven.

191. Mediterranean Shrimp Feta Pasta Recipe

Serving: 4 | Prep: | Cook: 20mins | Ready in:

Ingredients

- 1/4 cup olive oil
- 4 minced garlic cloves

- 1 lb uncooked meduim shrimp, peeled and deveined
- 1 8oz frozen artichoke hearts, thawed and halved
- 1 1/2 cups crumbled feta cheese
- 1/2 cup diced tomatoes
- 3 Tblsp lemon juice
- 3 Tblsp chopped parsley
- 2 Tblsp finely chopped oregano
- 12 ounces linguine or angel hair pasta

Direction

- Heat olive oil in heavy large skillet over medium heat. Add garlic and sauté 1 minute. Add shrimp and sauté 2 minutes. Add artichokes, feta, tomatoes, lemon juice, parsley and oregano.
- Sauté until shrimp are just opaque in center, about 3 minutes longer. Season sauce to taste with salt and pepper.
- Cook pasta in large pot of salted boiling water until tender but still firm to bite. Drain. Transfer past to large bowl
- Add shrimp mixture to the pasta and toss to coat. Season to taste with salt and pepper.
- Serve with a nice Chianti wine

192. Mediterranean Chicken And Pasta With Kalamata Olives Sun Dried Tomatoes And Pine Nuts Recipe

Serving: 6 | Prep: | Cook: 20mins | Ready in:

Ingredients

- Mediterranean chicken and pasta with kalamata olives, sun-dried tomatoes & pine nuts
- ½ - 1 cup sun-dried tomatoes, quartered with scissors
- ½ - 1 cup kalamata olives

- 2 boneless, skinless chicken breast halves, cut into bite sized chunks
- ¼ - ½ cup rosemary-Infused white wine vinegar
- ¼ c olive oil
- ½ small onion, chopped fine
- 2-3 cloves roasted garlic, mashed
- ½ t dried oregano or 1-2 t fresh oregano
- Coarsely cracked black pepper
- 1 green or red bell pepper, chopped
- 4 ounces crumbled feta cheese
- ½ - 1 cup pine nuts
- About 1 cup marinated artichoke hearts
- ½ - 1 cup fresh grated parmesan or asiago cheese
- 2-3 green onions, chopped
- 2 cups uncooked hearty pasta, like a gemelli or a penne

Direction

- First, soak the cut-up sun-dried tomatoes. Reserve all the soaking water. Set aside.
- For the marinade, combine the vinegar, 2 T of the tomato-soaking water, 2 T of Kalamata olive brine, 2T olive oil, the chopped onion, oregano, pepper, and one of the mashed roasted garlic cloves. Marinate the chicken for about thirty minutes.
- Cook the chicken in its marinade in a large heavy skillet. When the chicken is nearly cooked, toss in the bell pepper and garlic, continue cooking, turning frequently. Meanwhile combine the remaining tomato-soaking water with enough plain water to cook the pasta. Add a pinch of salt and bring to a boil in a large pan, add pasta. When pasta is al dente, drain and toss with a dash of olive oil. Add the chicken, peppers, and garlic and all remaining ingredients. Toss lightly and serve immediately with a salad of cucumbers and tomatoes. A Sauvignon Blanc is very nice with this.
- I change this recipe depending on my taste at the moment as well as what I have on hand. It's equally good with fresh tomatoes and

"regular" black olive, but the taste is very different.

193.   Mexican Chicken Fettuccini Alfredo Recipe

Serving: 6 | Prep: | Cook: 45mins | Ready in:

Ingredients

- 1 Rotisserie (sp?) whole chicken breast (the big-un)
- Fettuccini pasta (3/4 of the box)
- 1/2 a Pint half and half
- 1 Stick of butter
- 1 small onion finely chopped
- 1 8 oz. package of whipped cream cheese
- 1-1/2 TBS garlic powder
- 1 TBS ground cumin
- 1 tsp chilie powder
- 1 tsp. red pepper flakes
- 3/4 Cup parmesan cheese
- 1/4 Cup smooth salsa - none of that chunky stuff
- 1/4 Cup good quality ranch dressing
- salt and pepper to taste
- parsley flakes to garnish

Direction

- Debone chicken breast and cut into bite sized pieces, set aside.
- In a sauce pan over medium heat melt butter, add onion and cook until translucent.
- Start your water for your pasta.
- Add in cream cheese.
- Stir often and when cream cheese is completely softened, whisk to attain creamy texture.
- When water boils, add in pasta and cook to package directions.
- Slowly whisk in half and half, salsa and ranch dressing to the cream cheese mixture.
- Add seasonings and parmesan cheese, stir to blend thoroughly.

- Add in chicken to warm through.
- Drain pasta and plate, pouring Alfredo sauce over top.
- Serve and enjoy!

194.   Mexican Manicotti In The Microwave Recipe

Serving: 6 | Prep: | Cook: 18mins | Ready in:

Ingredients

- ½ pound ground sirloin (don't use a fatty ground beef for this)
- 1 cup refried beans or black beans
- ½ cup diced onion
- 1 or 2 tablespoon taco seasoning
- 8 manicotti shells, uncooked
- 1¼ cups water
- 8 ounces salsa
- 8 ounces sour cream
- ¼ cup chopped onions
- ¼ cup sliced black olives
- ½ cup shredded mexican cheese blend, or cheddar cheese
- sliced jalapeno peppers

Direction

- Combine uncooked meat, beans, 1/2 cup diced onions and taco seasoning; fill uncooked manicotti shells with mixture. Arrange filled shells in a 10x7 glass baking dish. Combine water and salsa; pour over shells. Cover with plastic wrap, poking a couple holes in it to allow steam to escape as it cooks. Microwave on High for 5 minutes; let it stand for 5 minutes. Cook on High for another 5 minutes. Using tongs, remove saran (BE CAREFUL of steam!) and turn shells over. Cover again, venting as before. Microwave on Medium for 10 to 18 minutes, until pasta is done. If your microwave does not have a turntable, be sure to turn baking dish every 5 minutes during all cooking times. Combine sour cream, ¼ cup chopped onions and olives; spoon down center of baked casserole. Top with cheese. Microwave on High, with just a piece of waxed paper on top to prevent splattering, for 1 minute, or until cheese begins to melt. Serve with jalapeno pepper slices on the side for anyone who likes more "heat".

195. Mexican Marinara Pasta Recipe

Serving: 4 | Prep: | Cook: 90mins | Ready in:

Ingredients

- 1 Lbs. ground chuck
- 1 small jalapeño pepper (finely chopped)
- 1 small (26 oz) jar of traditional Ragu spaghetti sauce
- 1 10 ounce can Mild rotel diced tomatoes & green chilies (drained) if more heat is desired, use regular or hot rotel.
- 1 4 ounce cans of Green Giant mushrooms (Pieces & Stems) (drained)
- ½ 6 ounce can tomato paste
- 1 8 ounce can tomato sauce
- 1 teaspoon Minced garlic
- 1 tablespoon Donnie's cajun seasoning mix (or equivalent) (Recipe on my recipe page)
- 1 tablespoon italian seasoning
- 1 pinch sugar
- 1 pinch ground oregano
- 1 pinch dried ground basil leaves
- 1 12 ounce packages of penne rigate pasta

Direction

- In a large 5 quart pot, brown beef over medium heat until no longer pink.
- Drain fat and return meat to pot.
- Combine all other ingredients into pot and bring to a low boil.
- Reduce heat and simmer for 1 hour.
- Cook the pasta according to the package instructions.
- Drain pasta and add to the Marinara Sauce pot and mix well.
- Serve and enjoy.

196. Mexican Pasta Casserole Recipe

Serving: 8 | Prep: | Cook: 15mins | Ready in:

Ingredients

- 24 ounce sour cream
- 2 cups cheddar cheese
- 2 cups colby jack cheese
- 1 can cream of mushroom soup
- 1 pound hamburger meat
- 1 pkg taco seosoning
- 3 cups cooked pasta rotini shaped
- 1 can rotel
- 1/2 green onions

Direction

- Brown and drain meat
- Add 1/2 pkg. of taco seasoning, rotel, 1/2 sour cream, mushroom soup,
- Mix thoroughly
- Mix with cooked pasta in casserole dish
- Top noodle mix with cheddar cheese
- Place in oven on 350 for 15 minutes or until cheese is melted and bubbly
- Mix the rest of the taco seasoning in the left over sour cream set aside
- Take out casserole let cool for 15 minutes
- Top casserole with sour cream mixture
- Top with Colby jack cheese
- Serve

197. Mexican Seafood Rollups Recipe

Serving: 12 | Prep: | Cook: 40mins | Ready in:

Ingredients

- 12 lasagna noodles, par cooked and drained and patted dry
- 16 oz. baby shrimp, frozen, defrosted patted dry
- 16 oz of claw meat, don't bother with lump, refrigerator section please
- 8 oz of cream cheese
- 8 oz of monterey jack cheese
- 8 oz of swiss cheese
- 2 tbsp. of butter
- 1 small green pepper minced
- 1 tsp ground oregano
- 1/2 teaspoon of cumin
- 1 tsp of seasoning salt (or adobo seasoning my favorite)
- 1 sm onion minced
- 2 tsp garlic minced
- 1 tsp of black pepper
- Las Palmas green enchilada sauce large can
- 1 cup of grated cheddar cheese
- Chopped black olives
- sour cream, guacamole, salsa as garnish

Direction

- Sautee the green pepper and onion and garlic until soft and wilted in some butter.
- Mix shrimp, crab, onion, garlic, green pepper, and seasonings, along with all the cheeses. Stir well.
- Spread a large spoonful on each lasagna noodle and roll up like a jelly roll.
- Place seam side down in a greased lasagna pan.
- Cover all rolls with a green enchilada sauce.
- Bake in 350 degree oven for 40 minutes.
- Pull out of oven and top with 1 cup of grated cheddar cheese.
- Put back in oven for 5 minutes more to melt the cheese.
- Serve individual rolls,
- Top with sour cream, olives, guacamole and salsa.

- A green salad with lots of avocado and chopped tomatoes and a citrus vinaigrette works great with this dish.
- I would make flan with caramel for dessert.

198.   Mexican Stuffed Shells Recipe

Serving: 8 | Prep: | Cook: 30mins | Ready in:

Ingredients

- 12-18 large pasta shells, cooked
- 1 lb ground beef
- 3 tablespoons taco seasoning,
- 1/2 cup water
- 1 onion, chopped
- 1 1/2 cups salsa, divided
- 1 cup grated cheese, divided (jalapeno Monterey Jack is especially good, but cheddar will work well too.)
- 750 ml tomato sauce
- chili powder, to taste
- green onions, for garnish

Direction

- Brown ground beef and drain.
- Add seasoning, water, onion, and 1/2 cup of salsa and 1/4 cup cheese.
- Mix together remaining salsa, tomato sauce, and chili powder.
- Spread a thin layer of sauce on the bottom of a 9 x 12 baking pan.
- Fill each shell with the ground beef mixture and place in pan.
- Pour remaining sauce on top. Sprinkle on the rest of the cheese on top and garnish with green onion. Cover and freeze at this point.
- Defrost overnight and bake at 350 degrees for 30 minutes. (Cook from frozen for 2 hours at 300 degrees.).
- If desired sprinkle additional cheese on top after baking and return to oven for 5 minutes longer or until cheese melts.

199. Minestrone Soup Recipe

Serving: 8 | Prep: | Cook: 40mins |Ready in:

Ingredients

- 5 cup chicken stock
- 1 small can tomato paste
- 1 (12 oz.) can no-salt tomato juice
- 2 -3 celery stalks chopped
- 2 carrots, sliced
- 1 large sweet onion, chopped
- 3 garlic cloves, minced
- 1 large zucchini, quartered, sliced
- 1 cup cut green beans or wax beans
- 2 large tomatoes, diced
- 1 Tbsp chopped Italian parsley
- 2 green onions, chopped
- 1 Tbsp fresh basil, chopped
- 1 tsp dried oregano
- 1 can garbanzo beans
- 1 can white kidney beans
- 1/3 cup elbow macaroni or broken spaghetti
- Dash of Tabasco or dried red pepper flakes
- 1 Tbsp grated parmesan cheese
- 1/4 cup grated parmesan cheese

Direction

- Add all but the 1/4 cup parmesan, pasta and the beans to a kettle
- Simmer until veggies are done...
- Drain the beans add this and the pasta to the pot
- If you have to add more stock or water to the pot to get it to the thickness you like.
- Add salt and pepper to taste
- Serve hot and offer the parmesan cheese.
- I love this soup, and it is good for you!

200. Mississippi Mays Shrimp Spaghetti Recipe

Serving: 10 | Prep: | Cook: 25mins |Ready in:

Ingredients

- 11/2 CUP OF butter (OR MORE)
- 1/2 CUP DICED bell pepper DICED FINELY (OR LESS)
- 1/2 CUP celery DICED FINELY (OR LESS)
- 1 LARGE DICED yellow onion
- 1 CUP CHOPPED green onions (TOPS & BOTTOMS)
- parsley
- A SHOT OF worcestershire sauce
- salt (TO YOUR TASTE)
- black pepper (TO YOUR TASTE)
- 1/2 TEASPOON EACH OF basil, thyme, garlic powder (MORE OR LESS, DEPENDS ON YOUR TASTE)
- 3 LBS OF MEDIUM fresh shrimp (NO FROZEN, GO TO YOUR LOCAL seafood MARKET) PEELED AND DEVEINED
- 1 (12 OZ) thin spaghetti, COOKED AND DRAINED
- 1 (80Z) PKG. OF VELVETTA CUT INTO 1/2 INCH PIECES
- 1 CAN PETITE diced tomatoes, DRAINED (OPTIONAL)
- mushroom pieces AND STEMS (OPTIONAL)

Direction

- PREHEAT OVEN TO 350 DEGREES
- IN A LARGE SKILLET, MELT BUTTER AND SAUTE ALL VEGETABLES
- ADD PARSLEY, WORCESTERSHIRE SAUCE, SALT, PEPPER, BASIL, THYME AND GARLIC POWDER.
- POUR MIXTURE INTO A CASSEROLE DISH OR BAKING PAN
- ADD SHRIMP, TOSS GENTLY TO COAT
- BAKE FOR 25 MINUTES, STIRRING OCCASIONALLY
- REMOVE FROM HEAT, STIR IN SPAGHETTI, CHEESE. THROW IN

TOMATOES AT THIS TIME IF YOU CHOSE THIS OPTION

- RETURN TO OVEN AND BAKE 5 MINUTES, OR UNTIL CHEESE IS MELTED, STIRRING TO COMBINE.

---

201. Mity Nice Grill Mac And Jack Recipe

Serving: 2 | Prep: | Cook: 10mins | Ready in:

Ingredients

- Mac and Jack Ingredients for the Sauce:
- 5 oz grated white cheddar cheese
- 3 cups heavy cream
- 1/4 teaspoon crushed red pepper
- 1/3 teaspoon of kosher salt
- 1/3 teaspoon ground white pepper
- 2 teaspoons parmesan cheese
- Ingredients for the Baked Mac and Jack:
- 2 1/2 cups of Mac and Jack Sauce
- 2 1/2 cups cooked Pipette (fancy macaroni)
- 2 pinches of kosher salt and pepper
- 1 cup shredded monterey jack cheese
- 1 1/2 cup shredded monterey jack cheese
- 4 tablespoons seasoned breadcrumbs
- 2 pinches chopped parsley

Direction

- Instructions for the Sauce:
- Bring all the ingredients to a boil, whisking until the cheeses are completely melted and well mixed.
- Do not reduce.
- Strain out the chili flakes.
- Set aside.
- Instructions for the Dish:
- Heat the sauce in a skillet until boiling.
- Heat the cooked pasta in boiling water for 15 seconds, drain and add to the sauce.
- Add the salt and pepper while tossing to combine.

- Pour about 1/4 of the pasta into 2 separate bowls and top each with 1/2 a cup of shredded Jack cheese.
- Add the remaining pasta, splitting between the two bowls and top with 3/4 cup of shredded Jack cheese each.
- Sprinkle half the breadcrumbs over each one and place under the salamander or broiler.
- Cook until golden brown, adding a pinch of chopped parsley to each bowl before serving.

---

202. Moroccan Harira Ramadans Soup Recipe

Serving: 8 | Prep: | Cook: 120mins | Ready in:

Ingredients

- * 1 lb. lamb, cut into small cubes
- * 1 teaspoon turmeric
- * 1 teaspoon pepper
- * 1 teaspoon cinnamon
- * 1/4 teaspoon ginger
- * 2 Tablespoons butter
- * 3/4 cup chopped celery and leaves
- * 2 onions, chopped
- * 1/2 cup parsley and cilantro, chopped
- * 1 2-lb. can of tomatoes, chopped
- * salt
- * 3/4 cup lentils
- * 1 cup chickpeas (canned are fine)
- * 1/4 cup fine soup noodles
- * 2 eggs, beaten with the juice of 1/2 lemon

Direction

- Put the lamb (or beef if lamb is unavailable), spices, butter, celery, onion, and parsley/cilantro in a large soup pot and stir over a low heat for 5 minutes. Add the tomato pieces, and continue cooking for 10-15 minutes. Salt lightly.
- Add the juice from the tomatoes, 7 cups of water, and the lentils. Bring to a boil, then

reduce heat, partially cover, and simmer for 2 hours.

- When ready to serve, add the chickpeas and noodles and cook for 5 minutes. Then, with the soup at a steady simmer, stir the lemony eggs into the stock with a long wooden spoon. Continue stirring slowly, to create long egg strands and to thicken the soup. Season to taste. Ladle into bowls and dust with cinnamon (optional). Squeeze in some lemon.
- Serve with some dates (Medjool dates are recommended)
- (You can use beef, if lamb is expensive or unavailable, just make sure the beef or lamb cubes are tender enough before serving)

203.   Mucho Gusto Mexican Style Pasta Bake Recipe

Serving: 6 | Prep: | Cook: 15mins |Ready in:

Ingredients

- 12 ounces dried bow tie pasta (about 5 cups)
- 1/2 cup chopped onion
- 1/2 cup chopped red sweet pepper
- 1-3 chopped jalapenos (as desired or omit)
- 3 tablespoons butter
- 1/3 cup all-purpose flour
- 1 teaspoon salt
- 1 teaspoon dried cilantro, crushed
- 1/2 teaspoon ground cumin
- 3 cups milk
- 6 ounces colby cheese, cubed
- 1-1/2 cups shredded monterey jack cheese (6 oz.)
- 1 cup bottled salsa
- 2/3 cup halved pitted green and/or ripe olives
- chili powder

Direction

- Preheat oven to 350 degree F.

- Butter six 12- to 16-ounce individual casserole dishes (or one 3-quart baking dish); set aside.
- In a 4-quart Dutch oven cook pasta according to package directions. Drain; return to pan.
- In a large saucepan cook onion and sweet pepper in butter over medium heat about 5 minutes or until tender.
- Stir in flour, salt, cilantro, and cumin. Add milk all at once.
- Cook and stir until mixture is thickened and bubbly.
- Reduce heat to low.
- Stir in Colby cheese and 1 cup of the Monterey Jack cheese; stir until cheese is melted.
- Pour over drained pasta; stir to combine.
- Layer half of the pasta mixture, all of the salsa, and the remaining pasta mixture in the prepared casserole(s.)
- Sprinkle with remaining 1/2 cup Monterey Jack cheese and olives. Sprinkle lightly with chili powder.
- Bake, uncovered, 15 to 20 minutes or until bubbly around edges and heated through. (If using large casserole, bake in a 400 degree F oven about 20 minutes.)
- Let stand 5 minutes before serving.

204.   Muffuletta Pasta Recipe

Serving: 8 | Prep: | Cook: 40mins |Ready in:

Ingredients

- 24 ounces penne
- 4 (10 ounce) cans seasoned chicken broth
- 1/4 cup minced garlic
- olive oil for sauteing
- 12 ounces genoa salami, finely chopped
- 12 ounces ham, finely chopped
- 1 pound provolone cheese
- 1 large jar olive salad, slightly drained
- 1 (4 ounce) can sliced black olives
- 12 ounces romano cheese, shredded

Direction

- Boil the pasta in the chicken broth in a large saucepan until al dente; drain.
- Sauté the garlic in olive oil in a skillet.
- Add the sautéed garlic, salami, ham, provolone cheese, olive salad, and mix well, adding additional olive oil if necessary.
- Spoon into a large baking pan.
- Bake at 350 degrees for 30 to 40 minutes or until all the cheese melts.

---

205.   Mushroom Stroganoff Recipe

Serving: 4 | Prep: | Cook: 15mins | Ready in:

Ingredients

- 3 tablespoons butter
- 1 large onion, chopped
- 2 cloves of garlic, minced
- 3/4 pound mushrooms, sliced (Note: I used Portobello and Baby Bella)
- 1 1/2 cups low sodium chicken stock (Note: You may also use vegetable or beef stock)
- 3/4 cup low-fat sour cream
- 3/4 cup non-fat yogurt (Note: You can use a combination of low or non-fat Greek yogurt (such as Fage) and light sour cream, or use one exclusively)
- 3 tablespoons all-purpose flour
- 1 teaspoon low sodium soy sauce
- 1 teaspoon worcestershire sauce
- 1/4 cup chopped fresh parsley and a lttle extra for garnish
- 8 ounces farfalle pasta (Note: Feel free to use whatever pasta you prefer, or even brown or white rice)
- salt and pepper to taste

Direction

- Bring a large pot of salted water to a boil. Add noodles, and cook according to your desired level of doneness. Remove from heat, drain, and set aside.
- While the pasta is cooking, melt the butter in a large heavy skillet over medium heat. Add onions and garlic, and cook, stirring until softened.
- Add the sliced mushrooms, cooking until they are softened and lightly browned.
- Next add the stock, soy and Worcestershire sauces. Bring the sauce to a boil, and cook until the mixture has reduced by 1/3.
- In a small bowl combine the sour cream and flour and parsley. Add this mixture to the pan and stir. Continue cooking over low heat, just until the sauce thickens. Pour the pasta into the sauce and cook until the dish is evenly heated through. Serve, seasoning with salt and pepper and garnish with additional parsley and a dollop of sour cream.

---

206.   My Moms Lasagna No Ricotta Recipe

Serving: 8 | Prep: | Cook: 55mins | Ready in:

Ingredients

- 1 lb lean ground beef
- 1 tablespoon onion powder
- 1 (28 ounce) jar traditional style spaghetti sauce
- 1 (15 ounce) can tomato sauce
- 1 teaspoon italian seasoning
- 9 dry lasagna noodles (I cook a few extra just in case a noodle or two self destructs)
- 2 (6 ounce) packages deli-style mozzarella cheese slices (you'll need 12 slices total)
- 1/4 cup grated parmesan cheese
- 1 (8 ounce) package shredded mozzarella cheese

Direction

- Preheat oven to 350 degrees.

- Cook lasagna noodles according to package directions.
- Meanwhile, brown ground beef in a large skillet; drain fat.
- Sprinkle meat with onion powder.
- Add spaghetti sauce, tomato sauce and Italian seasoning.
- Mix well. Set aside.
- Drain noodles.
- Spray a 13 x 9 inch baking pan with cooking spray.
- Add a layer of sauce to pan.
- Top sauce with 3 lasagna noodles.
- Top noodles with more sauce.
- Top sauce with enough mozzarella cheese slices to cover in a single layer (6 slices).
- Top cheese with 3 more noodles, sauce, and 6 more cheese slices.
- Top cheese with remaining 3 noodles and sauce.
- Sprinkle with Parmesan cheese. Top Parmesan with the shredded mozzarella cheese.
- Bake 35 to 45 minutes (watch closely after 30 minutes to make sure cheese does not over brown).
- Let sit 10-15 minutes before serving.

207.   My Simple Macaroni Salad Recipe

Serving: 8 | Prep: | Cook: 10mins | Ready in:

Ingredients

- 8 oz. (dry) cooked salad macaroni (you can use whatever pasta you prefer)
- Chopped roma tomatoes (I only had 2, but 3 would be better)
- 1/3 cup chopped sweet onion (approx. - I don't measure, sorry)
- bunch of ciilantro (leaves only) chopped (about 1/3 cup)
- 1 small can sliced black olives (drained)
- 1 tsp minced garlic

- 1/2 cup mayonnaise (more/less)
- 1 Tbls yellow mustard (Frenchs, I just squirted it in)
- 1/2 tsp dill weed - approx. (or you can use dill relish, or if you prefer, sweet)
- salt and pepper to taste
- olive oil (I drizzle with just before serving because it seems to soak up the mayo while in the fridge, just to moisten, and stir)

Direction

- Add chopped tomatoes, onions, cilantro, olives, and garlic to large bowl
- Add cooked macaroni (or pasta)
- Add mayo and mustard, stir in
- Add dill weed (or relish), salt and pepper
- Adjust seasoning and mayo to taste

208.   New Orleans Baked Pasta Recipe

Serving: 8 | Prep: | Cook: 45mins | Ready in:

Ingredients

- 1 lb penne pasta
- 2 eggs, beaten
- garlic
- 1/4 cup fresh parsley, minced
- 1 stick butter
- 1 cup onions, chopped
- 1/3 cup celery, chopped
- 1 cup half and half or light cream
- 2cups medium sharp cheddar, divided
- 1/2 cup swiss cheese, shredded
- 3/4 cup Velvetta
- 2 or 3 dashes louisiana hot sauce
- pinch white pepper
- salt, pepper

Direction

- Cook penne in boiling water seasoned with garlic and salt. Do not overcook. Drain and place in well-greased casserole dish. Cool slightly and add 2 beaten eggs and parsley. Mix well. Melt butter in saucepan and sauté onions and celery until wilted. Stir in cream and cook on medium heat until blended. Slowly add cheeses (reserve one cup cheddar) while stirring constantly until melted. Season with salt, white pepper and hot sauce. Pour over penne and mix well. Top with 1 cup grated cheddar. Bake at 350 for 35-45 minutes, until cheese is melted and barely starting to brown. Once browning starts it will brown fast. Do not burn.

209.   New Yorker Pasta Recipe

Serving: 2 | Prep: | Cook: 15mins |Ready in:

Ingredients

- 1 t. cracked pepper
- 1 lb. broccoli, cut up
- 1/2 c. Grated parmesan cheese
- 1/3 lb. Roquefort or blue cheese
- 2 clove Garlic, minced
- 3 T. butter
- 3/4 c. Thin Spagetti

Direction

- Cook pasta to al dente.
- Add the broccoli for the last 5 minutes.
- Melt butter in a saucepan. Add garlic and sauté over low heat about 2 minutes.
- Add Roquefort or Blue Cheese, stir until melted.
- Place drained pasta and broccoli in a large bowl.
- Add Garlic and Cheese sauce, toss to coat.
- Sprinkle with Parmesan Cheese and cracked pepper.

210.   No Name Casserole Recipe

Serving: 8 | Prep: | Cook: 40mins |Ready in:

Ingredients

- 2 lbs ground beef
- 2 cloves garlic, minced
- salt and pepper
- 1 28 oz. can tomato sauce
- 1 4 oz. can diced green chilies
- 8 oz cream cheese, softened
- 2 cups sour cream
- 1 onion, chopped
- 1 lb. egg noodles
- 3 cups shredded mozzarella cheese...I've used cheddar

Direction

- Preheat oven to 350
- Cook and crumble beef
- Drain grease
- Stir in garlic, salt, pepper, tomato sauce and chilies
- Reduce heat and simmer
- Combine cream cheese, sour cream and onions
- Cook noodles according to package directions
- Spray 9x13 baking dish
- Layer 1/3 meat sauce, 1/2 noodles, 1/2 cream cheese mixture then 1/2 cheese
- Cover with 1/3 meat sauce, remaining noodles, cream cheese, cheese then sauce
- Bake 40 minutes

211.   Noodle Bowl With Stir Fried Vegetables Tofu And Peanuts Recipe

Serving: 6 | Prep: | Cook: 10mins |Ready in:

Ingredients

- 1 oz vegetable oil
- 2 scallions chopped
- 1 garlic cloves finely chopped
- 1/2 tsp ginger root finely chopped
- 3 oz carrots cut julienne
- 3 oz red bell pepper cut batonnet
- 4 oz shiitake mushrooms caps, cut batonnet
- 1/2 lb bok choy cut into 1-in pieces
- 2 oz mung bean sprouts
- 4 oz snow peas trimmed
- 3/4 lb firm tofu pressed, cut in 1/2 inch dice
- 3 oz roasted peanuts shelled, skinless
- 1.5 fl oz soy sauce
- 1 fl oz hoisin sauce
- 2 fl oz vegetable stock or water
- 0.5 tbsp sesame oil or chili oil
- 1.5 lb egg noodles cooked hot (cooked Chinese wheat or egg noodles)

Direction

- Procedure:
- Heat the oil in a large sauté pan or wok over high heat.
- Add the scallions, garlic, and ginger.
- Stir-fry 1 minute.
- Add the carrots, peppers, and mushrooms.
- Continue to stir-fry another minute.
- Add the bok choy and bean sprouts.
- Stir-fry until the vegetables are wilted but still crisp.
- Add the snow peas and continue to cook about 30 seconds.
- Add the tofu and peanuts.
- Toss the mixture to blend, and cook until the tofu is hot.
- Pour in the soy sauce, stock or water, and oil.
- Toss to mix.
- 8Put the noodles into individual serving bowls and top with the vegetable mixture with its liquid.

212. Noodles Romanoff Recipe

Serving: 4 | Prep: | Cook: 15mins | Ready in:

Ingredients

- 3 cups cooked egg noodles
- 1 cup cottage cheese
- 1 cup sour cream
- 1/4 cup finely chopped white onion
- 1 clove garlic peeled and crushed
- 1-1/2 teaspoons worcestershire sauce
- 4 drops Tabasco sauce
- 1/2 teaspoon salt
- 1/2 cup grated sharp cheddar cheese

Direction

- Combine all of ingredients except cheddar cheese in a greased square baking dish.
- Sprinkle grated cheese over top/
- Heat uncovered in microwave for 14 minutes.
- Turn baking dish 1/4 turn after each 3 minutes.

213. Not Quite Just Another Chicken Salad Recipe

Serving: 8 | Prep: | Cook: 20mins | Ready in:

Ingredients

- The salad:
- • 1 lb (500g) pasta of your choice, cooked al dante, with two large bay leaves. Large elbow, rotini or rigatoni work well.
- • 1 large free range chicken or small duck cut into four pieces and cooked as below and then taken off the bone. This should give you 1 ½ to 2 lbs (700 to 900g) of boneless meat.
- • 4 hard boiled eggs, sliced.
- • ¼ cup chopped red bell pepper.

- • 1 tsp finely chopped medium chilies (jalapeño, problamo, etc) or chili flakes. (optional)
- • 2 Tsp chopped kalamata olives (optional but nice)
- • 4 fresh mushrooms, thin sliced.
- • ¼ - ½ cup frozen corn.
- • ¼ cup frozen green beans.
- 2 lg raddish, sliced
- • 1 stalk of celery, remove strings and coarse chop or thin slice.
- • ¼ cup finely chopped, mild onion.
- • ½ cup grated fresh carrot.
- The dressing:
- • 1 cup real mayonnaise, more or less to taste.
- • 6 Tbs. olive oil, I like the old fashioned kind for the flavor.
- • 1 Tbs good prepared mustard, your choice of type.
- • 2 - 4 Tbs dry white wine, or wine vinegar.
- • Pinch or two of basil, to taste.
- • 1 or 2 sprigs of parsley, chopped fine.
- • 1 sprig cilantro, chopped fine.
- • salt and fresh ground pepper to taste.
- • 1-2 Tbs fresh lemon juice, to taste.
- • 4 Tbs sour cream.
- • 1 tsp parmesan cheese, optional.
- • water or wine to adjust consistency.
- • 2 – 4 drops of liquid smoke, if you're cooking the bird in the oven (optional).

Direction

- Salad:
- 1. Cook the pasta, with the bay leaves, until al dente and drain. Remove the bay leaves. Rinse it if you like.
- 2. Boil eggs. It may be cheating but I boil the eggs with the pasta. If they are farm fresh, not store bought, scrub them good first.
- 3. Two ways to cook the chicken/duck, whatever. You can cook it in your Weber (or equivalent) BBQ/smoker or in the oven at say 350 deg. F until just done, about 1 ½ hours. If in the oven, put it on a rack with a little liquid in the bottom of the pan and cover. Please don't overcook. Who wants dry bird?

- 4. When the bird is cooked, debone it and rip, tear or hack the meat into bite size bits.
- 5. Put all of the salad ingredients, except the eggs in a large mixing bowl.
- Dressing:
- 1. Put all of the dressing ingredients, except the water or wine to adjust consistency, in a blender and blend until smooth, adjusting consistency to your liking with the water or wine; hay whatever.
- 2. Add the dressing to the salad and fold all the stuff together gently but completely. Put in the fridge to stand for an hour or more, folding occasionally to blend flavors.
- 3. Garnish with a dash of paprika and the sliced eggs. A sprig or two of parsley. Maybe, some chopped nuts and serve.
- For this dish you can do the cooking the night before and keep the cooked stuff in the fridge until you're ready to put the salad together. We like soft cooked corn tortillas with this. Manger avec appétit (Eat hearty)

214. Not Your Moms Mac And Cheese Recipe

Serving: 8 | Prep: | Cook: 25mins | Ready in:

Ingredients

- 3 Tbls flour
- 2 Tbls butter
- 1 1/2 tsp yellow mustard
- 3 tsp worchestershire sauce
- 1 can evaporated milk
- 1 10 oz block extra sharp white cheddar (like Crackerbarrel) cheese, shredded
- Just less than a 16 oz box of elbow pasta

Direction

- Preheat oven to 350*.
- Cook elbow macaroni according to box directions (drain and set aside).

- While pasta is cooking, melt the butter in a medium bowl.
- Combine butter w/all of the ingredients (EXCEPT the cheese) and microwave for 3 minutes, checking/stirring regularly as to not burn (cook time WILL vary w/microwave).
- Add cheese to thickened white sauce and microwave for 1 minute at 70% power (if cheese isn't completely melted upon stirring, microwave a little longer).
- Mix white sauce and pasta in a round 2 quart casserole dish, here's where mom and I differ. I prefer to serve now, all saucy and gooey while *mom prefers to bake for 20-30 minutes in the oven at 350 (until top is browned).

215. Old Fashioned Spaghetti Sauce Recipe

Serving: 6 | Prep: | Cook: 480mins |Ready in:

Ingredients

- One pound spicy italian sausage
- One large white onion, chopped
- Five cloves garlic, chopped
- One large green bell pepper, chopped
- Two cups sliced crimini mushrooms
- One large can crushed tomatoes
- One large can tomato sauce
- One medium can tomato paste
- extra virgin olive oil
- red wine
- salt & pepper
- One tablespoon oregano
- Two large bay leaves
- spaghetti noodles
- Fresh parmesan or asiago cheese, grated

Direction

- Heat about two tablespoons of olive oil in a large, heavy skillet over medium-high heat. Remove sausage from casings and chop roughly. Brown in the olive oil. While sausage is cooking, sauté onion and garlic in three tablespoons olive oil in a large pot. When sausage is completely cooked, drain and add to onion and garlic. Add tomatoes, bell pepper, and mushrooms. Stir thoroughly and bring to a boil. Add red wine to desired consistency and taste. Add oregano and bay leaves, and salt and pepper to taste. Reduce heat, cover, and simmer all day, stirring occasionally. Remove bay leaves before serving. Serve over hot cooked spaghetti and top with cheese.
- Recipe is easy to double

216. Olive Gardens Chicken Or Shrimp Carbonara Recipe

Serving: 8 | Prep: | Cook: 20mins |Ready in:

Ingredients

- Marinated chicken or shrimp
- 1 cup extra virgin olive oil
- 1 cup hot water
- 1 Tbsp italian seasoning
- 1 Tbsp chopped garlic
- 3 lbs chicken strips or large shrimp, peeled and deveined
- Sauce
- 1 cup butter
- 1 ½ tsp chopped garlic
- 3 Tbsp bacon bits
- 3 Tbsp flour (all purpose)
- 1 cup parmesan cheese (grated)
- 4 cups heavy cream
- 4 cups milk
- ¼ cup bacon base
- ½ tsp black pepper
- 2-14 oz boxes of any long pasta (spaghetti, linguine, etc.) cooked using instructions on package
- ¼ tsp salt
- Topping
- 3 Tbsp romano cheese, grated

- 3 Tbsp parmesan cheese, grated
- 1 ¾ cups mozzarella cheese, shredded
- ½ cup panko breadcrumbs
- 1 ½ tsp chopped garlic
- 1 ½ Tbsp melted butter
- 2 Tbsp parsley, chopped
- Marinated chicken strips (or shrimp) from step 1
- 1 ½ cups roasted red peppers, cut into small strips
- ¼ cup bacon bits

Direction

- Preheat oven to 350°F.
- Marinated Chicken (or Shrimp) - Whisk extra virgin olive oil together with hot water, seasoning and chopped garlic. Add the chicken strips (or shrimp). Cover and refrigerate for at least 30 minutes
- Sauce - Melt butter in a large saucepan over medium heat. Add garlic and bacon bits. Sauté for 5 minutes, stirring frequently. Add flour, Parmesan cheese, heavy cream, milk bacon base pepper and salt. Use a wire whisk to whip all ingredients together. Bring to a boil. Reduce heat and allow to simmer.
- Topping - Combine Romano, Parmesan, mozzarella, panko, chopped garlic, melted butter and chopped parsley in a mixing bowl. Stir until well blended. Set aside.
- Chicken (or Shrimp) - Preheat large skillet. Add chicken (or shrimp) to pan. Add red peppers and bacon bits. Cook for 3 more minutes or until cooked on both sides and internal temperatures reach 165°F for chicken and 155°F for shrimp. Add sauce (from above) Stir until well blended.
- Plating - Place hot, precooked pasta on a lager serving platter. Top with chicken (or shrimp) and sauce. Evenly distribute topping over top of chicken (or shrimp). Place in broiler until top is golden brown. Serve immediately and enjoy.

217. Orange Chicken Stir Fry Recipe

Serving: 4 | Prep: | Cook: 35mins |Ready in:

Ingredients

- 4 chicken breast halves, skinless and boneless, cubed
- 1 (6 oz) package crispy Chow-Mein noodles
- 1 tbsp grated orange zest
- 1 cup orange juice
- 1 tbsp brown sugar
- 2 tbsp all-purpose flour
- 1/4 cup soy sauce
- 3 garlic cloves, chopped
- 3 tbsp vegetable oil
- 1 tsp salt
- 1 cup bean sprouts (optional)

Direction

- Combine the orange zest, orange juice, brown sugar, soy sauce, garlic, and salt in a small bowl. Mix thoroughly.
- In a large skillet, or wok, heat the oil over a medium high heat. When it starts to bubble, add the chicken. Sauté until completely cooked (no longer pink inside), around 7-10 minutes.
- Add the orange sauce mixture to the chicken; cook until sauce the starts to bubble. Next, add the flour, slowly, to thicken the sauce to your desired consistency. Add the bean sprouts and cook for another minute. Finally, serve hot over chow mein noodles.

218. Our Chicken Milano Recipe

Serving: 45 | Prep: | Cook: 20mins |Ready in:

Ingredients

- 1 knob of butter

- 2 cloves garlic minced
- 1/2 c sundried tomatoes , chopped
- 1 C chicken broth
- 1 c heavy cream
- chicken breast halves
- salt n pepper to taste
- 2 Tbsp olive oil
- 2 Tbsp fresh basil
- 1 pkt fresh fettuccini

Direction

- 1. In a large saucepan melt butter over a low heat. Add garlic and cook briefly, combine Tomatoes and 3/4 c chicken broth, increase heat then bring to the boil. When you reach boiling point, reduce to a simmer for 10 mins leaving uncovered, or until tomatoes are tender.
- Add the cream, and bring to the boil again, stirring continuously, once boiling reduce heat to a simmer again and continue till sauce has thickened.
- 2. Season chicken with salt and pepper, and place in a large skillet with the added oil, cook until lightly golden and, and juice runs clear, roughly 4 mins per side.
- 3. Then add remaining chicken broth to deglaze pan, then add to the cream sauce, stir in basil and adjust seasoning to taste.
- 4. Bring to the boil a large pot of salty water and add fettuccini, cook till al dente or around 8mins, drain and remove to boil and toss thru 4-5, Tbsp. cream sauce to coat.
- 5. Cut chicken into strips and place on top of fettuccini, and pour over the remaining cream sauce, sprinkle with a little chopped basil or parsley, enjoy!

---

219.   Over The Rainbow Mac Cheese Recipe

Serving: 6 | Prep: | Cook: 35mins | Ready in:

Ingredients

- * Exported from MasterCook *
- Over the Rainbow macaroni & cheese
- Recipe By :Patti LaBelle
- Serving Size : 6 Preparation Time :0:00
- Categories : Side Dishes Starch
- Amount Measure Ingredient -- Preparation Method
- -------- ------------ -------------------------------
- 1 Tablespoon vegetable oil
- 1 pound elbow macaroni
- 1 stick butter
- 1 Tablespoon butter
- 1/2 cup Meunster cheese (2 ounces) -- shredded
- 1/2 cup mild cheddar cheese (2 ounces) -- shredded
- 1/2 cup sharp cheddar cheese (2 ounces) -- shredded
- 1/2 cup monterey jack cheese (2 ounces) -- shredded
- 2 Cups half and half
- 1 cup Velveeta (8 ounces) -- cut into small cubes
- 2 large eggs -- lightly beaten
- 1/4 teaspoon salt
- 1/8 teaspoon freshly ground pepper

Direction

- Preheat oven to 350º. Lightly butter a deep 2½ quart casserole.
- Bring a large pot of salted water to a boil over high heat. Add the oil, then the elbow macaroni, & cook until the macaroni is just tender, about 7 minutes. Do not overcook. Drain well. Return to the cooking pot.
- In a small saucepan, melt 8 T. of the butter (one stick). Stir into the macaroni. In a large bowl, mix the Muenster, mild & sharp Cheddar, & Monterey Jack chesses. To the macaroni, add the half-and-half, 1½ cups of the shredded cheese, the cubed Velveeta, and the eggs. Season w/ the salt & pepper. Transfer to the buttered casserole. Sprinkle w/

the remaining 1/2 c. of shredded cheese & dot w/ the remaining 1 T. of butter.

- Bake until it's bubbling around the edges, about 35 minutes. Serve hot.
- Per serving: 580 Calories (kcal); 31g Total Fat; (48% calories from fat); 14g Protein; 60g Carbohydrate; 139mg Cholesterol; 321mg Sodium
- Food Exchanges: 3 1/2 Grain (Starch); 1/2 Lean Meat; 0 Vegetable; 0 Fruit; 6 Fat; 0 Other Carbohydrates
- Serving Ideas: This is SURELY great w/ anything! Muenster is my fave cheese too. YUM.
- NOTES: Ask anyone who makes incredible macaroni & cheese for his or her recipe, & I bet you that Velveeta will be in there. But my recipe doesn't stop there. To make my special macaroni & cheese, I also us Muenster, mild & sharp Cheddar, & Monterey Jack cheeses, each one adding its own flavor & melting consistency. If you don't want to use all five cheeses, you can get away w/ just the Velveeta & sharp Cheddar-it won't be over the rainbow, but it will be pretty good. And, on special occasions, I sometimes add an extra stick of butter, in which instance, the macaroni goes over the moon! If you use two sticks of butter, substitute milk for the half-and-half.

---

220. PASTA AND SHRIMP Recipe

Serving: 6 | Prep: | Cook: 15mins | Ready in:

Ingredients

- 8 ounces uncooked dried linguine or spaghetti
- 6 tablespoons butter
- 1/2 cup chopped onion or shallots
- 12 ounces fresh medium raw WILD shrimp, peeled, deveined.
- 1 medium (1 cup) green bell pepper, coarsely chopped

- 1 teaspoon finely chopped fresh garlic
- 1/2 teaspoon salt
- 1/4 teaspoon coarsely ground pepper
- 1/4 cup heavy whipping cream or half & half
- 1 tablespoon all-purpose flour
- 5 to 6 (2 cups) roma tomatoes, cubed 1/2-inch
- 1 tablespoon chopped fresh basil leaves
- 1/2 cup freshly shredded parmesan cheese

Direction

- Cook linguine according to package directions. Drain. Set aside; keep warm.
- Melt butter in 10-skillet until sizzling; add onion, shrimp, bell pepper, garlic, salt and pepper. Cook over medium heat, stirring occasionally, until shrimp turn pink (6 to 7 minutes).
- Stir whipping cream and flour together in small bowl until smooth; stir into shrimp mixture.
- Continue cooking until mixture just comes to a boil (about 1 minute). Stir in tomatoes and basil.
- Place hot, cooked pasta in large pasta bowl or onto serving platter; top with shrimp mixture.
- Sprinkle with Parmesan cheese.
- ENJOY!

---

221. PASTA E FAGIOLI Recipe

Serving: 24 | Prep: | Cook: 25mins | Ready in:

Ingredients

- 4 tablespoons olive oil
- 2 garlic cloves, minced
- 1 16-ounce can Italian plum tomatoes, drained, chopped
- 2 tablespoons minced fresh parsley
- 1/2 teaspoon dried basil, crumbled
- 1/4 teaspoon dried oregano, crumbled
- 1 15-ounce can cannellini beans (white kidney beans), rinsed, drained

- salt and pepper
- 8 ounces elbow macaroni, freshly cooked
- Grated Parmesan

Direction

- Heat 3 tablespoons oil in heavy large skillet over medium heat.
- Add garlic and sauté until brown, about 2 minutes.
- Stir in tomatoes and cook 5 minutes.
- Add parsley, basil and oregano and simmer until tomatoes soften, stirring occasionally and breaking up tomatoes with back of spoon, about 15 minutes. Add beans and cook until heated through, about 5 minutes. Season with salt and pepper. Place pasta in bowl. Toss with remaining 1 tablespoon oil. Pour sauce over and toss thoroughly. Serve, passing Parmesan separately.

---

222.   Pad Thai Recipe

Serving: 2 | Prep: | Cook: 35mins | Ready in:

Ingredients

- 1/2 package(16oz)wide rice noodles
- 2 1/2 Tbsp. vegetable oil
- 2 cloves garlic
- 1/2 cup of fresh chive or sping onion long sliced
- 1/4 lb. shimp peeled and devined
- 3 Tbsp. dried shrimps, small size crushed
- 2 Tbsp. salted radish, chopped(optional)
- 2 Tbsp. fish sauce
- 1 Tbsp. thin soy sauce
- 2 1/2 Tbsp. sugar
- 1 Tbsp. lime juice
- 1 cup bean sprouts
- 1/2 cub of dice fried tofu or firm (optional)
- 1/4 cup unsalted roasted peanuts,
- break up in a mortar and pestle or chop with a chef's knife

Direction

- Boil 3 cups of water. Pour over noodles in a large bowl and soak for 20 minutes until softened. Drain.
- Heat oil in wok, until hot but not smoking. Add smashed garlic. Add shrimp, cook for about 4 to 5 minutes.
- Add noodles, dried shrimps, fish sauce, sugar, lime juice, chive and bean sprouts. Stir fry for another 3 to 4 minutes until mixed up and heated through.
- Add salted radish, if using (rinse if very salty). Stir fry another minute. Toss in the peanuts, tossing to mix or toping
- Remove to a platter or individual plates to serve. Garnish with cilantro or peanuts if desire.

---

223.   Pamelas Low Fat Chicken Piccata Recipe

Serving: 6 | Prep: | Cook: 25mins | Ready in:

Ingredients

- 6 boneless skinless chicken breasts, pounded thin
- flour (for dredging) (opt)
- veggie cooking spray
- 1 Tbs margarine
- 2 Tbs flour
- 15 ounces chicken broth
- 1/2 cup white wine (or you can use more chicken broth)
- juice of 1 lemon
- 1 Tbs parsley
- 1 Tbs capers
- artichokes (opt)
- mushrooms (opt)
- whole wheat pasta

Direction

- Coat large skillet with cooking spray & heat over medium-high heat
- Dredge chicken lightly with flour (I sometimes omit this step)
- Cook chicken until no longer pink (3-5 minutes)
- Remove chicken and keep warm on a plate
- Melt margarine in same skillet
- Stir in 2 Tbsp. flour
- Heat over medium 1-2 minutes
- Stir in chicken broth, wine and lemon juice and heat to boiling
- Stir until thickened (1-2 minutes)
- Reduce heat and simmer 15 minutes until sauce consistency
- Stir in parsley
- Return chicken to sauce over med-low heat, spooning sauce over chicken, until warmed through
- Serve over your favorite pasta
- **I sometimes add artichokes and mushrooms, and fresh garlic is delicious in it as well!
- PER SERVING: (without artichokes and mushrooms, using white pasta)
- 6 GRAMS FAT
- 301 CALORIES

---

224.   Pasta Carbonara Recipe

Serving: 6 | Prep: | Cook: 20mins | Ready in:

Ingredients

- 1 pound penne or linguine
- 2 tbsp flavourful olive oil
- 1/3 pound cooked ham or Canadian bacon
- 5 cloves garlic, crushed
- 1/4 cup white onion, diced
- 1/2 teaspoon crushed red pepper flakes
- 1/2 cup dry white wine
- 2 large egg yolks
- 3 tablespoons freshly grated asiago cheese
- A liberal sprinkle of black pepper

Direction

- Cook pasta to an al dente texture and drain, setting aside 1/4 cup pasta water.
- Heat large skillet over moderate heat.
- Sauté ham in a drizzle of oil until it warms through and begins to brown.
- Add measured olive oil, garlic, onion and crushed pepper flakes and sauté 3-4 minutes.
- Add wine to the pan and reduce by half, 2 minutes.
- Separately, beat together egg yolks, cheese and pepper.
- While whisking vigorously, stir in a ladle of the boiling pasta water.
- Add hot pasta to pan containing garlic mixture.
- Toss pasta with ham, add egg mixture and stir well 1 minute. Take off heat.
- Continue to mix pasta well until sauce is thickly coating the pasta.
- Adjust seasonings with salt and pepper and serve.

---

225.   Pasta Chicken In A Garlic Cream Sauce Recipe

Serving: 4 | Prep: | Cook: 35mins | Ready in:

Ingredients

- 1 pack vermicelli noodles or pasta of your choice
- 5 cloves garlic rough chopped (at least this many, depends on how much you like garlic, personally I use more)
- 4 chicken breasts (Think one per person you are serving)
- 1 cup milk or heavy cream
- 2-3 cups chicken broth
- 1- package mushrooms, washed and sliced
- 1/2 large white onion preferably vidalia
- 1 large jar marinated artichoke hearts drained
- 2-3 Tbsp butter

- 2-3 Tbsp flour
- salt
- pepper
- olive oil
- fresh parmesan cheese

Direction

- Boil pasta in large pot.
- While pasta boiling preheat large deep skillet to medium low.
- Cube chicken to bite size pieces
- Coat pan with olive oil and add chicken, salt and pepper
- Cook until chicken is almost done
- Dice onions, mushrooms and garlic and add in with chicken (you don't add it at the beginning or you will burn your garlic.)
- Move chicken to the outside of the pan and add butter and flour to center of pan, whisk until butter/flour mixture turns the color of toasted bread or a light golden color, this creates a roux.
- Mix chicken into your roux and add in the first cup of chicken stock raising heat to medium high, stir until thickens. Sauce will be very thick
- Whisk in second cup of stock, up to three until desired consistency.
- . Taste sauce at this point and add in more salt and pepper to taste. Heavy pepper is good in this dish.
- Add in artichoke hearts, reduce heat to low and allow sauce to continue cooking and thickening.
- . At the very end add in your milk or cream starting with a half a cup first.
- Drain pasta and add to sauce, coating pasta with chicken and cream sauce.
- Top with Parmesan cheese and enjoy.
- If sauce gets to thick it is better to add more stock then milk, as milk or cream will make the dish to rich and take away from the flavor of mushrooms, and artichokes. If your sauce is not thick enough turn up the heat and quickly whisk in more flour.

- **If you have a gluten or wheat intolerance, you can make this same dish by mixing about 2 Tbsp. of cornstarch in with 1/2 cup cold chicken stock and adding that in place of flour and butter. This will also cause your sauce to thicken just as well. Like the roux, if it isn't thick enough simply dissolve more cornstarch in chicken sauce and add in. Both of these need heat to activate.
- ** You can make this same recipe vegetarian, by eliminating the chicken and using vegetable broth. I use thick chunked Portabello mushrooms in place of chicken for my recipe.

226.   Pasta Puttanesca Recipe

Serving: 34 | Prep: | Cook: 10mins | Ready in:

Ingredients

- 2 tablespoon olive oil
- 1 tablespoon anchovy paste
- 3 cloves garlic, minced
- 1 tablespoon red pepper flakes
- 1 can whole tomatoes
- 1 can crushed tomatoes
- ¼ cup flat leaf parsley, chopped
- 1 dozen kalamata olives, pitted and chopped
- 3 tablespoon capers
- freshly ground pepper
- parmesan, for garnish

Direction

- Over medium heat cook the garlic, chillies and anchovy paste in the oil. Stir it around until the paste dissolves and garlic is tender - about 3 minutes.
- Add the tomatoes, olives, capers, parsley and pepper and cook for about 10 minutes.
- Toss with pasta and garnish with parmesan cheese.

227.   Pasta Salad With Spinach Olives And Mozzarella Recipe

Serving: 6 | Prep: | Cook: 25mins | Ready in:

Ingredients

- 1 pound orecchiette or conchiglie pasta
- 8 ounces fresh mozzarella cheese, drained, small dice
- 3 ounces baby spinach (about 4 cups), thoroughly washed and dried
- 1 1/2 cups pitted and halved kalamata olives
- 1 cup finely grated parmesan cheese
- 3 tablespoons red wine vinegar
- 2 teaspoons kosher salt
- 1 teaspoon freshly ground black pepper
- 6 tablespoons olive oil

Direction

- Bring a medium pot of heavily salted water to a boil over high heat. Cook pasta according to the package instructions, or until al dente.
- Drain, then rinse under cold water until cool.
- Transfer pasta to a large bowl and add mozzarella, spinach, olives, and Parmesan. Toss to combine.
- In a separate, nonreactive bowl, combine vinegar, salt, and pepper.
- Whisking constantly, slowly add oil by pouring in a thin stream down the side of the bowl. Whisk until completely incorporated.
- Pour vinaigrette over salad, and toss until pasta is coated. Taste, adjust seasoning as desired, and serve.

228.   Pasta Shells With Portobello Mushrooms Amd Aparagus In Boursin Sauce Recipe

Serving: 6 | Prep: | Cook: 25mins | Ready in:

Ingredients

- 1 tbps. butter
- 1 tbps. olive oil
- 1 pound portobello mushrooms, stems removed
- 1/2 tps. salt
- 1 1/4 cup chicken broth
- 1 (5.2 ounce) package pepper boursin cheese
- 3/4 pound uncooked pasta shells
- 1 pound freah asparagus, trimmed

Direction

- 1. In a large skillet over medium heat, melt the butter and heat the olive oil. Cut the mushrooms caps in half, and sliced 1/4 inch thick. Cook mushrooms in the skillet 8 minutes, or until tender and lightly browned. Season with salt. Stir in the chicken broth and Boursin cheese. Reduce heat and simmer stirring constantly, until well blended.
- 2. Bring a large pot of lightly salted water to a boil. Add shell pasta and cook for 5 minutes. Place the asparagus into pot, and continue cooking 5 minutes, until the pasta is al dente and the asparagus is tender; drain. Toss with the mushrooms sauce to serve.

229.   Pasta With Cream Sauce

Serving: 0 | Prep: | Cook: | Ready in:

Ingredients

- 1 package (16 ounces) bow tie pasta
- 1 small red onion, chopped
- 3 tablespoons olive oil

- 4 large garlic cloves, minced
- 3/4 cup chicken broth
- 1-1/2 teaspoons minced fresh basil
- 1-1/2 teaspoons minced fresh oregano
- 1/4 teaspoon salt
- 1/4 teaspoon pepper
- 1 cup heavy whipping cream

Direction

- Cook pasta according to package directions. Meanwhile, in a large skillet, saute onion in oil until tender. Add garlic; cook 1 minute longer. Stir in the broth, basil, oregano, salt and pepper. Bring to a boil; cook for 8 minutes or until reduced by about half. Stir in cream.
- Cook, uncovered, 8-10 minutes longer or until sauce is reduced to 1-1/4 cups. Drain pasta; toss with sauce.
- Nutrition Facts
- 3/4 cup: 358 calories, 17g fat (8g saturated fat), 41mg cholesterol, 181mg sodium, 44g carbohydrate (2g sugars, 2g fiber), 8g protein.

230.   Pasta With Lemon Cream Sauce Asparagus And Peas Recipe

Serving: 4 | Prep: | Cook: 15mins | Ready in:

Ingredients

- 8 ounces uncooked long fusilli
- 13/4 C (about 1 lb) asparagus cut into 1 1/2" pieces
- 1 C frozen peas, thawed
- 1 Tbl butter
- 1 garlic clove, minced
- 1 C vegetable broth
- 1 tsp cornstarch
- 1/3 C heavy cream
- 3 Tbl fresh lemon juice
- 1/2 tsp salt
- 1/4 tsp pepper

- Dash of cayenne
- Coarsely ground pepper (optional)
- lemon slices(optional)

Direction

- Cook pasta according to package directions, omitting any fat or salt
- Add asparagus during last minute of cooking time
- Place peas in a colander; drain pasta mixture over peas and set aside
- Melt butter in a skillet over medium-high heat
- Add garlic to the pan; sauté 1 minute
- Combine broth and cornstarch in a small bowl; stir until well blended.
- Add broth mixture to pan; bring to a boil
- Cook 1 minute or until thickened, stirring constantly
- Remove from heat
- Stir in cream, juice, salt, the 1/4 tsp. black pepper and the cayenne
- Add pasta mixture to broth mixture; toss gently to coat
- Garnish with coarsely ground black pepper and lemon slices if desired

231.   Pasta With Olives And Tuna Recipe

Serving: 4 | Prep: | Cook: 15mins | Ready in:

Ingredients

- 1 pound spaghetti or other pasta
- 2 tablespoons olive oil
- 1 small onion, diced
- 2 cloves of garlic, minced
- 1/2 teaspoon crushed red pepper
- 2 anchovies, minced (optional)
- 1/4 cup Italian parsley, chopped
- 1 tablespoon tomato paste
- 2 6 ounce cans of tuna packed in oil, lightly drained

- 1/2 cup coarsely chopped kalamata olives
- 1 tablespoon capers
- 1 tomato chopped (optional)

Direction

- Bring 4 quarts of well-salted water to a boil. Add the pasta and cook until al dente. Drain thoroughly, reserving 1 cup of the pasta cooking water. Set the pasta aside in a warm place.
- Heat the olive oil over medium heat in a large pan. Add the onion and cook for about 2 to 3 minutes until the onion is softened. Add the garlic, crushed red pepper flakes, and anchovies and cook for another minute. Add about 1/4 cup of the pasta cooking water and continue to cook for another 2 to 3 minutes. Add the parsley and tomato paste and stir to dissolve the tomato paste. Add another 1/4 cup of the pasta cooking water. Cover and simmer the sauce for about 5 minutes to allow the flavors to develop, adding more pasta cooking water if it becomes too dry.
- Remove the tuna from the can and break apart into bite-sized pieces. Add the tuna, olives, and capers to the sauce along with the pasta and enough of the pasta cooking water to allow the sauce to coat the noodles but without being too watery. Stir to reheat the pasta and coat it evenly in the sauce. Season with salt if necessary. Serve garnished with additional chopped parsley or cut tomatoes.

232.   Pastitsio Greek Casserole Recipe

Serving: 8 | Prep: | Cook: 120mins | Ready in:

Ingredients

- 1 1/2 lbs lg tubular pasta (such as ziti #2)
- 1 c olive oil
- 1-2 cloves of garlic, finely minced
- 1 1/4 c chopped onions
- 1 1/2 lbs ground beef
- 2 1/2 c peeled, chopped plum tomatoes
- 1 1/2 t ground cinnamon
- 6 whole cloves
- sea salt
- 20 or more ground peppercorns (to taste)
- 1 1/4 c grated kefalotyri cheese (or pecorino)
- 1/2 c breadcrumbs
- béchamel sauce w/cheese or basic béchamel

Direction

- Sauté onions till translucent in 2 T olive oil in large heavy-bottomed frying pan.
- Add meat & continue to stir till lightly brown.
- Add tomatoes, spices, garlic, salt, & pepper & stir well to combine. Reduce heat & simmer till liquid has been absorbed, about 30-35 min. This is very important - the meat mixture should be as dry as possible without sticking to the bottom of the pan. Set meat mixture aside, uncovered, & allow to cool.
- Preheat oven to 350F. Lightly grease a baking or roasting pan approximately 11 X 14 X 3 in. high.
- While the meat is simmering, prepare pasta. Cook till slightly underdone, drain, toss w/couple T. olive oil to prevent sticking, & set aside.
- Make the béchamel sauce with cheese or 6 c. of basic béchamel.
- Spread the breadcrumbs evenly on bottom of an 11x15x3-in. baking pan.
- Use 1/2 the pasta for first layer & sprinkle with 1/2 c. of the grated cheese.
- Add meat sauce evenly over the pasta, & sprinkle w/1/2 cup of the grated cheese.
- Add remaining pasta on top. Carefully pour béchamel over the top & use a spatula to spread evenly.
- Bake at 350F for 30 min., then sprinkle remaining 1/4 c. grated cheese on top, & continue to bake for another 15-30 min. till sauce rises & turns golden brown.
- Remove pan from oven & allow to cool before serving (Pastitsio is served warm, not hot). Serves 6-8

- This dish can be prepared the day before, all the way to the béchamel sauce, refrigerated overnight, & cooked the next day after adding sauce.

233.   Pastitsio Recipe

Serving: 8 | Prep: | Cook: 40mins | Ready in:

Ingredients

- coarse salt and ground pepper
- 1 lb. penne,cooked and drained
- 2lbs ground lamb or beef
- 2 medium onions,diced
- 1/2 c red wine
- 1 can (6 oz) tomato paste
- 1/2 tsp ground cinnamon
- 6 Tbs butter
- 1/2 c flour(spooned and leveled)
- 3 c milk
- 1/8 tsp cayenne pepper (optional),I double this
- 1/4 c parmesan cheese

Direction

- Preheat oven to 375 degrees. Cook pasta, reserve. Meanwhile, in a large saucepan over medium heat, cook lamb, breaking apart pieces with a spoon, until no longer pink, 6 to 8 mins. Cook, stirring occasionally, until translucent, about 5 mins.
- Transfer to colander; drain fat, and discard. Return lamb to pan; add wine. Cook over medium heat till liquid has evaporated, about 5 mins. Stir in tomato paste, cinnamon and 2 cups water, simmer, stirring occasionally, until thickened, 15 to 20 mins. Season with salt and pepper
- Make Parmesan cheese sauce while mixture is simmering. In medium saucepan, melt butter over medium heat; whisk in flour until incorporated, about 30 seconds. In slow, steady stream, whisk in milk till there are no

lumps. Cook, whisking often, until mixture is thick and bubbly and coats the back of a wooden spoon, 6 to 8 mins. Stir in cayenne, if desired and Parmesan.
- Add pasta to lamb mixture; transfer to a 9x13" baking dish. Pour sauce over, smooth with back of spoon till level. Bake till browned in spots, 35 to 40 mins.
- Remove from oven; let cool 15 mins before serving.

234.   Pecan Pesto Recipe

Serving: 1 | Prep: | Cook: | Ready in:

Ingredients

- 1c basil leaves, packed
- 1/2 c pecans
- 3 cloves garlic
- 1 Tbsp lime juice or balsamic vinegar
- 2/3 c olive oil
- 1/2 tsp salt
- 1 Tbsp black pepper
- 4 Tbsp parmesiano reggiano

Direction

- Combine all ingredients except cheese in a blender.
- After blended well, stir in cheese.

235.   Penne Pasta Salad Recipe

Serving: 4 | Prep: | Cook: 10mins | Ready in:

Ingredients

- 16 ounces penne pasta - cooked and drained
- 8 ounces feta cheese - crumbled (use sun dried tomato flavor!)
- 2 ripe tomatoes, large - chopped
- 1/4 cup capers

- 1/4 cup parsley - chopped
- 3 ounces package of sun dried tomatoes , chopped
- Your favorite Zesty Italian dressing
- salt and pepper to taste

Direction

- Cook pasta according to package directions, drain and put into a large bowl.
- While pasta is cooking, prepare salad dressing and pour over the warm, drained pasta. Let cool before adding the rest of the ingredients.
- Add drained capers, crumbled feta cheese, chopped parsley, and chopped sun dried tomatoes.
- Add salt and pepper to taste.
- Refrigerate for 4 to 6 hours so ingredients absorb the flavors.
- Just before serving, add the tomatoes. Instead of using capers, chopped Kalamata olives can be substituted.
- To use this as an entrée, add one chicken breast per person. This recipe doubles and triples easily.

236.   Penne Pasta With Bacon And Cream Southern Living Recipe

Serving: 6 | Prep: | Cook: 25mins |Ready in:

Ingredients

- 15 bacon slices
- 1 (8oz) package sliced fresh mushrooms
- 2 garlic cloves, minced
- 16 oz penne pasta, cooked
- 1 cup freshly grated parmesan cheese
- 2 cups whipping cream
- 1/2 teaspoon pepper
- 4 green onions, sliced

Direction

- Cook bacon in a large skillet over medium heat until crisp; remove bacon, reserving 2 tablespoons drippings in skillet.
- Coarsely crumble bacon.
- Sauté sliced mushrooms and garlic in reserved drippings 3-5 minutes or until tender.
- Stir in pasta and next 3 ingredients; simmer over medium-low heat, stirring often, until sauce is thickened.
- Stir in bacon and green onions. Serve hot.
- Per serving: Calories 772 (53% from fat); Fat 45.4g (sat 23.3g, mono 15.3g, poly 2.7g); Protein 26.4g; Carb 63.4g; Fiber 2.8g; Chol 146mg; Iron 3mg; Sodium 852mg; Calcium 348mg

237.   Penne With Pancetta And Garlic Cream Recipe

Serving: 6 | Prep: | Cook: 30mins |Ready in:

Ingredients

- 1 pound fresh penne or other ridged pasta tubes (we used dried organic penne from Trader Joe's that is excellent)
- 1 tsp. kosher salt
- 1 tsp. olive oil
- 1/4 pound pancetta, diced
- 1 head garlic, roasted
- 3 cloves garlic, chopped
- 3 roma tomatoes, seeded and diced
- 1/2 cup dry white wine
- 1 1/2 cups heavy cream
- 1/2 cup grated parmigiano-reggiano cheese
- kosher salt & freshly ground black pepper to taste
- 6 large fresh basil leaves, chiffonade

Direction

- Bring 8 cups salted water to a boil in a large pot. Add the penne. Return the water to a boil and cook the pasta for 2 or 3 minutes, or until al dente. Drain the pasta, toss with the olive oil, and set aside.

- In a very large sauté pan over med-high heat, cook the diced pancetta for 6-8 minutes, or until crisp. Remove the pancetta from the sauté pan and set it aside.
- Squeeze the pulp from the head of roasted garlic. Add it, and the chopped garlic to the pancetta oil in the pan and sauté until the mixture begins to give off its aroma, 2-3 minutes. Add the tomatoes and sauté for 1-2 minutes. Add the wine and cook for 3-4 minutes, or until about 2 tablespoons of the liquid remain. Add the cream and cook for 4-5 more minutes, or until the cream thickens. Add half the Parmesan cheese and season the mixture with salt & pepper. Add the pasta and pancetta, mix together, and cook just until the pasta is heated through.
- Place the pasta on a serving platter and top with the remaining cheese and basil leaves.
- NOTE: If you can't find pancetta easily, substitute pepper bacon.

238.   Pesto Recipe

Serving: 1 | Prep: | Cook: | Ready in:

Ingredients

- 2 c fresh basil leaves, packed
- 1/2 - 3/4 c fresh Romano or Parmesean
- 1/2 - 3/4 c virgin olive oil
- 1/2 c pine nuts or walnuts
- 2 cloves garlic
- salt & white pepper

Direction

- If you are using walnuts, pulse them in the processor to make them small enough.
- Put basil in the processor (with the pine nuts if you are using pine nuts) and pulse a few times.
- Add garlic, pulse a few times

- Turn the food processor on, and add oil in a slow, steady stream.
- Stop occasionally to scrape the sides of the processor with a spatula.
- Add the cheese and pulse until well blended.
- Add salt and white pepper to taste.
- NB: If you are going to freeze the sauce, do not add the cheese. When you are ready to use the frozen pesto, thaw it, and add the cheese at that point in the processor.

239.   Phad Thai Recipe

Serving: 2 | Prep: | Cook: 10mins | Ready in:

Ingredients

- 2 portions of Thai dried phadt hai noodles, soaked in warm water 100 grams of pork, finely sliced (or sea food)
- 2 eggs
- 200 grams of bean sprouts & chinese chives
- 1 tbs of minced shallot (small red onion)
- 1 tbs of minced garlic
- 1 tbs of minced chilli
- 50 grams of roasted peanuts
- 1 tbs of sugar
- 1 tbs of fish sauce
- 1 tbs of soy sauce
- 1 tbs of oyster sauce
- 2 tbs tamarind juice
- cooking oil

Direction

- In a wok, fry the shallots and garlic in 3 tbsp. of oil over medium heat until fragrant. Add noodles and water, stir until tender. Season with sugar, fish sauce and tamarind juice/vinegar. Stir well, then push the noodles to the side of the wok.
- Heat the wok, add a little oil and brown the pork.
- Add shallots, garlic and chili; keep stirring. Sauté until very fragrant.

- Add eggs; stir to break the eggs.
- Add pad Thai noodles; add fish sauce, soy sauce, oyster sauce and tamarind juice
- Stir well to mix everything together.
- Add the bean sprouts. Toss well, do it as soon as possible because we still want the bean sprouts to be crunchy.
- Sprinkle with roasted peanuts and a squeeze of lime juice, serve.

240. Philadelphia Stroganoff Recipe

Serving: 4 | Prep: | Cook: 60mins | Ready in:

Ingredients

- 1 lb round beef steak, cut in thin strip, deer & moose can also be used
- 3 tbsp margarine
- 1/3 cup chopped onion
- 1 can sliced mushrooms, drained
- 1/4 tsp dry mustard
- 1/2 tsp salt
- pepper to taste
- 1 - 8 oz pkg cream cheese, cubed
- 2/3 cup milk
- Hot parsley noodles

Direction

- Brown the beef slowly in margarine. Add onions, mushrooms and seasonings. Cook until beef is tender.
- Add cream cheese and milk; continue cooking, stirring until cheese melts. Serve over hot noodles.

241. Philly Cheese Steak Casserole Recipe

Serving: 6 | Prep: | Cook: 50mins | Ready in:

Ingredients

- (6 oz) wide egg noodles
- 1-1/2 lb. beef, boneless sirloin steak, about 3/4 inch thick
- 1/2 teaspoon pepper
- 2 medium onions, chopped
- 2 garlic cloves, minced or finely chopped
- 1 green bell pepper, chopped
- 1 (14 oz.) can fat-free and sodium reduced beef broth
- 1/4 cup Gold Medal all-purpose flour
- Note: The recipe calls for 1/4 cup but I find a couple of Tablespoons do the trick.
- 1/2 cup half-and-half, fat-free or regular
- 1 Tablespoon Dijon mustard
- 1 cup cheddar cheese, reduced-fat or regular, shredded

Direction

- Heat oven to 350 degrees F.
- Spray an 11 x 7 inch (2 quart) glass baking dish with cooking spray.
- Cook and drain noodles as directed on package.
- Meanwhile, remove any fat from beef.
- Cut beef into 3/4 inch pieces.
- Heat a 12 inch non-stick skillet over medium heat.
- Cook beef and pepper in skillet 3-4 minutes, stirring occasionally, until beef is lightly brown.
- Stir in onions and bell pepper.
- Cook 2 minutes, stirring occasionally.
- Spoon into baking dish.
- In medium bowl, beat broth and flour with wire whisk until smooth.
- Add to skillet and heat to boiling.
- Cook, stirring constantly, until mixture thickens.
- Remove from heat.
- Stir in half-and-half and mustard.
- Spoon over beef mixture.
- Stir in cooked noodles.
- Cover and bake for 40 minutes.
- Sprinkle with cheese.

- Bake uncovered about 10 minutes longer or until cheese is melted and casserole is bubbly.
- Makes 4-6 servings (1-1/3 cups each)
- From: Betty Crocker, Quick-to-Fix Casseroles

242. Pizza Casserole Recipe

Serving: 68 | Prep: | Cook: 30mins | Ready in:

Ingredients

- 1 pound lean ground beef, browned and drained
- 1 small onion, chopped
- 1/3 green pepper, chopped
- 1 clove garlic, minced
- 1 (4-ounce) can mushrooms, drained
- ½ cup chopped pepperoni
- ½ cup sliced black olives
- 1 (6-ounce) can tomato paste
- 2 cups cooked noodles
- 2 cups water
- 1 teaspoon salt
- 1/8 teaspoon pepper
- 1/8 teaspoon basil
- 1/8 teaspoon oregano
- ¼ cup grated parmesan cheese
- mozzarella cheese, for topping

Direction

- Preheat the oven to 350 degrees F. In a large bowl, mix all ingredients together, except the mozzarella. Pour the mixture into a casserole dish and bake for 30 to 40 minutes. When done, sprinkle with mozzarella cheese and let melt.

243. Pork And Cabbage Halushki Recipe

Serving: 8 | Prep: | Cook: 120mins | Ready in:

Ingredients

- 3 pounds pork chops
- Note: You can use smoked sausage or kielbasa in place of pork chops
- 1-1/2 - 2 cups flour, mixed with 2 tsp. garlic powder, 2 tsp. onion powder, 1/2 tsp. cumin, salt and pepper to taste
- 1 large onion, chopped
- 1 head of cabbage, either cut into chunks or thickly sliced
- 1 pound large egg noodles
- 2 Tablespoons of butter
- a pinch of caraway seeds tossed into the cabbage water (optional)

Direction

- Shake pork chops in a plastic bag with flour, garlic powder, onion powder, cumin, salt and pepper.
- Place them in a LARGE greased sauce pan or a LARGE deep skillet and fry until browned and cook completely.
- Add chopped onion during the last 10-15 minutes of cooking.
- It is fine if the pork chops stick a little, as the scrapings are necessary in this dish.
- When they are done, remove chops and onions and set aside.
- Add a little water to the saucepan or skillet and mix up the drippings/scrapings a bit.
- Place cabbage into the pot, and allow to cool down completely.
- In a separate large saucepan, boil the egg noodles until cooked to your liking.
- Drain noodles and mix in butter.
- Cut up the pork chops into chunks and set aside.
- When the cabbage has cooked down, add pork and cooked noodles and mix completely adding more butter if you wish.
- Note: You require a LARGE skillet or Dutch oven for this recipe.

244. Pork Chops Smothered In Red Gravy Recipe

Serving: 2 | Prep: | Cook: 30mins | Ready in:

Ingredients

- cajun seasoning mix
- 4 ½-¾ inch bone in pork chops
- 2 tablespoons of olive oil
- 1 tablespoon of butter
- 2 cups of prepared pasta sauce (Ragu')
- 1 tablespoon of worcestershire sauce
- 2 teaspoons of brown sugar
- ½ cup of water
- 3 cloves of garlic, minced
- 1 small onion, diced
- 1 small bell pepper, diced (optional)
- 1 4 ounce can of sliced mushrooms

Direction

- Wash and pat dry the pork chops.
- Lightly sprinkle some Cajun seasoning both sides of the chops and let rest at room temperature for about 15 minutes.
- Mix together the pasta sauce, brown sugar and Worcestershire sauce and set aside.
- In a deep 10 inch skillet, heat the olive oil and butter on medium heat and brown the chops on both sides then set them aside. (About 1 minute on each side)
- Deglaze the same pan with a little water if necessary then sauté the onion and bell pepper (if being used) until they are soft, (About 3 minutes).
- Add the mushrooms and sauté for another minute.
- Add the garlic and sauté for one more minute.
- Remove the onion, bell pepper, garlic and mushrooms, add to the pasta sauce and mix well.
- Add the chops and pasta sauce mixture to the same pan and bring to a low boil, stirring frequently.
- Lower the heat to medium low, cover and simmer for 20-30 minutes, until chops are tender. (Be sure to stir frequently so that the red sauce doesn't burn)
- Remove from heat and serve over steaming white rice.

245. Pork Lo Mein Recipe

Serving: 4 | Prep: | Cook: 30mins | Ready in:

Ingredients

- olive oil
- 1/2 lb spaghetti, cooked al dente, drained and set aside
- 1 lb   pork tenderloin, sliced thinly into strips
- 1   medium onion, sliced
- 4-5   cloves garlic, minced
- crushed red pepper flakes, to taste
- 3 cups cole slaw mix, or about 2 cups thinly sliced cabbage and 1 cup matchstick carrots
- 2   stalks bok choy, sliced
- 2 red, yellow or orange bell peppers, sliced
- 1/3 cup   soy sauce

Direction

- Heat about 3 TBSP olive oil in a large skillet.
- Sauté pork, onion, garlic and pepper flakes just until meat is no longer pink.
- Pour this mixture into a plate and keep warm.
- Add a bit more oil to the pan and sauté cabbage, bok choy, carrots and peppers to desired doneness.
- Add pasta to the pan.
- Stir in soy sauce and add the pork mixture the pan.
- Cook for about 5 minutes, or longer, if you like the noodles darker.

246. Pork And Peas Macaroni Medley Recipe

Serving: 4 | Prep: | Cook: 10mins | Ready in:

Ingredients

- 3 white onions chopped
- 2 small green peppers chopped
- 2 small red peppers chopped
- 2 celery ribs chopped
- 3 tablespoons olive oil
- 1/4 cup cooked peas
- 1 cup chopped pieces of pork
- 1 pound macaroni
- 1 teaspoon salt
- 1 teaspoon freshly ground black pepper
- 1 cup buttered bread crumbs

Direction

- Sauté onions, peppers and celery in oil until soft.
- Add peas and meat.
- Cook macaroni until al dente then drain well and place in a baking dish.
- Stir in the vegetable meat sauce and sprinkle with salt and black pepper then stir well.
- Top with buttered bread crumbs then place under broiler for 7 minutes.

247. Potato Gnocchi And Tail On Shrimp Scampi With A Garlic Sauce Recipe

Serving: 4 | Prep: | Cook: 1mins | Ready in:

Ingredients

- 2 pounds of yukon gold potatoes scrubbed baked and cooled.
- 1 14 cups of flour
- 1 teaspoon of salt
- Sauce:

- 1 pound of jumbo tail on shrimp
- 4 tablespoons of butter
- ¼-cup olive oil
- 8 large cloves of garlic pealed
- Pinch of red pepper flakes
- fresh ground black pepper
- 1 teaspoon of thyme
- 1 teaspoon of basil
- salt to taste
- Fresh grated Parmigianino cheese.

Direction

- Bake the potatoes until a fork can pierce the skin and the potatoes are tenders no need for a crispy skin.
- Cool potatoes to room temperature and peal skins.
- Remove flesh and pass through a ricer.
- Add potatoes to a mixing bowl then the teaspoon of sale and the flour.
- Mix by hand to combine if sticky add a teaspoon of flour and mix again do not knead like bread dough.
- Place on a lightly floured surface and form a ball.
- Slice or break off a small ball and roll into a ¾-inch thick log, repeat the process until all the dough is used up.
- Slice logs into ¾-inch pieces, roll each piece against the tines of a fork, and roll onto a cookie sheet.
- For the sauce rough, chop the peeled garlic
- In a sauté pan, add the butter the olive oil and heat on medium high.
- Add the garlic and sauté for a few minutes until fragrant.
- Add the thyme and basil then half the shrimp sate until shrimp turn pink.
- Remove shrimp and sauté the remaining shrimp.
- Bring a large pot of salted water to a medium boil and add a half dozen gnocchi at a time cook them until they float and remove to a warmed dish with a little scampi sauce keep warm.

- After all the Gnocchi are cooked transfer, those to the sauté pan with the shrimp and heat thoroughly.
- Plate them, sprinkle some Parmigianino cheese, and serve at once.
- * serve with crusty bread and a wine of your choice.

---

248. Potatoe Gnocchi Johns Way Recipe

Serving: 46 | Prep: | Cook: 45mins |Ready in:

Ingredients

- 6 IDAHO POTATO'S--(OR 4 IDAHO,AND 2 SWEET POTATO,) IF YOU LIKE A NICE COLOR AND A SLIGHTLY SWEET TASTE. (I ALWAYS USE THE sweet potatoes)
- 1 TSP. salt
- ¼ TSP OF WHITE ground pepper
- 2 eggs BEATEN
- 3 TO 4 CUPS OF flour ((I USE 1 1\2 CUP OF DURUM, AND 1 1\2 CUP OF ITALIAN flour.)) ((I ALSO MAKE THIS WITH ONE CUP OF chestnut, AND 2 CUPS OF ITALIAN flour-WITCH YOU CAN GET FROM KING ARTHUR flour CO ON LINE - ALSO SOME SUPER MARKETS CARRY IT - AND SO DOES TRADER JOE) ITS THE BEST flour IN THIS COUNTRY (MY OPINON)
- 1/4 CUP OFGRADED parmigiano cheese.
- (IF USING SWEET POTATOE-- ADD A GOOD DASH OF nutmeg,)

Direction

- Gnocchi can be made up to 48 hours ahead. Before cooking the gnocchi, set up ice bath with 6 cups ice and 6 cups water. As the gnocchi cook and are floating in the boiling water, remove them with a spider or skimmer and place them into the ice bath. Let sit several minutes in bath and drain from ice and water. Toss with 1/2-cup canola oil and store covered in refrigerator up to 48 hours until ready to serve.
- BAKE THE POTATOS AT 375 TILL DONE ABOUT AN HOUR--WHEN COOL ENOUGH TO HANDLE REMOVE SKINS PUT IN A RICER, AND SPREAD THEM OVER A LARGER TABLE TO DRY OUT FOR A HOUR OR TWO, (THE DRYER THE BETTER).
- GATHER UP THE POTATO'S MAKE A MOUND WITH A WELL IN THE MIDDLE. BEAT THE EGG'S WELL.
- ADD THE SALT AND PEPPER, POUR THE MIXTURE INTO THE WELL, AND WITH YOUR HANDS MIX THE EGG MIXTURE INTO THE POTATOES ADDING A LITTLE FLOUR AT A TIME UNTIL IT'S ALL INCORPORATED INTO THE POTATO MIXTURE, YOU MAY NOT USE ALL THE FLOUR AND THATS OK. (WORK FAST THIS SHOULD NOT TAKE MORE THAN 10 MIN OR THE GNOCCHI WILL BECOME HEAVY IF YOU OVER KNEED IT.) SHAPE THE DOUGH INTO AN OVAL MOUND AND CUT INTO 6 EQUAL PARTS, TAKING ONE PART AT A TIME WITH FLOURED HANDS ROLL DOUGH INTO A LONG ROPE ABOUT 1\2 INCH ROUND, THEN CUT AT 1\2 INCH INTERVALS. CONTINUE THIS UNTIL ALL THE DOUGH IS USED UP, PUT THE GNOCCHI IN A POT OF BOILING WATER AND COOK UNTIL THEY FLOAT TO THE TOP (ABOUT 3 OR 4 IN) WHEN ALL ARE DONE, SERVE WITH YOUR FAVORITE SAUCE. THIS IS GOOD WITH JUST A PLAIN MARINARA SAUCE, SO YOU CAN SAVOR THE GNOCCHI WITHOUT DISTRACTIONS.

---

249. Pumpkin Ravioli W Hazelnut Cream Recipe

Serving: 6 | Prep: | Cook: 45mins |Ready in:

Ingredients

- 2 1/2 cups pumpkin puree

- 2 large carrots, cooked and pureed
- 2 onions, diced
- 1 clove garlic, minced
- 2 teaspoons ground coriander seed
- 1/2 teaspoon ground mace
- 1/2 teaspoon ground allspice
- 1 pinch ground cardamom
- 1 cup unsalted butter
- 1/3 pound grated parmesan cheese
- 2 tablespoons real maple syrup
- 1 egg, beaten
- 2 1/2 pounds fresh pasta sheets
- salt to taste
- ground black pepper to taste
- 1 cup hazelnuts
- 3 cups heavy whipping cream
- 3 cloves garlic, minced
- 1 pinch cayenne pepper
- 1 pinch white pepper
- salt to taste
- 2 cups shredded sorrel, stems removed

Direction

- Preheat the oven to 400 degrees F (205 degrees C). Toast the hazelnuts in a shallow pan on the middle rack for 10 to 12 minutes, or until brown and fragrant. When they are cool enough to handle, wrap the nuts tightly in a lint-free towel, and vigorously rub nuts against the towel. Continue rubbing until the nuts are almost blond.
- Sauté the onions, garlic, and spices in butter or margarine until the onions are soft. Stir together with the pureed vegetables. Add cheese, maple syrup, egg, salt, and black pepper. Adjust seasoning. Set the filling aside.
- Cook the cream, garlic, cayenne, and white pepper over high heat; stir often, and adjust heat to keep the cream from boiling over. When the cream is thick enough to coat the back of a spoon, add a pinch salt. Adjust seasoning. Remove sauce from heat until you're ready to use it.
- Lay one sheet of Fresh Pasta out on a flat surface. Spray with water to prevent drying, and to make it more flexible. Place half

tablespoons of filling along the bottom edge of the pasta about 1/2 inch apart. For larger ravioli, use 1 tablespoon of filling, and leave 1 inch between dollops. Fold the pasta sheet over the filling, and cut apart with a ravioli cutter. Set the finished ravioli aside, and cover with a damp cloth. Repeat until filling and/or pasta is completely used.

- Cook the ravioli in salted boiling water until al dente. Drain.
- Meanwhile, reheat the sauce. Add the shredded sorrel to the sauce; cook just until it wilts -- about 30 seconds. Add half the hazelnuts, turn the heat off, and add the cooked ravioli. Stir gently, and serve immediately. Garnish with remaining hazelnuts.

250. Quick Cajun Shrimp Recipe

Serving: 4 | Prep: | Cook: 10mins | Ready in:

Ingredients

- 1/2 cup olive oil
- 2 TBS cajun seasoning
- 2 TBS lemon juice - fresh
- 2 TBS parsley - fresh - chopped
- 1 TBS honey
- 1 TBS soy sauce
- 1/8 tsp cayenne pepper
- 1 lb. uncooked, large shrimp
- cooked spaghetti or pasta of your choice
- parmesan cheese

Direction

- Combine first seven ingredients in an ungreased 13x9 inch baking pan.
- Add shrimp and toss to coat.
- Bake at 450 degrees for 8 to 10 minutes.
- Toss shrimp with pan juices.
- Serve over cooked spaghetti or pasta.
- Sprinkle Parmesan cheese on top if desired.

251. Quick N Easy Balsalmic Sirloin And Pasta Saute Recipe

Serving: 4 | Prep: | Cook: 8mins | Ready in:

Ingredients

- 1 t olive oil
- 1 t butter or margarine
- 10 oz boneless beef sirloin steak, cut into 2 1/2 inch strips
- 1/2 t dried basil
- 3 T water
- 2 T balsamic vinegar
- 1 T chopped garlic
- 1 (1lb) package garlic frozen vegetables with pasta
- 1 c diced seeded tomatoes
- *** I add 1 T Kikomans Stir Fry Sauce and 1 T Worcestershire
- *** I add 1 small can mushrooms, drained,
- 1 red pepper, seeded and diced, 1 small onion - chopped, and 1 small can water chestnuts, drained if I have it on hand (broccoli, squash, zuchini, etc, I add whatever needs to be used!).

Direction

- Heat oil and butter in large non-stick skillet over medium high heat
- Add beef strips, basil and garlic (onion & pepper)
- Cook until beef is browned
- Stir in water and vinegar and sauces
- Add frozen veggies with pasta, mushrooms and water chestnuts
- Bring to boil
- Reduce heat to medium and simmer 4 minutes, stirring once
- Add tomatoes, cover and cook 1 minute, or until thoroughly heated
- Garnish with fresh grated parmesan

252. Quick And Easy Thrown Together Baked Spaghetti Casserole Recipe

Serving: 8 | Prep: | Cook: 20mins | Ready in:

Ingredients

- 1 lb angel hair pasta noodles
- 1 lb lean ground beef
- 1 small onion, chopped
- 1/2 green pepper, chopped
- 1 teaspoon minced garlic
- 1 teaspoon basil
- 1/2 teaspoon oregano
- 1/2 teaspoon salt
- 1/2 teaspoon ground pepper
- 1 (10 ounce) can cream of mushroom soup
- 1 (10 ounce) can cream of tomato soup
- 1 1/2 cups water
- 2 cups mild cheddar cheese, shredded

Direction

- Preheat oven to 350 degree.
- Prepare noodles according to directions on package.
- Drain well.
- In a large skillet, add beef, onion, peppers and garlic.
- Brown until pink is gone out of the beef. Drain.
- In a large bowl, mix together the meat mixture with the soups, water, seasonings, and spaghetti noodles.
- Spray a 9x13 inch glass dish with Pam and spread mixture into dish.
- Top with shredded cheese.
- Bake in oven 20 minutes or until cheese is golden brown.

253. Ramen Skillet Supper Recipe

Serving: 4 | Prep: | Cook: 20mins | Ready in:

Ingredients

- 1 bl. extra lean ground beef
- 2-1/2 cups water
- 1 (3-oz.) pkg. oriental-flavored ramen noodle soup mix
- 1/2 cup purchased stir-fry sauce
- 3 cups frozen broccoli florets, carrots and cauliflower

Direction

- Brown ground beef in large skillet over medium high heat until thoroughly browned, stirring frequently, and drain
- Add water, contents of the soup mix seasoning pkg. stir-fry sauce and frozen vegetables, mix well.
- Bring to a boil, reduce heat to medium low cover and cook 5 minutes or until vegetables are tender, stirring occasionally.
- Break up Ramen noodles, add to skillet.
- Cover and cook 8 minutes or until sauce id of desired consistency, stirring occasionally and separating the noodles as they softened.

254. Ramen Stir Fry Recipe

Serving: 4 | Prep: | Cook: 15mins | Ready in:

Ingredients

- 1 pound beef boneless sirloin
- 1 tablespoon vegetable oil
- 2 cups water
- 1 package (3 ounces) Oriental-flavor ramen noodle soup mix
- 1 package (16 oz) fresh stir-fry vegetables (broccoli, cauliflower, celery, carrots, snow pea pods and bell peppers) (4 cups)
- 1/4 cup stir-fry sauce

Direction

- Remove fat from beef. Cut beef into thin strips.
- In 12-inch skillet, heat oil over medium-high heat. Cook beef in oil 3 to 5 minutes, stirring occasionally, until brown.
- Remove beef from skillet; keep warm.
- In same skillet, heat water to boiling. Break up noodles from soup mix into water; stir until slightly softened.
- Stir in vegetables.
- Heat to boiling. Boil 5 to 7 minutes, stirring occasionally, until vegetables are crisp-tender.
- Stir in contents of seasoning packet from soup mix, stir-fry sauce and beef. Cook 3 to 5 minutes, stirring frequently, until hot.

255. Ravioli Casserole In The Crockpot Recipe

Serving: 4 | Prep: | Cook: 480mins | Ready in:

Ingredients

- 1-1/2 pounds lean ground beef
- 1 medium white onion chopped
- 2 garlic cloves minced
- 28 ounce can peeled tomatoes in thick puree
- 15 ounce can tomato sauce
- 2 teaspoons Italian herb seasoning
- 1/4 teaspoon freshly ground black pepper
- 1 pound bow tie pasta freshly cooked
- 10 ounces frozen chopped spinach thawed and squeezed dry
- 2 cups ricotta cheese
- 1/2 cup freshly grated imported parmesan cheese

Direction

- In a large skillet over medium high heat cook the ground beef, onion and garlic stirring often to break up lumps for 5 minutes. Tilt pan to drain off excess fat then transfer beef mixture to a small slow cooker. Add tomatoes with their puree, tomato sauce, Italian seasoning and pepper stirring to break up tomatoes with the side of a spoon. Cover and slow cook for 8 hours on low. Skim the fat from the surface of the meat sauce then stir in the cooked pasta, spinach, ricotta and Parmesan cheese and slow cook for 5 minutes.

256.   Ravioli With Balsamic Butter Recipe

Serving: 2 | Prep: | Cook: 30mins |Ready in:

Ingredients

- 18 to 20 oz store bought (frozen works great here) ravioli - ie mushroom spinach is nice.
- 6 Tbsp unsalted butter
- 1/2 tsp salt
- 1/4 tsp fresh ground black pepper
- 1/3 cup toasted, chopped walnuts
- 1/4 cup grated parmesan
- 2 Tbsp balsamic vinegar. (make it a good one)

Direction

- Place the walnuts on a small baking pan, and toast in the oven on broil for a few minutes... not much. Judgement call on this one. Then set aside.
- Bring large pot of salted water to a rapid boil over high heat. Add the ravioli and cook 4 - 5 minutes, until tender but firm to the bite.
- Drain ravioli and place in large platter.
- While the ravioli is cooking, melt and cook the butter in a medium saucepan over medium heat stirring occasionally. When the butter's foam subsides and begins to turn a golden brown (~ 3 minutes) turn off the heat. Let the butter cool ~ 1 minute, then stir in the balsamic vinegar, salt, and pepper.

- Transfer the ravioli to the saucepan with the balsamic brown butter and coat the ravioli thoroughly.
- Sprinkle the toasted walnuts and Parmesan over the Ravioli.
- Serve immediately.

257.   Red Beefy Bow Ties Made With Chuck Roast Recipe

Serving: 8 | Prep: | Cook: 150mins |Ready in:

Ingredients

- 3-4 Lb. chuck roast
- onion powder
- garlic powder
- worcestershire sauce
- Donnie's cajun seasoning Mix (or equivalent) (Recipe on my profile page)
- salt & pepper
- 1 gal size zip loc bag
- 45 oz. jar of Ragu' traditional pasta sauce
- ½ teaspoon of sugar
- Pam cooking spray
- 12 oz. bag of bow ties pasta

Direction

- Remove as much fat as possible from the chuck roast then cut it into large pieces. (1 ½ to 2 inches)
- Sprinkle the pieces of roast with the onion powder, garlic powder, Worcestershire sauce, Cajun seasoning mix, salt and pepper.
- Mix and coat the seasonings on the meat well and put all of the pieces into the Ziploc bag and seal the bag.
- Let meat stand at room temperature for 30 minutes.
- Preheat oven to 300.
- Spray a 5-6 qt. Dutch oven with PAM.
- On medium heat, brown the meat until all sides are brown.

- Add Ragu' and sugar to the meat and cook until the Ragu' starts to bubble.
- Cover the Dutch oven and put into the 300 deg. oven for 2 ½ hours, or until the meat is tender, stirring every ½ hour.
- Remove from oven and cook the bow ties pasta according to the package instructions while the gravy and meat rest.
- Mix the gravy, meat and pasta and enjoy.

258. Rib Sauce For Pasta Recipe

Serving: 8 | Prep: | Cook: 120mins |Ready in:

Ingredients

- onions, diced, 1 large
- garlic, minced, 2-3 cloves
- celery, diced, 2 ribs
- carrots, diced, 2 or 3
- banana peppers, diced, 2
- beer, 1 bottle
- tomatoes, canned diced, 19 ounces or 540 ml
- tomato sauce, about 14 ounces or 400 ml
- pork ribs, you can use Spare Ribs but they are kind of big I use Back ribs or sometimes they sell something called Sweet and Sour cut (I think that they are just Spare Ribs that have been chopped smaller-or you can do it yourself if you own a cleaver)
- bouillon cube, chicken
- oil, for sautéing

Direction

- Sauté the prepared vegetables together in some oil after a few minutes add the meat and brown it up a bit. This will take around 10 minutes
- Add salt and pepper to taste.
- Add the beer and the diced tomatoes along with the tomato sauce and the bouillon cube.
- Bring to a quick boil and then turn way down to a simmer and cook for about 2 hours.

Alternately I brown everything on top of the stove and then put it into a slow oven, covered, and let it simmer there. If I used the oven then I would set it at about 275 or 300F

259. Romanos Macaroni Grill Grilled Salmon With Spinach Orzo Recipe

Serving: 4 | Prep: | Cook: 10mins |Ready in:

Ingredients

- 4 Bias Cut salmon Filets (2 lbs total)
- 1oz canola oil
- 1oz soy sauce
- 8oz Teriyaki glaze (posted below)
- 16oz garlic olive oil sauce
- 4oz Diced red bell peppers
- 24oz orzo pasta, precooked
- 8oz spinach, julienned
- TERIYAKI GLAZE:
- 2 cups soy sauce
- ¾ cups Italian dressing
- 4 cups honey
- ¾ cups lemon juice
- 2 TBSP red pepper, crushed
- 1/8 cup cayenne pepper

Direction

- Dip salmon in soy sauce then the oil.
- Place the salmon on hot grill silver side up.
- Grill salmon evenly until done, approximately 6-7 minutes or until the internal temperature reaches 145 F.
- Slowly ladle the teriyaki glaze over the salmon while still on the grill.
- In a hot sauté pan, add olive oil garlic mix, red bell peppers and orzo.
- At home, an ounce or two of chicken stock will help the orzo during this step.
- Sauté for approximately one minute until orzo is almost dry, stirring to prevent sticking.

- Remove pan from heat and add spinach.
- Toss for approximately three seconds until spinach is incorporated but is not wilted.
- Place spinach and orzo on a plate, then add salmon and additional honey teriyaki glaze if needed.
- TERIYAKI GLAZE
- Mix all ingredients together by hand whisk. Sauce will remain for 48 hours so it needs to be prepared fresh or the day before.

260.   Rosemary Pasta In Butter Garlic Sauce Recipe

Serving: 6 | Prep: | Cook: 15mins |Ready in:

Ingredients

- 6 Tbsp unsalted butter
- 1/2 cup finely chopped onions
- 6 garlic cloves, coarse chop
- 1 cups chicken stock
- 2 Tbsp chopped fresh rosemary
- 1 pound fettuccine or spaghetti
- 1/4 cup grated parmesan cheese plus more for table
- 3 Tbsp kosher salt
- ground pepper to taste

Direction

- Melt 4 Tbsp. butter in large pan over medium heat.
- Add onions and cook until well caramelized - about 7-10 min.
- Add garlic and cook and additional 2 min.
- In large pot bring 3 quarts of water to a boil and add pasta, cook 7-10 min. until al dente.
- While pasta is cooking add 1 cup of chicken stock and chopped rosemary to the onions. Increase the heat to medium-high and cook until reduced by about a third, 6-8 minutes.
- When pasta is done drain well and add to onion-garlic-rosemary pan with remaining 2 tbsp. butter and cheese. Mix well until butter

is incorporated and add salt and pepper to taste.

261.   Rotisserie Chicken Pasta From Italian Market And Grill Recipe

Serving: 6 | Prep: | Cook: 8mins |Ready in:

Ingredients

- 5 oz. rotisserie chicken
- 2 T. roasted red peppers, diced
- 2 T. diced red onions
- 1 T. minced garlic
- ** 1 T capers, drained and 2 T. kalamata olives
- 2 oz. lemon butter
- 2 T. butter
- 1 tsp. salt
- 1-1/2 tsp. pepper
- 1 oz. olive oil
- 1/2 T. rosemary
- 6 oz. penne pasta, cooked
- 2 pinches kosher salt
- 2 T olive oil

Direction

- Cook pasta according to package directions in boiling water that has been salted with kosher salt and also has 2 T olive oil added.
- Cook until al dente, drain and rinse
- Meanwhile, heat oil in pan.
- Add chicken, garlic, peppers, onion, rosemary, salt & pepper.
- ** Add capers and olives here **
- Sauté until hot on high heat, then add lemon butter, pasta and adjust with salt and pepper.
- Heat until hot, then finish with whole butter-- add and combine--ready to serve.

262. Rustic Lasagne Recipe

Serving: 8 | Prep: | Cook: 130mins | Ready in:

Ingredients

- Sauce:
- =====
- 1 Liter milk
- 1 egg
- 1 tbsp flour
- 1 tin tomato puree (large)
- Dish:
- ====
- olive oil
- 2-3 x onions
- 2-3 x green peppers
- 1kg Lean Minced Meat (beef) (Chopped meat)
- Italian herbs to taste
- salt and black pepper to taste
- Lasagne sheets
- Enough Grated cheddar cheese

Direction

- Pour a glass of your favourite wine & get a fire going.
- Sauce:
- =====
- Mix all sauce ingredients. Ensure that there are no lumps
- Dish:
- ====
- Place olive oil in black pot
- Fry onions and green pepper until onions are transparent.
- Transfer onion & pepper mixture to reserve bowl
- Fry the minced meat in the black pot and add some Italian herbs, salt & pepper
- When browned, add onion & pepper mixture & stir well
- Taste and add some more herbs/salt/pepper as required
- Transfer mixture in reserve bowl
- Move some of the coals in order to create coals with low heat.

- Starting with the minced meat, place layers of minced meat, lasagne, cheese and sauce in black pot.
- End off with a layer of sauce & cheese
- Put on the "low heat" coals for about 1 hour.
- Serve with a green salad and enjoy.

263. SMOKED MOZZARELLA AND PENNE SALAD From The Whole Foods Cookbook Recipe

Serving: 8 | Prep: | Cook: 10mins | Ready in:

Ingredients

- THE PARMESAN DRESSING
- 1/4 cup grated parmesan cheese
- 1/2 cup chopped parsley
- 1/2 cup mayonnaise
- 1/4 cup white wine vinegar
- 3 cloves garlic, minced (1 and 1/2 tsp.)
- Pinch of cayenne pepper
- salt and freshly ground pepper to taste
- THE SALAD
- 1/2 pound penne pasta
- 2 cups packed baby spinach, washed and stemmed
- 2 small jarred roasted red pepper, diced
- 1/2 pound smoked mozzarella cheese, diced

Direction

- TO PREPARE THE PARMESAN DRESSING
- Combine the Parmesan cheese, parsley, mayonnaise, vinegar, garlic, cayenne pepper, and salt and pepper with a hand mixer or in the bowl of food processor or in a blender until the dressing is smooth.
- TO PREPARE THE SALAD
- In a large pot of boiling salted water, cook the pasta until it is al dente. Drain the pasta into a colander, run cold water over it or submerge it in ice water until chilled through, and drain

well. IN a large mixing bowl, combine the cooked pasta, spinach, roasted red peppers, and smoked mozzarella.

264. SPICY MIDDLE EASTERN PASTA AND CHICKPEA CASSEROLE Recipe

Serving: 6 | Prep: | Cook: 60mins | Ready in:

Ingredients

- 2 Tbs olive oil
- 2 medium onions, minced
- 3 cloves garlic, crushed or minced
- 1/4 cup chopped fresh cilantro OR 1 Tbsp dried
- 1 small hot pepper, minced OR 1 tsp ground cayenne
- 2 cups fresh or canned tomatoes, chopped with the juice or canning liquid
- 2 cups well-cooked chickpeas
- 1 1/2 cups raw macaroni or small shell pasta (wholewheat is fine)
- 1 cup water
- 1 tsp salt
- 1/2 tsp black ground pepper
- 1/2 tsp ground allspice
- 1/2 tsp ground cumin

Direction

- Preheat the oven to 350 degrees F.
- Heat the oil in a large skillet and sauté the onions and garlic over medium heat until they begin to brown.
- Stir in the cilantro and hot pepper and sauté a few minutes more.
- Mix in the remaining ingredients, mix well, and scoop into a 2 qt. oiled casserole dish.
- Cover and bake for 1 hour.

265. Salisbury Steak With Onion Gravy Recipe

Serving: 4 | Prep: | Cook: 20mins | Ready in:

Ingredients

- 1 egg
- 1 can condensed French onion soup divided
- 1/2 cup dry bread crumbs
- 1/4 teaspoon salt
- 1/2 teaspoon freshly ground black pepper
- 1-1/2 pounds lean ground beef
- 1 tablespoon all purpose flour
- 1/4 cup water
- 1/4 cup ketchup
- 1 teaspoon worcestershire sauce
- 1/2 teaspoon prepared mustard
- 6 cups hot cooked egg noodles

Direction

- In a large bowl beat the egg then stir in 1/3 cup of the soup, bread crumbs, salt and pepper.
- Add the beef and mix gently.
- Shape into six oval patties.
- Brown the patties in a skillet over medium heat for 4 minutes on each side then remove and set aside.
- Discard the drippings.
- In the skillet combine flour and water until smooth.
- Add ketchup, Worcestershire sauce, mustard and remaining soup then bring to a boil and cook and stir 2 minutes.
- Return patties to skillet then cover and simmer 15 minutes.
- Serve patties and gravy over noodles.

266. San Moritz Pasta Recipe

Serving: 4 | Prep: | Cook: 12mins | Ready in:

Ingredients

- 4 cups cooked pasta (penne or rotini work best)
- 3/4 cup chicken stock
- 1 T. sun dried tomatoes, plumped & chopped
- 1 clove garlic, minced
- 1 tsp. black olives, chopped
- 1 cup spinach leaves, cleaned & stemmed
- 3/4 cup fresh asparagus tips, blanched
- 3 oz. fresh mozzarella, diced
- 2 oz. grated parmesan cheese
- 3/4 cup heavy cream
- 2 T. fresh basil
- pinch oregano
- salt & freshly ground black pepper to taste

Direction

- In shallow saucepan, bring chicken stock to boil.
- Add tomato, garlic; cook 2 minutes.
- Add cream; cook 1 minute.
- Add spinach, asparagus and cheeses.
- Allow cheeses to melt through.
- Add pasta, toss and warm through.
- Add herbs and olives, salt and pepper to taste.
- Present on warm serving platter.

267. Saucy Slim Noodles Recipe

Serving: 1 | Prep: | Cook: 10mins | Ready in:

Ingredients

- 10 asparagus spears, woody ends removed, cut in half widthwise
- 25 cocktail shrimp, thawed and de-tailed

- 2 tbsp fat-free cream cheese
- 1 tbsp fat-free sour cream
- 1/4 tsp red pepper flakes
- 1/4 tsp dried oregano
- 1/4 tsp dried basil
- 1 tsp garlic powder
- 1/4 tsp onion powder
- 1 8-oz pkg fetuccine-shaped tofu Shirataki noodles, drained

Direction

- Steam asparagus spears 5 minutes, then add shrimp and steam 1 more minute. Remove and keep warm.
- In a microwaveable bowl, heat cream cheese until runny.
- Stir in sour cream and spices until well blended.
- Heat noodles in microwave about 1-2 minutes, until steaming hot.
- Add asparagus and shrimp, then pour sauce over the mix and toss.
- Serve immediately, sprinkled with parmesan if desired.

268. Sausage Spinach Pasta Casserole Recipe

Serving: 6 | Prep: | Cook: 20mins | Ready in:

Ingredients

- 12 oz. baby spinach
- 8 oz italian sausage, remove from casings and crumble
- 2 cloves garlic, minced
- 1 medium onion, chopped
- 1 TB flour
- 1 c. chicken stock
- 1 (14.5oz) can of diced tomatoes in juice
- 1 (16oz) can kidney beans, drained and rinsed
- 1/2 tsp. crushed red pepper flakes

- 1 lb. rigatoni, penne or ziti pasta cooked and drained
- 1/4 c. freshly grated parmesan cheese or more to suit taste

Direction

- Wash spinach and set aside to drain.
- In a large non-stick skillet, cook the sausage over medium heat until browned. Remove sausage and set aside.
- Sauté the minced garlic and onion until fragrant.
- Put the spinach in the skillet and toss for no longer than 45 seconds. (You just want to wilt it.)
- In a small bowl, stir the flour into the broth. Add to the spinach and bring to a boil.
- Add the tomatoes, beans and crushed red pepper.
- Simmer for about 6 minutes, stir in sausage and simmer for 1 minute longer.
- Toss the sauce with the hot pasta and parmesan cheese.
- Serve immediately with extra parmesan cheese to sprinkle on.

269.   Sauteed Light Chicken Scampi Recipe

Serving: 4 | Prep: | Cook: 15mins | Ready in:

Ingredients

- 1/4 cup extra virgin olive oil
- 6 tbsp butter
- 2 tbsp chopped garlic
- 1 cup white wine
- 1/2 tbsp garlic powder
- 1/2 tsp salt
- 1/2 tsp fresh ground pepper
- 2 tbsp lemon juice
- 1.5 lb boneless, skinless chicken, cut into 1 inch cubes
- 2 tbsp capers (optional)

- 1 lb linguine

Direction

- Cook linguine according to instructions, set aside. In a skillet sauté garlic, olive oil and 3 tbsp. of butter over medium heat, until garlic is tender- about 5 minutes.
- Add wine, chicken, salt, pepper, garlic powder, and lemon juice and capers to pan, and cook on medium/high heat for 7-10 minutes, or until juices run clear from the chicken.
- Pour over the linguine and serve immediately.
- Recently I purchased a George Forman grill and I have made the chicken on it and simply sliced and added it to the pasta and sauce at the end. It is really good this way too- but you must marinade the meat overnight in 2-3 tbsp. balsamic vinegar, Italian spices of your choice, and 2 tbsp. olive oil. I used Mrs Dash garlic +herb for the marinade. If you are making it this way, do everything the same but add the chicken in the pan at the end with the linguine and sauce. YUM!
- *optional- Add more lemon for an extra zesty summer flavor or use less wine for a richer sauce.

270.   Scallops And Pasta With Fresh Tomato Cream Sauce Recipe

Serving: 4 | Prep: | Cook: 30mins | Ready in:

Ingredients

- 2 ripe tomatoes
- 1 gallon boiling water
- 1 1/2 pounds bay scallops
- 1 tablespoon butter
- 1/2 cup dry white wine
- 2 tablespoons minced shallots
- 1 tablespoon chives
- 1 teaspoon minced garlic

- 2 tablespoons minced red bell pepper
- 1/4 cup shredded fresh basil
- 1 cup heavy cream
- 2 cups cooked pasta shells
- salt and pepper, to taste

Direction

- Plunge the tomatoes into the water for 20 to 30 seconds or until the skin just begins to show a tiny split or two.
- Remove and let cool for a second or two.
- Peel the tomato under running water.
- Slice into halves and gently squeeze the tomato to force out the seeds.
- Chop the tomato quickly into a glass bowl until ready for use.
- (Glass is for the acid, it won't react with glass.)
- Rinse the scallops.
- Heat the butter in a pan and add the scallops.
- Cook and toss for a minute.
- Add the wine, shallots, chives, garlic and bell pepper.
- Cover the pan and let simmer for three minutes or until the scallops are just done.
- Remove the scallops with a slotted spoon and set aside.
- Add the basil to the liquid from the cooked scallops and put into a separate bowl.
- Put the cream and chopped tomato into the pan and reduce over high heat buy one-half.
- Add the reserved liquid and reduce by half again.
- Add the pasta to this to heat through and then the scallops for just a minute.
- IF YOU USE REGULAR SCALLOPS... CUT IN HALF AS THEY ARE BIGGER.
- Serve with freshly grated Parmesan cheese. I would serve it on the side if it was me. I don't like cheese on lots of seafood dishes. It's just the way I was raised with Italian foods.
- Enjoy!

271. Scrumptious Baked Chicken Parmesan Recipe

Serving: 46 | Prep: | Cook: 60mins | Ready in:

Ingredients

- 4 - 6 med/large Boneless, skinless chicken breasts
- Seasoned salt
- garlic pepper
- italian seasoning
- 1 med. white onion, sliced in thin rings
- 4 - 6 pads margarine or butter
- 1 (or 2 - depending on size of chicken breasts) Jar(s) Classico garlic & ripe olive spaghetti Sauce (or Homemade tomato sauce)
- 1 tub fresh whole mushrooms, brushed clean
- 1 t garlic
- 2 bay leaves
- 2 cups shredded parmesan cheese, halved
- 1 cup shredded italian blend cheese, halved
- 1 package spaghetti noodles
- olive oil
- 2 T margarine
- kosher salt
- *SAUCE note: I always make my own sauce for spaghetti, etc, but the jarred sauce works really well in this one, tastes homemade after being combined and cooked with the other ingredients. A real time saver!

Direction

- Preheat oven to 350
- Season both sides of chicken breasts with seasoned salt, garlic pepper, and Italian Seasoning
- Drizzle with olive oil
- Place in casserole dish and cover with lid or foil
- Bake 25 minutes
- Remove from oven
- Turn chicken
- Sprinkle half of each of the cheeses over chicken
- Lay onion rings on top of chicken

- Add pad of butter to each piece of chicken
- Smother with sauce
- Add bay leaves
- Return to oven, and bake until juices run clear - about 30 more minutes, depends on size of chicken breast (bake uncovered, or the sauce will be watery)
- While chicken is baking, bring large pot of water to boil
- Add a little olive oil, slight palmful of kosher salt and butter
- Add spaghetti and cook according to directions
- (Most of the cooks on FN, etc. don't do this, but, I always rinse my pasta in a colander with cool water. I just don't love that starchy taste!).
- While pasta is boiling, brush mushrooms clean and sauté in some evoo, butter, 1 t garlic, and white wine or white wine Worcestershire.
- Remove chicken from oven when done, top with remaining cheese
- Layer noodles, chicken, sauce and mushrooms on plate.
- Serve with salad and great Italian bread with garlic & herb butter

272. Seafood Lasagna Recipe

Serving: 8 | Prep: | Cook: 65mins | Ready in:

Ingredients

- 5 c. mozzarella cheese, shredded
- 1 c. freshly grated parmesan cheese
- 3 c. milk
- 3 tbls. all-purpose flour
- 3 tbls. butter
- 1 lb. fresh crab meat
- 1 lb. cooked salad shrimp
- 16-oz. package of lasagna noodles

Direction

- Preheat oven to 350 degrees F (175 degrees C).

- Cook lasagna noodles according to package directions. Drain well.
- In a medium-sized size saucepan melt butter or margarine over medium heat. Then stir in flour and let it brown slightly. Add the milk slowly, stirring constantly until the sauce thickens. Stir in the parmesan cheese and mix well.
- Spread a thin layer of the white sauce into a 9x13 baking dish, followed by a layer of the cooked lasagna noodles. Now put a 1/4 of the shrimp, 1/4 of the crabmeat and 1 cup of the grated mozzarella on top of the lasagna noodles. Repeat this process, until you have four layers of the lasagna. Add sauce to the final layer and top with mozzarella cheese. Bake until dish is heated thoroughly and the top is golden brown, approximately 45 minutes.

273. Seafood Linguine Recipe

Serving: 4 | Prep: | Cook: 15mins | Ready in:

Ingredients

- 1 lb. linguine pasta
- 1/2 c. extra virgin olive oil
- 1/2 c. unsalted butter
- 4 cloves garlic, minced (or more to taste)
- 1 lb. bay scallops
- 1 lb. shrimp, peeled and deveined
- 8 oz. clam juice
- 1/3 c. sundried tomatoes
- 1/2 jar of artichoke hearts
- 1/4 c. chopped fresh parsley
- 2 1/2 tsp. lemon zest
- 1/4 tsp. salt
- 1/4 tsp. dried red pepper flakes

Direction

- In a large pot of boiling water cook pasta 8-10 minutes until al dente, drain.

- In a large skillet add olive oil and butter. Heat until butter is melted.
- Add garlic and sauté until garlic is just tender.
- Add scallops and shrimp. Cook until shrimp are pink, about 10 minutes, taking care not to burn garlic. Add clam juice, salt and red pepper flakes. Cook 3 minutes more.
- To the cooked pasta add; tomatoes, artichoke hearts, parsley and lemon zest. Pour seafood mixture over linguine and serve.

274. Seafood Linguine With Herbed Wine And Clam Broth Recipe

Serving: 8 | Prep: | Cook: 30mins | Ready in:

Ingredients

- 1/2 cup (1 stick) unsalted butter
- 6 tablespoons olive oil
- 3 onions, chopped
- 8 garlic cloves, peeled, smashed
- 4 medium roma tomatoes, cored, chopped
- 4 cups dry white wine
- 2 cups fish stock or clam juice (have a little extra clam juice or fish stock on hand in case you need it)
- 24 small littleneck clams, scrubbed (I asked for two dozen and my seafood guy gave me 27, bless him - and they were all good...so I used 27)
- 1 lb. 21-25 count shrimp, shelled and deveined
- 1 lb. medium sea scallops
- 8 oz. cooked jumbo lump crab meat
- 2/3 cup thinly sliced fresh basil leaves
- 1/2 cup chopped fresh parsley
- 1/4 cup chopped fresh oregano
- 1 teaspoon of dried crushed red pepper
- salt and cracked black pepper to taste
- 16 ounces linguine

Direction

- Melt butter with 4 tbsp. of olive oil in heavy large pot over medium heat. (I like to cook the butter out a bit until it stops foaming and starts to slightly brown in the oil. Don't let it go too far or it will get bitter. Stir a lot while this is happening.) Add onions and cook until soft, stirring occasionally, about 5-7 minutes.
- Add garlic and cook 1 minute. Add tomatoes and cook until they begin to soften, stirring often, about 2-3 minutes.
- Add white wine and 2 cups of fish stock/clam juice and bring to boil. Reduce heat to low, cover, and simmer 20 minutes to blend flavors.
- DO AHEAD: Broth can be made 1 day ahead. Cool slightly, then cover and refrigerate.
- Heat a separate heavy skillet over medium high heat. Add 2 tbsp. of olive oil and sauté/lightly brown sea scallops. Only cook about 2 minutes per side. You want them slightly underdone as they will cook a bit more in the final addition to the pasta. **Be sure and cook in batches - I think I had three or four batches. Overcrowding the pan will cause the scallops to steam and not brown. It's not the worst thing in the world if you do that - but be patient and cook in batches for best color, flavor and presentation. Plate and save. I loosely covered my platter of scallops with foil and stuck the platter in a preheated 200 F oven. That way they stay warm and out of the drafts.
- Add the shrimp to the same pan in batches (don't overcrowd) and cook about 2 minutes per side. You want them to be slightly underdone as well - they will also finish in the final dish). They will just start turning pink on both sides.
- Add shrimp to scallop platter and re-cover loosely with foil - return to oven.
- Bring your broth to boil. Add clams, cover, and cook until the clams open, 3 to 5 minutes (discard any clams that do not open). Transfer clams to large bowl; tent with foil and move to oven to keep warm.
- Stir basil, parsley, oregano, and crushed red pepper into broth in pot. Add linguine. Boil gently over medium high heat until pasta is

almost tender but still very firm to the tooth (timing will vary depending on what brand of linguine you use - I think mine went for about 9 minutes to this point). Stir often and add broth/clam juice by tablespoonfuls if too dry. With about 1 minute to go, I gently folded in the lump crab meat with tongs. Be gentle here - try not to break the crab up.

- Return clams, scallops, and shrimp with any accumulated juices to top of pasta in pot. Cover and reduce heat to low. Simmer until seafood is heated through and pasta is tender but still al dente, about 3 minutes longer. Season to taste with salt and pepper.
- Transfer linguine and seafood mixture to large shallow platter and serve. Sprinkle with parsley.

---

275.   Seafood Stroganoff Over Old Bay Buttered Noodles Recipe

Serving: 6 | Prep: | Cook: 32mins | Ready in:

Ingredients

- 1 pound fresh shrimp, peeled and deveined
- 1 pound bay scallops, rinsed and drained
- 1 tablespoon olive oil
- 1 teaspoon creole seasoning
- 1/2 teaspoon ground black pepper
- 1 tablespoon butter
- 3 cups fresh mushrooms, sliced
- 2/3 cup sour cream
- 1 tablespoon cornstarch
- 1 can Rotel tomatoes or 1 can diced tomatoes with green pepper
- 1 (8 ounce) bottle clam juice or shrimp broth
- 1 tablespoon pimientos
- 1/3 cup frozen peas
- •
- OLD BAY buttered noodles
- 8 ounces medium egg noodles
- 3 tablespoons butter

- 1 teaspoon Old Bay Seasoning
- 1 teaspoon paprika

Direction

- Combine peeled shrimp, scallops, oil, Creole Seasoning, and teaspoon ground black pepper in a medium bowl. Set aside.
- Meanwhile, melt butter over medium heat in a large frying pan. Cook mushrooms until tender.
- Add the can of diced tomatoes, pimientos and peas to the pan, and bring to a boil.
- In a separate pan cook shrimp and scallops; cook and stir for 3-4 minutes until shrimp turn pink.
- In a small bowl, stir together sour cream and cornstarch; mix in 1 cup clam juice. Stir into the frying pan with shrimp and scallops. Cook and stir until thick and bubbly. Cook 1 minute more.
- Add tomato-mushroom mixture, stir and heat through. Serve over Old Bay Buttered Noodles.
- OLD BAY Buttered Noodles
- Bring a large pot of lightly salted water to a boil. Add egg noodles and cook according to package directions (about 12-14 minutes) or until done; Drain well; return noodles to hot pot. Add butter, Old Bay seasoning, and paprika; toss to combine.

---

276.   Seared Scallops With Asian Noodle Salad Recipe

Serving: 4 | Prep: | Cook: 5mins | Ready in:

Ingredients

- Salad:
- 4 ounces bean thread noodles (cellophane noodles)
- 4 ounces snow peas, thinly sliced on diagonal (about 1 1/3 cups)
- 1 cup bean sprouts

- 1 cup matchstick-size strips seeded peeled cucumber
- 1/4 cup chopped fresh mint
- 1/4 cup chopped fresh basil
- 1/4 cup chopped fresh cilantro
- 1/4 cup chopped roasted salted peanuts
- 2 tablespoons finely shredded carrot
- 1/3 cup water
- 1/4 cup Thai fish sauce (nam pla)
- 3 tablespoons sugar
- 2 tablespoons fresh lime juice
- 1 garlic clove, minced
- 1 teaspoon minced serrano chili
- 1 teaspoon chili-garlic sauce
- ****
- Scallops:
- 1 pound sea scallops
- 1/2 teaspoon sugar
- 2 tablespoons vegetable oil
- 2 shallots, thinly sliced
- 1 tablespoon finely chopped lemongrass*
- 1 large garlic clove, chopped

Direction

- For salad:
- Pull noodles apart; place in large bowl. Pour enough boiling water over to cover generously. Soak noodles until tender, stirring occasionally, about 1 hour. Drain; return to same bowl. Cut noodles in half (or in thirds if very long).
- Add snow peas, bean sprouts, cucumber, herbs, peanuts, and carrot to noodles and toss to blend.
- Combine 1/3 cup water and all remaining ingredients in small bowl; whisk to blend. Season dressing to taste with salt and pepper. Stir dressing into noodle mixture.
- Let stand 15 minutes, tossing occasionally.
- ****
- For scallops:
- Sprinkle scallops with sugar, salt, and pepper.
- Heat oil in large skillet over medium-high heat.

- Add shallots, lemongrass, and garlic; stir 1 minute. Add scallops; sauté until just opaque in center, about 3 minutes.
- Divide salad among 4 plates; top with scallops and serve.

277. Sesame Chicken And Noodles Recipe

Serving: 4 | Prep: | Cook: 8mins | Ready in:

Ingredients

- 8 oz uncooked spaghetti
- 1/2 cup chicken broth
- 1/4 cup natural creamy peanut butter
- 2 TB sesame seeds, divided
- 1 TB brown sugar
- 2 TB rice vinegar
- 2 TB low sodium soy sauce
- 1 TB fresh lime juice
- 1/2 tsp hot pepper sauce
- 2 TB canola oil
- 3/4 lb chicken tenders, cut in one inch pieces
- 1/4 tsp salt
- 2 cups matchstick carrots
- 1 1/2 cups sliced green onions

Direction

- Cook pasta according to package directions, drain--reserving 2 TB cooking liquid.
- Combine broth through hot sauce and mix in a small bowl.
- Heat the oil in a large skillet over med-high heat.
- Sprinkle the salt over the chicken and cook chicken for 3 minutes.
- Add carrots and green onions, cook for 2 more minutes.
- Add sauce mixture to the pan.
- Add reserved cooking liquid and pasta to the pan, and toss to coat.

- Top with remaining sesame seeds and serve immediately.

278. Shrimp And Garlic Pasta For Two Recipe

Serving: 2 | Prep: | Cook: 10mins | Ready in:

Ingredients

- 2 tablespoons extra-virgin olive oil
- 2 tablespoons butter
- 6 cloves of garlic, sliced as thinly as possible
- dash of Old Bay Seasoning
- dash of sea salt
- dash of fresh ground black pepper
- Enough pasta for 2 servings (about 4 ounces of spaghetti or linguini or fettuccini)
- 10 jumbo shrimp or prawns, raw, shells removed and de-veined
- 1 or 2 tablespoons chopped fresh chives, if desired
- Fresh grated good quality parmesan cheese

Direction

- About 1 hour before serving, place the olive oil and butter in a large skillet; add sliced garlic and seasonings to the pan.
- Simmer at a VERY LOW heat to allow the garlic and seasonings to infuse into the oil and butter. Keep the temperature very low - you do not want to brown the garlic.
- When ready to prepare the meal, remove shells from shrimp and de-vein, if necessary; set them aside.
- Prepare pasta as directed on package.
- While pasta is boiling, turn the heat up a bit on the oil/butter mixture and add the shrimp in a single layer.
- Cook shrimp until done, which should only take about 2 minutes max per side. I have found that once I flip the shrimp in the pan, I cook the other side only for 1 minute longer then remove them to a plate and cover them -

the heat will continue to cook them, without over-cooking them and making them tough.
- Drain pasta and add it to the oil/butter in the pan; add the shrimp.
- Toss pasta and shrimp to coat with the oil and butter mixture.
- Place pasta and shrimp on serving plate and top with fresh chives and parmesan; serve immediately.

279. Shrimp Dijon Over Linguini Recipe

Serving: 6 | Prep: | Cook: 20mins | Ready in:

Ingredients

- 1lb uncooked shrimp, shelled, detailed and deveined
- 2 cloves garlic, minced
- 1/2 stick butter, plus 2T
- 1/4 cup Dijon mustard
- 1/4 cup fresh lemon juice
- 3 cups heavy cream
- 1T white wine
- 1t Old Bay Seasoning
- dash of cayenne
- fresh ground pepper
- 6oz Parmesan, shredded
- 1/4 cup fresh parsley, chopped
- 1lb linguine, just cooked to al dente
- 1/2 cup seasoned bread crumbs

Direction

- Melt 1/2 stick butter with garlic over low heat in large saucepan
- Add Dijon, lemon juice, cream, Old Bay and peppers and continue to cook on low/med low until warmed through and sauce begins to thicken.
- Add Shrimp and continue to cook until just turning pink.
- Add Parmesan, wine and parsley and cook until cheese is melted and well blended.

- In broiler safe single serve, or large soufflé dish, place linguini in bottom and top with a generous portion of the shrimp/sauce mixture.
- Sprinkle the top with bread crumbs and drizzle with melted butter
- Broil for about 5 minutes until warm and tops are golden brown

280. Shrimp Lo Mein Recipe

Serving: 4 | Prep: | Cook: 15mins | Ready in:

Ingredients

- 1/2 tablespoons soy sauce
- 16 oz large shrimp, peeled, deveined
- 16 ounces spaghetti noodles, cooked
- 1 1/2 tablespoons dark toasted sesame oil, divided
- 3 cups thinly vertically sliced onion
- 5 cups broccoli florets (about 1 pound)
- 8 oz sliced fresh mushrooms
- 1 tablespoon minced fresh garlic
- 1 tablespoon minced peeled fresh ginger
- 3/4 cup fat-free, less-sodium chicken broth
- 1/4 teaspoon salt
- sesame seeds to taste (optional)

Direction

- Combine the soy sauce and shrimp; cover and refrigerate 30 minutes. Drain through a sieve over a bowl, reserving soy sauce. Prepare noodles according to package directions, omitting the salt and fat. Drain and rinse; drain well. Toss noodles with 1 teaspoon sesame oil. Set aside. Heat 2 teaspoons sesame oil in a large non-stick skillet over medium-high heat. Add onion; stir-fry 3 minutes. Add broccoli and mushrooms; stir-fry 3 minutes. Add garlic and ginger; cook 1 minute, stirring constantly. Remove vegetable mixture from pan. Heat 1 1/2 teaspoons sesame oil in pan. Add shrimp, and stir-fry 1 minute. Add the

reserved soy sauce, broth, and salt, and bring to a boil. Add noodles, vegetable mixture, and sesame seeds, and toss well to combine.

281. Shrimp Scampi Primavera Recipe

Serving: 2 | Prep: | Cook: 30mins | Ready in:

Ingredients

- 2tablespoons of sweet butter
- 3tablespoons olive oil
- 6 cloves of fresh garlic
- Fresh oregano
- fresh basil
- Fresh chives
- chive flowers for garnish
- fresh ground black pepper
- A splash of white wine
- 2 tablespoons sea salt for the water teaspoon salt
- A pinch of red pepper flakes
- 1/3 cup of mixed vegetables
- 1 pound of 16 – 20count shrimp de-veined shells left on.

Direction

- In a large pot bring to a boil 6 quarts of water and add the sea salt
- Add the fussily and cook until extra firm, "you will finish cooking it to al dente in the sauce pan"
- In a large skillet, add butter with the oil.
- Add the garlic and sauté for one minute
- Add the vegetables, herbs and the shrimp
- Cook until the shrimp just turns pink no longer remove the shrimp with a slotted spoon.
- Peal the shrimp completely or leave on the tails for decoration
- Add the wine and 4 ladles of the pasta water cook a few minutes until some of the water is absorbed into the pasta.

- Taste for seasoning, and adjust if necessary.
- When the fussily is al dente remove to plates.
- Add the shrimp and garnish with chive flowers or fresh chives

282.   Shrimp Scampi Drenched In Garlic Butter Recipe

Serving: 8 | Prep: | Cook: 35mins | Ready in:

Ingredients

- 14 tablespoons butter (no margarine please!), divided
- 2 tablespoons garlic, peeled and minced, divided
- 1 cup clam juice
- 1/4 cup all-purpose flour
- 2 tablespoons flat-leaf parsley, minced, divided
- 2/3 cup dry white wine, divided
- juice of 1 1/2 lemons, divided
- 2 teaspoons dried basil, divided
- salt and ground black pepper to taste
- 1/2 cup light cream or half and half
- 1/3 cup olive oil
- 1/2 teaspoon crushed red pepper flakes
- 3 pounds large shrimp, peeled and deveined
- 1 1/2 to 2 pounds linguine, cooked and drained
- Additional fresh parsley for garnish (optional)

Direction

- In large saucepan, melt 12 tablespoons butter. Add 1 tablespoon garlic and sauté 1 minute or until fragrant.
- In separate bowl, whisk together clam juice, flour and 1 tablespoon fresh parsley.
- Pour into saucepan and stir until smooth.
- Stir in 1/3 cup wine, juice of 1/2 lemon, 1 teaspoon dried basil, salt and pepper. Cook, stirring constantly until thickened.
- Gradually add cream or half and half. Stir until combined.

- Simmer 20 to 30 minutes over low heat.
- Meanwhile, in large skillet, melt remaining 2 tablespoons butter with oil. Add 1 tablespoon garlic, juice of 1 lemon, 1 tablespoon parsley, red pepper flakes, 1 teaspoon dried basil, 1/3 cup white wine, salt and pepper.
- At last minute before sauce is finished cooking, add shrimp to skillet and sauté just until shrimp turn pink.
- Combine shrimp with sauce.
- Serve over pasta sprinkled with additional parsley.

283.   Shrimp Vermicelli Recipe

Serving: 8 | Prep: | Cook: 20mins | Ready in:

Ingredients

- 1/2 cup butter (I use diet butter)
- 1 bunch green onions, chopped
- 3/4 lb. fresh mushrooms, chopped or sliced
- You can use canned mushrooms also
- 2 cloves chopped garlic
- 1 lb. medium shrimp, peeled
- 8 oz. pkg of vermicelli noodles
- 1 cup grated parmesan cheese (I use reduced)
- creole seasoning, salt & pepper to taste

Direction

- Cook vermicelli according to package directions. Drain.
- Melt butter in large skillet.
- Sauté green onions, mushrooms and garlic until tender.
- Add raw shrimp and sauté until pink and firm.
- Season to taste.
- Add cooked vermicelli to the skillet.
- Mix to coat well with the butter
- Add parmesan cheese and toss to mix.
- Cover and cook on very low just to heat for a few minutes
- This is delicious!

284.   Six Can Casserole Recipe

Serving: 6 | Prep: | Cook: 35mins | Ready in:

Ingredients

- 1 large can mushrooms
- 1 can mushroom soup
- 1 can chicken-rice soup
- 1 can evaporated milk
- 1 can boned chicken or tuna
- 1 can chinese noodles
- bread crumbs

Direction

- Mix all ingredients except bread crumbs.
- Sprinkle crumbs over top.
- Bake at 325 for 35 minutes.
- Six to eight servings.

285.   Slow Cooker Lasagna Recipe

Serving: 6 | Prep: | Cook: 480mins | Ready in:

Ingredients

- 1 lb Italian turkey sausage
- 1 medium onion, chopped
- 1 large (28 oz) jar spaghetti sauce
- 2 tsp italian seasoning
- 1/4 tsp thyme
- 1 15oz container part skim ricotta cheese (can use fat free - you won't taste the difference)
- 1/2 to 1 c shredded parmesan or romano
- 2 c shredded mozzarella
- 12 uncooked lasagna noodles

Direction

- Spray slow cooker with cooking spray

- In a large skillet, sauté sausage and onion over medium heat until browned
- Drain
- Add sauce and seasonings, mix well, reduce heat to low
- In a bowl, combine ricotta, parmesan, and 1 cup of mozzarella
- Spoon 1/4 of the sausage mixture into the slow cooker, top with noodles, broken to fit
- Top with half the cheese mixture
- Continue building layers until all ingredients are used
- Cover and cook on low 6-8 hours or high 3-4 hours
- Sprinkle with remaining mozzarella, cover and cook 15 minutes more until cheese is melted

286.   Soba Noodles With Chicken Recipe

Serving: 6 | Prep: | Cook: 30mins | Ready in:

Ingredients

- 2 chicken breasts, skinless and boneless
- 1 c water
- 1 tbsp each: soy sauce, hoisin sauce, oyster sauce, sugar
- 1 package buckwheat noodles, cooked according to package, drained
- 1/2 c carrots, thinly sliced, bias cut
- 3 stalks of green onions, bias cut
- 1/2 c shredded cabbage
- 1 garlic clove, chopped
- 1 inch grated ginger
- Slurry: 2 tbsp water + 1 tbsp cornstarch
- black pepper, to taste
- toasted sesame seeds, garnish
- Chopped cilantro, garnish
- sesame oil
- Chopped cilantro

Direction

- In a medium pan, heat water and chicken with seasonings (soy sauce, hoisin sauce, oyster sauce and sugar.) Let it boil and turn down heat. Cover and simmer for 15 minutes. Remove chicken and thinly shred meat. Reserve seasoned broth.
- Cook noodles in boiling water for 5 minutes. Drain and set aside.
- In a large heated sauté pan, add some oil and sauté together carrots, green onions, cabbage, ginger and garlic for 2 minutes.
- Add shredded chicken to the vegetables and sauté for 1 minute. Taste and season with black pepper.
- Pour slurry and stir until desired thickness.
- Add noodles and gently stir mixture.
- To serve, sprinkle noodles with sesame seeds, cilantro, and a drop of sesame oil.

287.   Southern Penne Pasta With Chicken Recipe

Serving: 4 | Prep: | Cook: 20mins | Ready in:

Ingredients

- 3/4 pound penne pasta
- 2 tablespoons butter
- 2 skinless boneless chicken breast halves, sliced 1/2" thick
- 3 cloves garlic, minced
- 1 bunch green onion, chopped
- 2 tablespoons cajun seasoning
- 1 teaspoon freshly ground black pepper
- 1 teaspoon ground cayenne pepper
- 8 ounces heavy cream
- 1 green bell pepper, julienne
- 1 red bell pepper, julienne
- 8 ounces fresh mushrooms, quartered
- 3/4 cup Parmesan Reggiano cheese, grated

Direction

- Cook penne pasta according to package directions. Drain; set aside. Meanwhile, melt

butter in a large skillet over medium-high heat. Add chicken; cook, stirring frequently, until browned, about 6 to 8 minutes. Add garlic, onions, Cajun seasoning and ground black and cayenne peppers. Add bell peppers and mushrooms; stir to combine. Cover and cook for 5 minutes. Uncover; Stir in cream and let simmer another 2-3 minutes. Stir in Parmesan cheese. Remove sauce from heat, stir in cooked pasta and serve immediately.

288.   Spaetzle Homemade Noodles Recipe

Serving: 8 | Prep: | Cook: 10mins | Ready in:

Ingredients

- 3 cups flour
- 1 tsp salt
- 4 large eggs, beaten
- cold water as needed
- 1/4 cup butter

Direction

- Put flour and salt in a mixing bowl. Pour eggs and 1/4 cup cold water into flour mixture. Beat with a wooden spoon, adding more water as needed, until mixture shows air bubbles. Dough should be slightly sticky, yet elastic.
- Using a spaetzle machine or colander with medium holes, press noodles into a large pot of boiling, salted water. Repeat process until all the dough is used.
- Cook noodles about 5 minutes or until they rise to the top. Watch that they don't boil over. Drain noodles in a colander, and run cold water over them. I place a clean dish cloth over a cookie sheet and let the noodles cool dry slightly.
- Melt butter in frying pan and brown noodles in butter.

289. Spaghetti Bake Recipe

Serving: 4 | Prep: | Cook: 30mins | Ready in:

Ingredients

- 1 pound of ground chuck
- ½ cup of diced onion
- ½ cup of diced green bell pepper
- ½ teaspoon of chili powder
- 1 10 ¾ ounce can of condensed tomato soup
- ½ can of water
- 2 shots of worcestershire sauce
- ¼ teaspoon oregano
- ¼ teaspoon basil
- ½ teaspoon garlic powder
- 6 ounces of #3 or #4 spaghetti
- 1 cup of grated cheddar cheese
- salt and pepper to taste

Direction

- Sauté ground beef, onion, bell pepper, chili powder, salt and pepper until ground beef is browned.
- Drain excess liquid and place meat mixture into a 2.5 quart round casserole dish.
- To the meat mixture, add all of the other ingredients except for the spaghetti and the cheese and mix well.
- Break the spaghetti in half and cook according to the package instructions.
- Add the spaghetti to the meat mixture and mix well.
- Cover the casserole dish and put it into the refrigerator for 4 to 6 hours. (This allows for all of the flavors to blend)
- Remove from refrigerator and allow 30 minutes to come to room temperature.
- Preheat oven to 350 degree.
- Uncover and sprinkle the cheese all over the top of the mixture.
- Cook UNCOVERED for 30 minutes.
- Remove from oven, cover and let set for 10 minutes.
- Serve and Enjoy :)

290. Spaghetti Carbonara Recipe

Serving: 4 | Prep: | Cook: 15mins | Ready in:

Ingredients

- 1 Package of spaghetti
- 1cup of Chopped bacon (pancetta is the best)
- 3 garlic cloves, minced
- 1tbs olive oil
- 1/4 Cup white wine
- 1/3 Cup Cream
- 1 egg yolk
- 2/3 Cup parmesan cheese, Grated
- salt & pepper
- 2 Tbs Fresh, Finely Chopped parsley

Direction

- Cook the pasta until al dente.
- Over medium heat cook the pancetta and garlic until golden.
- Add wine to skillet and cook until it has bubble
- Remove from the heat and add the cream.
- Whisk together the egg yolk, parsley and cheese.
- Add cooked pasta into the skillet
- Pour the cream mixture and add the egg mixture mix thoroughly.
- Add salt and pepper to taste, mixing well. Serve

291. Spaghetti N Spinach Pie Recipe

Serving: 8 | Prep: | Cook: 30mins | Ready in:

Ingredients

- 6 ounces uncooked angel hair pasta
- 2 eggs, lightly beaten
- 1/3 cup parmesan cheese
- 1 lb 93% lean ground beef
- 1/2 cup chopped onions
- 1/4 cup chopped red or green peppers
- 1 (14 ounces) jar meatless sauce
- 1 teaspoon creole seasoning
- 3/4 teaspoon garlic powder
- 1/2 teaspoon basil
- 1/2 teaspoon oregano
- 1 (8 ounces) package cream cheese, softened
- 1 (10 ounces) package frozen spinach, thawed and squeezed dry
- 1/2 cup shredded mozzarella cheese

Direction

- Cook pasta according to package directions; drain.
- Add eggs and Parmesan cheese.
- Press onto the bottom and up the sides of a greased 9-inch deep dish pie plate.
- Bake at 350 degrees for 10 minutes.
- Meanwhile, in a skillet, cook the beef, onion and green pepper over medium heat until meat is no longer pink; drain.
- Stir in spaghetti sauce and seasonings.
- Bring to a boil.
- Reduce heat; cover and simmer for 10 minutes.
- Between two pieces of waxed paper, roll out cream cheese into a 7 inch circle.
- Place in the crust.
- Top with spinach and meat sauce.
- Sprinkle with mozzarella cheese.
- Bake at 350 degrees for 20-30 minutes or until set.

292. Spaghetti With Sausage And Peppers Recipe

Serving: 4 | Prep: | Cook: 30mins | Ready in:

Ingredients

- 1 tablespoon olive oil
- 1 lb italian sausage (mild or hot)
- 1 onion, chopped
- 2 red bell peppers, cut into 1 inch pieces
- 1 3/4 teaspoons salt
- 3 cloves garlic, minced
- 1 cup canned crushed tomatoes, in thick puree
- 1 cup low-sodium chicken stock
- 2 tablespoons dry vermouth or dry white wine
- 3 tablespoons chopped flat leaf parsley
- 3/4 lb spaghetti
- 2 tablespoons grated parmesan cheese, plus more for serving

Direction

- *In a large frying pan, heat the oil over moderate heat.
- *Add the sausage and cook, turning, until browned and cooked through, about 8 minutes.
- Remove from pan.
- *When cool enough, cut into 1/2 inch slices.
- *Add the onion, peppers and 3/4 teaspoon of the salt to the pan.
- *Cook, stirring frequently until the vegetables begin to brown, about 5 minutes.
- *Cover and cook, stirring occasionally until the vegetables are soft, about 3 minutes longer.
- *Add the garlic and cook, stirring, for about 30 seconds.
- Add the tomatoes, broth, vermouth, the reserved sausage and any accumulated juices, the parsley and the remaining 1 teaspoon of salt, and bring to a simmer.
- In a large pot of boiling salted water, cook the spaghetti until just done, about 12 minutes.
- Drain and toss with the sausage and pepper mixture and the Parmesan.
- Serve with more Parmesan.

293. Spaghetti With Shrimp Tomatoes And Feta Recipe

Serving: 8 | Prep: | Cook: 15mins | Ready in:

Ingredients

- 1 lb. large fresh, wild shrimp, peeled and deveined
- 2 tablespoons butter
- 1 tablespoon fresh lemon juice
- 2 green onions, chopped (include some of the tops)
- 2 tablespoons olive oil
- ½ cup dry white wine
- ½ cup clam juice
- 1 garlic clove, minced
- 3-4 organic roma tomatoes, seeds removed, coarsely chopped
- 2 teaspoons chopped organic fresh oregano
- 1 teaspoons chopped organic fresh basil
- 1 teaspoons chopped organic fresh Italian parsley
- 1 cup crumbled feta cheese (greek)
- 1/2 cup heavy cream
- 1 package organic spaghetti

Direction

- Prepare pasta according to package. Keep warm in covered pot until shrimp mixture is ready to add.
- Melt butter in a large skillet over medium heat. Add shrimp, garlic and lemon juice. Sauté 2-3 minutes or just until shrimp turn pink. Remove shrimp from skillet.
- Heat olive oil in skillet and add onion, cooking until just tender. Add wine and clam juice. Reduce heat and simmer 10 minutes. Add tomato and heavy cream; simmer 5 more minutes.
- Stir in shrimp, oregano, basil, and parsley. Gently toss with cooked pasta. Serve on warm plates and top with feta cheese and additional herbs.

294. Spaghetti With Asparagus And Shrimp Recipe

Serving: 4 | Prep: | Cook: 20mins | Ready in:

Ingredients

- 2 pounds of medium shrimp, peeled and deveined
- salt
- 1 tsp of paprika
- 1 tsp. of chile flakes
- 1 dozen asparagus spears, wood parts trimmed and then cut into 1 inch pieces
- 1/3 cup olive oil
- 3 cloves of garlic, smashed
- 1 small red onion, diced
- 1/4 cup white wine (Chardonnay)
- zest of 1/2 lemon
- 2 T. lemon juice
- some pasta water
- 2 handfuls of spaghetti

Direction

- Get a large pot of water boiling for your pasta. When the water begins to boil, add a generous amount of salt and cook your pasta according to the package's instructions.
- In a bowl, toss your shrimp with some salt, paprika and chili flakes. Place a skillet on a burner on medium high-heat and pour in your olive oil. Add the shrimp and sauté until they've just turned pink (about 3 to 4 minutes). Remove your shrimp with a slotted spoon and reserve.
- In the same skillet add your garlic, onions and asparagus and sauté them on medium heat for about 5 minutes (or enough to soften).
- Add your wine and reduce until there's barely any liquid left. Take the skillet off the heat and reserve (you may remove the garlic, if you wish).
- As soon as your spaghetti is cooked, reserve some pasta water and strain the spaghetti.

- Place you skillet back on the burner (heat off) and add your pasta, shrimp, zest and lemon juice and toss to coat the pasta with the remaining ingredients. Add some pasta water if the sauce is too dry.
- Serve with a nice Chardonnay.

295. Spaghetti With Pancetta And Mushrooms Recipe

Serving: 4 | Prep: | Cook: 30mins | Ready in:

Ingredients

- 1 1/2 lbs. Dried spaghetti
- 1/2 lb. pancetta or Cured bacon, diced
- 1 28 oz. can San Marzano tomatoes, crushed and juices reserved
- 3 Tbsp. extra virgin olive oil + more for drizzling
- 1 Large sweet onion, finely chopped
- 4 cloves fresh garlic, thinly sliced
- 1/2 tsp. Crushed red chili Flakes
- 2 cups Button or cremini mushrooms, thinly sliced
- 1 cup dry, non-oaky white wine
- 2 Tbsp. Fresh thyme
- 1/2 cup freshly grated Parmesan or pecorino romano cheese

Direction

- In a large stock pot, prepare 6 quarts cold water + 1 Tbsp. kosher salt for the pasta. Add pasta to boiling water and cook until al dente, about 7-8 minutes.
- Meanwhile in a separate stock pot or large skillet, heat the 3 Tbsp. oil until just lightly smoking. Add the pancetta and render until brown. Add the onion, garlic, and chili flakes, season with salt, and cook until the onions are translucent and just barely browning, about 5-6 minutes. Add the mushrooms, season with salt, and cook until the mushrooms start to get tender, about 2-3 minutes. De-glaze the pan

with the white wine and reduce by half. Add the tomatoes and the thyme, bring to a light boil then reduce heat to a simmer and cook until the sauce thickens slightly and the flavors meld, about 15 minutes.
- Remove the pasta from the boiling water and drain, but do not rinse. Season the sauce to taste with salt and pepper. Add the pasta to the sauce and toss thoroughly off the heat, about one minute. Divide the pasta evenly into four bowls, drizzle with the extra virgin olive oil and sprinkle with cheese.

296. Spaghetti Pizza Casserole Recipe

Serving: 6 | Prep: | Cook: 20mins | Ready in:

Ingredients

- 1 (16-oz) package spaghetti
- 1 cup milk
- 2 eggs
- 1 pound ground beef (I used ground turkey)
- 1 medium onion, chopped
- 1 medium-size green pepper, chopped
- 1 (32-oz) jar spaghetti sauce
- 1 (4-oz) can sliced mushrooms, drained
- 1 (12-oz) package sliced pepperoni
- 2 cups (8 oz) shredded mozzarella cheese
- 1 cup (4 oz) shredded cheddar cheese

Direction

- Cook spaghetti according to package directions; drain and place in a lightly greased 13" x 9" x 2" baking dish.
- Combine milk and eggs, stirring well; pour over spaghetti.
- Cook ground beef, onion, and bell pepper in a large skillet, stirring until beef crumbles; drain well. Stir in spaghetti sauce; spoon over spaghetti. Place mushrooms and pepperoni on top.

- Bake at 350° for 20 minutes. Sprinkle with cheeses; bake an additional 10 minutes. Yield: 8 servings

---

297. Special Chow Mein Recipe

Serving: 4 | Prep: | Cook: 15mins | Ready in:

Ingredients

- 3 tblspns vegetable oil
- 2 cloves garlic - thinly sliced
- 1 tsp fresh ginger root - chopped fine
- 2 red chillies - chopped fine
- 4 oz ham - sliced into thin strips
- 1 boneless chicken breast - sliced into thin strips
- 16 uncooked tiger prawns - peeled & deveined. tails left on
- 4 oz fresh green beans
- 8 oz bean sprouts
- 2 oz chives (garlic chives if you can get them)
- 1 lb Chinese egg noodles - cooked in boiling water til tender
- 2 tblspns soy sauce
- 1 tblspn oyster sauce
- salt & black pepper to taste
- 1 tblspn sesame oil
- 2 spring onions for garnish

Direction

- Heat 1 tbsp. of the oil in a wok or large frying pan.
- Stir-fry the garlic, ginger & the chillies for just a few seconds.
- Add the ham, chicken, prawns & beans & stir-fry for about 2-3 mins on high heat or until the chicken & prawns are cooked.
- Transfer to a bowl & set aside.
- Heat the rest of the oil in the same wok & stir-fry the chives & the beansprouts for 1 - 2 mins.
- Add the noodles, soy sauce, oyster sauce, salt & pepper & toss.

- Return the prawn/chicken mixture to the wok & toss all together with the sesame oil.
- Serve, garnished with the slivered spring onions.

---

298. Spicy Beefy Noodles Recipe

Serving: 6 | Prep: | Cook: 38mins | Ready in:

Ingredients

- 1 1/2 lbs. ground beef
- 1 small onion, minced
- 1 clove garlic, minced
- 1 tablespoon chili powder
- 1 teaspoon paprika
- 1/8 teaspoon dried basil leaves
- 1/8 teaspoon dill weed
- 1/8 teaspoon dried thyme leaves
- 1/8 teaspoon dried marjoram
- salt
- black pepper
- 1 can (10oz) dieced tomatoes with green chilies, undrained
- 1 can (8oz) tomato sauce
- 1 cup water
- 3 tablespoons worcestershire sauce
- 1 package (about 10 oz) egg noodles, cooked according to package directions
- 1/2 cup shredded cheddar cheese
- 1/2 cup mozzarella cheese
- 1/2 cup pepper-jack cheese
- 1/2 cup provolone cheese

Direction

- Preheat oven to 350.F
- Cook and stir ground beef, onion and garlic in a large skillet over medium heat until meat is no longer pink, stirring to separate meat. Pour off drippings. Add chili powder, paprika, basil, dill, thyme and marjoram. Season with salt and pepper. Cook and stir 2 minutes.

- Add tomatoes with juice, tomato sauce, water and Worcestershire sauce; mix well. Cover and simmer 5 minutes.
- In a lightly greased 2-quart casserole, combine meat mixture and noodles. Bake 25 minutes.
- Mix cheeses and sprinkle evenly over top. Bake 5 minutes more or until cheese melts and casserole is bubbly

299. Spicy Chicken Over Angel Hair Pasta Recipe

Serving: 6 | Prep: | Cook: 35mins | Ready in:

Ingredients

- 3 to 4 Tbsp. olive oil
- 4 cherry peppers, seeded & chopped
- 1 Italianelle or bell pepper, chopped
- 1 onion,chopped
- 11/2 lbs. boneless,skinless chicken breasts, cut in bite-size pieces
- 2 garlic cloves,chopped
- 1 (141/2 ounce) can chopped or diced tomatoes
- 1 lb. angel hair pasta
- Parmesan or romano cheese

Direction

- Heat oil in a large heavy skillet over med.-high heat
- Add cherry peppers, onion and italianelle pepper.
- Sauté 2 min.
- Add chicken; sauté 3 to 4 min.
- Add garlic and sauté 1 min. longer.
- Add tomatoes, reduce heat to medium and simmer a while.
- Cook pasta according to package directions; drain
- Divide pasta among 6 serving plates.
- Spoon chicken mixture on top.
- Sprinkle with Parmesan or Romano cheese.
- Serves 6

300. Spicy Garlic Shrimp And Penne Pasta Recipe

Serving: 4 | Prep: | Cook: 25mins | Ready in:

Ingredients

- 1 15 oz can Italian diced tomatoes
- 1 Tbsp italian seasoning
- 1 tsp dried basil
- ¼ tsp sea salt
- 8 oz. penne pasta
- 1/3 cup olive oil
- ½ cup chopped onion
- ½ cup chopped yellow or green bell pepper
- 1 Tbsp minced garlic (more if desired)
- 1 lb medium pre-cooked shelled shrimp
- ¼ cup favorite hot sauce (Franks)
- ¼ cup Parmesan or romano cheese Plus extra to sprinkle on finished dish

Direction

- In a covered sauce pan simmer diced tomatoes, Italian seasoning, basil and sea salt.
- Allow to sauce to simmer while the pasta is cooked according to directions on package. Drain.
- While sauce and pasta are cooking:
- Heat oil over medium heat in large skillet or pan, add onion and peppers. Cook until soft.
- Add garlic, stir and add shrimp, toss to coat with oil.
- Add hot sauce when shrimp is hot.
- Add pasta to shrimp lightly toss to coat pasta with oil and hot sauce.
- Add tomatoes and quickly toss again.
- Add Parmesan cheese, toss.
- Sprinkle extra cheese on top of pasta just before serving.
- Serving suggestion: Serve with warmed garlic bread, buttered with Italian Spread.

301. Spicy Lo Mein Noodles Recipe

Serving: 4 | Prep: | Cook: 10mins |Ready in:

Ingredients

- 1 pound linguine
- 1/2 tsp- 1 tsp, (or more if you like it hot) cayenne pepper
- 3 cloves garlic minced
- about 3-4 tablespoons extra virgin olive oil
- about 3 tsp.toasted sesame seed oil
- 3/4 cup light soy sauce
- 2 tsp. peanut butter
- chopped chives
- 2 tsp sesame seeds
- Optional: peanuts, cashews, water chestnuts, bean sprouts,sauteed veggies, or cooked shrimp or beef

Direction

- Toast sesame seeds, (can be done in toaster oven, or the sauce pan)
- While water is cooking for linguine
- Heat oils in sauce pan
- Add garlic and sauté until garlic is soft
- Add toasted sesame seeds and cayenne pepper
- Add soy sauce and peanut butter, simmer on low.
- Cook linguine until al dente, drain and put in a big pasta bowl.
- Pour sauce over pasta and toss, top with chives. If need more sauce, add a little water to it before pouring over pasta.
- Add any optional ingredients depending on whom you are feeding!
- WARNING: Make sure no one eating this is allergic to peanuts, or have an epipen on hand...

302. Spicy Romano Chicken With Artichoke Hearts And Sundried Tomatoes Recipe

Serving: 8 | Prep: | Cook: 20mins |Ready in:

Ingredients

- THE SAUCE
- 1 pint heavy cream
- 4 T butter
- 2 t salt
- 1 T pepper
- 1/4 cup romano cheese
- 1/4 cup parmesan cheese
- 2 t cayenne pepper
- *for extra zip add 1 to 2 tsps red pepper flakes in addition to cayenne
- INGREDIENTS
- 10 ounce package of bowtie pasta cooked and drained according to package directions - al dente.
- 1 1/2 T melted butter
- 1/2 cup sliced mushrooms
- 1/4 cup sliced green onions
- 1 small jar artichoke hearts - drained
- 1 7-8 ounce precooked sliced grilled chicken, sliced
- 1/8 cup sundried tomatoes, chopped
- 1 oz heavy cream

Direction

- To Prepare The Sauce:
- Melt butter in sauté pan or skillet. Add cream, salt and pepper, heat to a boil. Remove from heat and fold in cheeses and cayenne pepper. Set aside.
- For Ingredients:
- In a large skillet over medium heat, melt butter, then add mushrooms, green onions and sundried tomatoes. Stir for one minute. Next add artichokes and chicken. Stir. Stir in 1 ounce heavy cream and 1/2 of the sauce. Add bowtie pasta followed by rest of the sauce. Stir gently. Serve.

303. Spicy Tarragon Chicken In Wine Sauce Recipe

Serving: 6 | Prep: | Cook: 60mins |Ready in:

Ingredients

- 1/3 cup flour
- 2 tsp or more tarragon
- 1 tsp salt
- 1/2 tsp paprika
- 1 tsp ground ginger
- 3 lbs. chicken (I like using the tenders)
- oil & butter
- 1 cup chopped onion
- 3 garlic cloves minced
- 1/2 cup chicken broth
- 2 oz white wine
- 2 oz sherry wind
- 1 can mushrooms
- 1 pkg wide egg noodles

Direction

- Combine flour, tarragon, salt, paprika, and ginger in a plastic bag.
- Add chicken to coat.
- In skillet heat oil & butter and add coated chicken and brown well on all sides. Transfer cooked chicken to plate as you continue till all chicken is cooked.
- In same skillet sauté onion and garlic till tender.
- Add the wines, broth and bring to boil.
- Add mushrooms and salt & pepper to taste.
- Add cooked chicken, and cook for about 15 minutes to incorporate taste.
- If you like, you can add more tarragon & ginger for taste. And if too dry add more wines & broth. No too much as the sauce should be a slightly thick sauce
- In meantime, boil salted water and cook wide noodles. When al dente drain and serve under chicken & sauce.

304. Spicy White Lasagna Recipe

Serving: 8 | Prep: | Cook: 60mins |Ready in:

Ingredients

- 12 lasagna noodles
- 1 lb pork sausage. crumbled
- 3-4 boneless, skinless chicken breasts, cut into 1-1/2" pieces
- 1 tbsp chili Seasoning
- 1 chopped medium onion
- 2 minced garlic cloves
- 2 (16 oz) jars of garlic alfredo sauce
- 1/2 cup chicken broth
- 1/2 cup grated asiago cheese
- 1 (15 oz) container ricotta cheese
- 1 large egg
- 1 tbsp dried basil
- 1 (9 oz) bag fresh spinach
- 1-2 cans drained, canned mushrooms
- 2 cups shredded mozzarella cheese
- salt & pepper

Direction

- Preheat oven to 350
- Lightly grease a 13 x 9 baking dish
- Cook noodles according to package, drain
- In large skillet, combine sausage and cook over medium high heat until lightly pink
- Add chicken and continue cooking till no longer pink
- Remove meat from skillet, leaving as much grease in pan as possible
- Add onion & garlic to skillet, cook for 5 minutes or till tender
- Remove pan from heat
- Stir meat back in and add Chili Powder
- Stir in ONE jar of Alfredo sauce, chicken broth and Asiago Cheese
- In medium bowl, combine ricotta, egg & basil.
- Spread a thin layer over bottom of prepared pan

- Top with half of remaining jar of Alfredo sauce
- Arrange 4 noodles over sauce
- Spread 1/3 of meat mixture over noodles
- Arrange half of spinach & mushrooms over meat mixture
- Sprinkle with 1/2 cup mozzarella cheese & dot with 1/2 of ricotta mixture
- Repeat procedure with remaining ricotta mixture, Alfredo sauce, noodles, meat mixture, spinach & mushrooms & mozzarella
- Bake 45 minutes or until hot and bubbly
- Let stand 10 minutes before serving
- Tip: I used more of ricotta & mozzarella, our family likes CHEESE

305. Spinach Artichoke Pasta Salad Recipe

Serving: 6 | Prep: | Cook: 5mins | Ready in:

Ingredients

- kosher salt
- 1 pkg cheese tortellini
- 1/2 lb fresh baby spinach
- 1 can baby artichoke hearts in water, drained and chopped
- 1 roasted red pepper, drained and chopped
- 1/2 small red onion, chopped
- 1 garlic clove
- 1 lemon, zested
- 2 tsp fresh lemon juice
- 2 Tbs red wine vinegar
- 1/2 cup EVOO
- 1 Tbs fresh thyme leaves, chopped (or 1/2 tsp dried)
- pepper
- handful sundried tomatoes, packed in oil, chopped

Direction

- Bring pot of water to boil and add pasta

- Cook 3-4 minutes
- Drain and cool pasta
- Chop spinach
- Combine with artichoke pieces, roasted red pepper and onion
- Chop garlic, add salt to it and make into a paste with the back of your spoon or a flat knife
- Transfer garlic paste to small bowl and add lemon zest, lemon juice and vinegar
- Whisk in oil, thyme and pepper
- Add pasta and sun-dried tomatoes
- Dress salad and gently toss
- Serve or refrigerate!
- **you could add cubed or shredded rotisserie chicken and make it a meal! Fabulous!!

306. Spinach Bacon And Parmesan Pasta Recipe

Serving: 4 | Prep: | Cook: | Ready in:

Ingredients

- 1/2 box of penne pasta, preferably Barilla plus
- 6 slices bacon or turkey bacon
- 2 T garlic butter, divided
- 1/2 yellow onion, diced
- 2 garlic cloves, minced
- 1 pkg button mushrooms, sliced
- garlic salt to taste
- 1/2 bag of baby spinach
- 1 T flour
- 1 c half and half
- 1/2 c fresh grated parmesan cheese

Direction

- Cook penne pasta and set aside.
- Meanwhile, in a big skillet, cook the bacon. (If you're using real bacon, you'll need to drain most of the extra grease off.) Set the cooked bacon aside on a plate and crumble once cool.

- In the leftover fat and 1 T of the garlic butter, sauté the garlic and onion over medium-low until very well browned, 20-30 min.
- Add mushrooms, season with garlic salt, and cook until reduced, 10 or so minutes.
- Add the spinach and cook over medium for about 5 minutes, stirring frequently.
- Mix together the pasta, bacon and the sautéed vegetables in a large serving bowl.
- In the still hot pan, melt the remaining T of garlic butter. Add flour and make a paste.
- Add a couple of ounces of half and half and stir well until no lumps remain. Slowly add the rest of the half and half, stirring constantly.
- Once smooth, boil 30 to 60 seconds until just slightly thickened, still stirring constantly.
- Add the parmesan to the sauce and stir just until melted.
- Pour sauce over pasta, bacon and veggie combo, and mix well.
- Serve with additional parmesan cheese if desired.

307. Spinach Lasagna Recipe

Serving: 8 | Prep: | Cook: 50mins | Ready in:

Ingredients

- 1 tablespoon plus 1 teaspoon margarine
- 1 tablespoon plus 1 teaspoon olive oil
- 6 each garlic cloves, minced
- 1 cup canned Italian tomatoes (with liquid), drain and dice tomatoes reserving liquid 1 bay leaf
- 1/2 teaspoon pepper, divided
- 1 teaspoon each of oregano and basil leaves, divided
- 2 packages 10 oz package frozen chopped spinach
- 1 egg, beaten
- 11 ounces shredded Jack cheese divided pieces)
- 3 cups sliced mushroom

- 1 cup chopped onion
- 1 1/2 cups tomato sauce
- 1 1/2 teaspoons salt, divided
- 2 cups part-skim ricotta cheese
- 8 ounces uncooked lasagna macaroni (12x3 inch, cooked according to directions.

Direction

- 1. In a 10-inch skillet heat margarine over medium heat until bubbly and hot; add mushrooms and sauté occasionally, until mushrooms are lightly browned and cooked through (2 to 3 minutes).
- 2. Remove from heat and set aside. In 3-quart saucepan heat oil over medium heat; add onions and garlic and sauté until onions are softened.
- 3. Add tomato sauce, tomatoes, 3/4 teaspoon salt, ¼ teaspoon pepper, basil, and oregano, and bay leave; mix well.
- 4. Reduce heat to low, cover and simmer stirring occasionally, for 25-30 minutes; remove and discard bay leaf.
- 5. In medium mixing bowl combine spinach, ricotta cheese, egg, remaining 3/4 teaspoon salt and ¼ teaspoon pepper, mixing well. Preheat oven to 350°F.
- 6. In 13x9x2-inch baking dish spread ½ cup tomato mixture; arrange half of the lasagna macaroni lengthwise in dish, overlapping edges slightly. Spread half of the spinach mixture evenly over macaroni and top with half of the mushrooms; spread ½ cup of the tomato mixture over mushrooms and sprinkle with half of the Monterey Jack Cheese.
- 7. Arrange remaining macaroni crosswise in dish cutting macaroni to fit and overlapping edges slightly.
- 8. Spread remaining spinach mixture, over macaroni, top with remaining mushrooms, tomato mixture, and Monterey Jack Cheese.
- 9. Bake until lasagna is cooked through and cheese is lightly browned, 40-50 minutes.

308. Spinach Feta Orzo Recipe

Serving: 4 | Prep: | Cook: 20mins | Ready in:

Ingredients

- 1 (16-ounce) package orzo pasta, uncooked
- ½ cup evoo
- 2 tbsp butter
- 1 garlic clove, minced
- ½ tsp dried basil
- ½ tsp crushed red pepper flakes
- 1 cup pine nuts
- 1 (10-ounce) bag baby spinach
- 1/8 cup balsamic vinegar
- 1 (8-ounce) package crumbled feta cheese
- ½ a large tomato, chopped
- salt and pepper, to taste

Direction

- Bring a large pot of lightly salted water to a boil, add orzo and cook for 8-10 minutes (just under al dente)
- Drain, transfer to a mixing bowl, set aside
- Heat olive oil and butter in a skillet over medium-high heat, stirring to blend.
- Stir in garlic, basil, and red pepper flakes, and reduce heat to medium.
- Stir in pine nuts and cook until lightly browned.
- Add spinach and cover, and cook on low heat for 5 minutes, or until spinach is wilted.
- Toss spinach mixture with orzo, add salt and pepper to taste.
- Portion onto serving plates, drizzle with vinegar, and top with feta cheese and chopped tomatoes.

309. St Louis Blues Recipe

Serving: 6 | Prep: | Cook: 20mins | Ready in:

Ingredients

- 1 lb. penne or other medium pasta shape
- 1/2 lb. bacon
- 4 cloves garlic, chopped
- 1 cup onion, chopped
- 1 tsp. salt
- 1 lb. collard greens, chopped and rinsed (I use spinach)
- 1 14.5 oz. can chicken broth
- 1 tbsp. wine vinegar
- 1 tsp. hot pepper sauce
- 1/2 cup parmesan cheese, grated

Direction

- Cook pasta according to pasta directions, drain.
- Meanwhile, cook bacon in large skillet until crisp.
- Remove from pan, crumble and reserve bacon.
- Pour off all but 1 tbsp. bacon drippings.
- Sauté garlic and onion in remaining drippings.
- Sprinkle with salt.
- Add greens and stir to coat with bacon drippings.
- Add chicken broth.
- Cover pan and simmer until greens are tender but not mushy, about 15 minutes.
- Stir in vinegar and hot pepper sauce.
- Mix collard greens and pan juices with the cooked pasta.
- Sprinkle with parmesan cheese and chopped bacon.
- Serve immediately.

310. Stuffed Shells With Artichoke Spinach And 3 Cheeses Recipe

Serving: 8 | Prep: | Cook: 20mins | Ready in:

Ingredients

- 1 box jumbo pasta shells (barilla)
- evoo

- 1 onion, minced
- 2 garlic cloves, minced
- 1 box frozen artichoke hearts, thawed
- 1 box frozen chopped spinach, thawed
- ½ cup basil, chopped
- 4 tbsp parsley, chopped
- 1 ½ cups ricotta cheese
- 1 cup each mozzarella and parmesan cheese, grated (plus 3 tbsp each for topping)
- 2 eggs
- 3 cups marinara sauce
- salt and pepper

Direction

- Cook pasta according to directions on the package
- While pasta water boils, do all of the chopping for the onion and garlic, chop the artichoke hearts, basil, and parsley.
- Grate the cheeses and drain the excess water off the spinach
- Once pasta is in the water, heat evoo to a medium skillet and add the onions and garlic cook for 3 minutes.
- Add the artichoke hearts and salt and pepper. Sauté for 2 minutes longer. Cool
- Drain pasta and run under cold water to cool.
- In a medium bowl, combine onion mixture, basil, parsley, all cheeses, eggs, salt and pepper, stir to combine.
- Place a thin of marinara sauce on the bottom a baking pan
- Fill the shells with the mixture all the way to the brim, and place in baking pan.
- Drizzle remaining marinara sauce over the top and sprinkle with mozzarella and parmesan cheeses.
- Place in a 350 oven for 20 minutes.

311.   Stuffed Shells With Arrabbiata Sauce Recipe

Serving: 810 | Prep: | Cook: 45mins | Ready in:

Ingredients

- 12 ounces (1 box) jumbo pasta shells (approximately 36 shells)
- 2 tablespoons olive oil, plus extra for greasing baking sheet
- 6 ounces thinly sliced pancetta, diced
- 2 teaspoons dried crushed red pepper flakes
- 2 garlic cloves, minced
- 5 cups marinara sauce
- 2 (15-ounce) containers whole milk ricotta cheese
- 1 1/3 cups grated Parmesan
- 4 large egg yolks
- 3 tablespoons chopped fresh Italian parsley leaves
- 3 tablespoon chopped fresh basil leaves
- 1 teaspoon chopped fresh mint leaves
- 1 1/2 teaspoons salt
- 1/2 teaspoon freshly ground black pepper
- 1 cup shredded mozzarella cheese

Direction

- Preheat the oven to 350 degrees F.
- Lightly oil a 12 by 9 by 2-inch baking dish and set aside.
- Lightly oil the baking sheet and set aside.
- Partially cook the pasta shells in a large pot of boiling salted water until slightly tender but still quite firm to the bite, about 4 to 6 minutes.
- You will continue cooking the shells in the oven after they have been stuffed.
- Using a slotted spoon, drain pasta shells and place on oiled baking sheet, spreading them out so that they don't stick together and allow to cool.
- Heat the oil in a heavy medium saucepan over medium heat.
- Add the pancetta and sauté until golden brown, about 5 minutes. Add the red pepper flakes.
- Add the garlic and sauté until tender, about 1 minute.
- Add the marinara sauce.
- Bring the sauce to a simmer, stirring often.

- In a medium bowl, stir the ricotta, Parmesan, egg yolks, basil, parsley, mint, salt, and pepper. Set aside.
- Spoon 1 1/4 cups of the sauce over the prepared baking dish.
- Fill the cooked shells with the cheese mixture, about 2 tablespoons per shell.
- Arrange the shells in the prepared dish.
- Spoon the remaining sauce over the shells, then sprinkle with the mozzarella.
- Bake in the lower third of your oven until the filling is heated through and the top is golden brown, about 25 to 30 minutes.

---

312.   Succulent Sour Cream Pot Roast Recipe

Serving: 6 | Prep: | Cook: 210mins | Ready in:

Ingredients

- * 5 lb bonless rolled chuck roast
- * 2 tb unbleached flour
- * 1 tb cooking oil
- * 1/2 ts salt
- * 1/4 ts pepper
- * 3/4 c water
- * 1 ea clove garlic, pressed
- * 2 ea small onions, chopped
- * 1/2 c tomato sauce
- * 1 ea bay leaf
- * 1/8 ts thyme leaves
- * 1/2 lb fresh mushrooms, sliced
- * 2 tb butter
- * 1 c dairy sour cream
- * 1 hot buttered noodles
- * 1 paprika

Direction

- Dredge pot-roast in flour; brown all sides in cooking oil in Dutch oven.
- Slip rack under meat; sprinkle with salt and pepper.

- Add water, garlic, onion, tomato sauce, bay leaf and thyme. Cover and cook in slow oven (325 degrees F.) 3 1/2 hours or until tender.
- Cook sliced mushrooms in butter in small frying-pan until tender and golden.
- When meat is tender, remove to cutting board. Remove bay leaf.
- Thicken cooking liquid with 2 T flour combined with 1/4 c water, if desired.
- Add mushrooms and sour cream to cooking liquid; cook over moderate heat but do not allow to boil.
- Slice beef; serve with hot buttered noodles sprinkled with paprika. Pass the cream sauce separately.

---

313.   Sukiyaki Traditional Recipe

Serving: 5 | Prep: | Cook: 12mins | Ready in:

Ingredients

- For the Sukiyaki:
- 14 oz good beef tenderloin, sliced paper thin
- 1/2 block fresh tofu
- 6 Shiitaki mushrooms
- 1 Medium onion or 2 leeks
- 4 oz fresh spinach
- beef suet (optional)
- 2 packets udon noodles or 1/2 package vermicelli
- For the Warishita Broth:
- 6 Tbs Soy
- 6 Tbs sake (rice wine)
- 5 Tbs sugar
- 2 cups soup broth with a bit of dashi (or substitute beef bullion)
- Dipping Sauces:
- 1 raw organic egg for each person, broken and slightly beaten into small individual bowls
- 1 bottle Japanese Sesame dipping sauce (also used for shabu shabu) called Shiro Neri Goma

(see my recipe) poured into small individual bowls.

Direction

- Slice up and arrange all the Sukiyaki ingredients on a platter to put by your cook top.
- Cook the noodles and keep warm in an attractive bowl.
- Mix the Warishita Broth and heat in the microwave for 1 min.
- Heat the suet or a little vegetable oil in a large skillet.
- Fry the onion till browned, push aside.
- Fry the meat until barely pink, push aside.
- Fry the mushrooms.
- Add the tofu and the broth.
- Place each ingredient next to each other in separate attractive groups in the pan, getting broth on all bits.
- Add the spinach.
- Cover and simmer for about 5 mains till ingredients are all softened.
- Uncover and serve the meal right from the skillet at the table with the dipping sauces and the noodles.

---

314.   Super Cheesy Mac And Cheese Recipe

Serving: 6 | Prep: | Cook: 37mins | Ready in:

Ingredients

- 1 tbsp. olive oil
- 1 lb. elbow macaroni
- 1/2 cup butter
- 1/2 cup shredded swiss cheese
- 1/2 cup shredded muenster cheese
- 1/2 cup shredded mild cheddar cheese
- 1/2 cup shredded sharp cheddar cheese
- 1/2 cup shredded monterey jack cheese
- 1/2 cup shredded asiago cheese
- 2 cups half and half

- 1 cup velveeta cut into small pieces
- 2 lg eggs beaten lightly
- 1/4 tsp seasoning salt
- 1/8 tsp fresh ground black pepper

Direction

- Preheat oven to 350. Lightly butter a deep 2.5 quart casserole.
- Bring a large pot of water to a boil over high heat, add the oil then the elbow macaroni and cook until the macaroni is just tender
- Drain well and return to pot.
- Add the butter and mix it into the macaroni.
- In a large bowl mix the Muenster, mild and sharp cheddar cheese, asiago, Monterey jack cheese and the Swiss cheese together.
- Then to the macaroni add the half and half, 1.5 cups of the shredded cheeses, the Velveeta and the eggs and mix well.
- During this time you should season with salt and pepper to your own liking.
- Then layer the macaroni mixture and remaining cheese.
- Place in the oven and bake for 30 minutes or until bubbling around the edges.

---

315.   Swedish Meatballs Recipe

Serving: 8 | Prep: | Cook: 60mins | Ready in:

Ingredients

- 2lbs lean ground beef
- 1 1/2 cups fine bread crumbs
- 1/4 cup beef stock
- 3-4t fresh grated nutmeg, divded
- 4t Dijon, divided
- 2 eggs
- salt and pepper
- 2 cloves garlic
- 8-12 oz fresh mushrooms, sliced
- 1 small onion, chopped
- 1/4 cup flour
- 1 1/2 cups chicken stock

- 1 cup half and half
- 2T olive oil
- 2T butter
- 1 bag egg noodles, cooked and drained

Direction

- Combine meat, beef stock, bread crumbs, salt, pepper, 1t nutmeg, 2t Dijon and eggs together.
- Form into about 1 inch meatballs and brown lightly in olive oil and butter.
- About halfway through browning, add mushrooms, garlic and onion and finish browning.
- When done, remove them from pan with slotted spoon and place them in a 9X13 dish.
- In browning pan, add flour to drippings and stir on low heat to make a roux.
- Add chicken stock and stir till thickens.
- Add 2t nutmeg and salt and pepper, remaining Dijon and half and half and stir to combine and thicken
- Pour over meatballs and bake at 350 for about 30 minutes.
- Serve over cooked egg noodles.
- **this can also be made as a casserole by slightly undercooking the noodles and placing them in a large casserole dish, then the meatballs, then the cream mixture and bake about the same time. Add a couple T more of chicken stock if you do it this way, though.

316. Swedish Meatballs With Egg Noodles Recipe

Serving: 8 | Prep: | Cook: 20mins | Ready in:

Ingredients

- 2 pounds ground chuck
- 2 eggs
- 2 cups bread crumbs
- 1/2 teaspoon salt
- 1 teaspoon freshly ground black pepper
- 1 white onion finely chopped

- 2 tablespoons canola oil
- 1 can cream of celery soup
- 1 can cream of mushroom soup
- 1 cup sour cream
- 1/2 cup milk
- 1 package medium egg noodles
- 1/2 teaspoon Greek seasoning
- 1 teaspoon granulated sugar
- 6 quarts boiling water
- 2 tablespoons salt

Direction

- Mix together ground chuck, eggs, breadcrumbs, salt, pepper, Greek seasoning, sugar and onion.
- Shape mixture into small meatballs.
- Put canola oil in large skillet then add meatballs and brown on all sides.
- Cover and cook over low heat for 10 minutes.
- Blend soups, sour cream and milk then cover and simmer 10 minutes.
- Bring water and salt to a rapid boil.
- Gradually add noodles to water and cook until noodles and tender.
- Drain well then serve meatballs over noodles.

317. Sweet Potato Gnocchi With Maple Cinnamon Sage Brown Butter Recipe

Serving: 8 | Prep: | Cook: 90mins | Ready in:

Ingredients

- For the Gnocchi:
- 2 pounds sweet potatoes
- 2/3 cup whole milk ricotta cheese
- 1 1/2 teaspoons salt
- 1 teaspoon ground cinnamon
- 1/4 teaspoon freshly ground black pepper
- 1 1/4 cups all-purpose flour, plus 1/3 cup for the work surface
- For the Maple cinnamon sage Brown Butter:

- 1/2 cup unsalted butter (1 stick)
- 20 fresh sage leaves
- 1 teaspoon ground cinnamon
- 2 tablespoons maple syrup
- 1 teaspoon salt
- 1/2 teaspoon freshly ground black pepper

Direction

- For the Gnocchi:
- Preheat the oven to 425 degrees F.
- Pierce the sweet potato with a fork. Bake the sweet potatoes until tender and fully cooked, between 40 to 55 minutes depending on size. Cool slightly.
- Cut in half and scoop the flesh into a large bowl. Mash the sweet potatoes and transfer to a large measuring cup to make sure the sweet potatoes measure about 2 cups.
- Transfer the mashed sweet potatoes back to the large bowl.
- Add the ricotta cheese, salt, cinnamon, and pepper and blend until well mixed.
- Add the flour, 1/2 cup at a time until a soft dough forms.
- Lightly flour a work surface and place the dough in a ball on the work surface.
- Divide the dough into 6 equal balls.
- Roll out each ball into a 1-inch wide rope.
- Cut each rope into 1-inch pieces.
- Roll the gnocchi over the tines of a fork.
- Transfer the formed gnocchi to a large baking sheet.
- Continue with the remaining gnocchi.
- Meanwhile, bring a large pot of salted water to a boil over high heat.
- Add the gnocchi in 3 batches and cook until tender but still firm to the bite, stirring occasionally, about 5 to 6 minutes.
- Drain the gnocchi using a slotted spoon onto a baking sheet.
- Tent with foil to keep warm and continue with the remaining gnocchi.
- For the Brown Butter sauce:
- While the gnocchi are cooking melt the butter in a large sauté pan over medium heat.

- When the butter has melted add the sage leaves.
- Continue to cook, swirling the butter occasionally, until the foam subsides and the milk solids begin to brown.
- Remove the pan from the heat.
- Stir in the cinnamon, maple syrup, salt, and pepper. Careful, the mixture will bubble up. Gently stir the mixture.
- When the bubbles subside, toss the cooked gnocchi in the brown butter.
- Transfer the gnocchi to a serving dish and serve immediately.

318.   Sweet Potato Gnocchi With Sage Brown Butter Recipe

Serving: 4 | Prep: | Cook: 10mins | Ready in:

Ingredients

- 2 large local sweet potatoes, cooked through, peeled
- 1 12-ounce container organic ricotta cheese, drained
- 1 cup high quality parmesan cheese, grated finely
- 2 tbsp (packed) organic light brown sugar
- 2 tsp sea salt
- 1/2 tsp freshly ground nutmeg
- 1/2 tsp pumpkin pie spice
- 1/4 tsp cinnamon
- 2 3/4 cups all purpose flour
- 1 cup (2 sticks) unsalted, local butter
- 6 tbsp fresh sage, chopped

Direction

- Mash sweet potato in a medium-sized bowl.
- Add ricotta cheese gradually.
- Add Parmesan cheese, brown sugar, salt, nutmeg, pumpkin pie spice, and cinnamon.
- Mash everything together. Mix in flour gradually until a dough forms.

- Turn dough out onto floured surface and divide into six equal pieces.
- Rolling between palms and floured work surface, form each piece into 20-inch-long rope, sprinkling with flour as needed if sticky.
- Cut each rope into 20 pieces.
- Make an imprint with a fork on each piece.
- Bring large pot of water to boil, add a handful of salt, and return to boil.
- Don't overcrowd the pot and boil pasta until it floats to the top, about five minutes.
- Melt butter in heavy large saucepan over medium-high heat. Cook for about five minutes and then add sage.
- Top gnocchi with sage butter and serve immediately
- From Planet Green

319.   Sweet Potato Gnocchi With Sweetened Brown Butter Recipe

Serving: 10 | Prep: | Cook: 50mins | Ready in:

Ingredients

- 2 1-pound red-skinned sweet potatoes (yams), rinsed, patted dry, pierced all over with fork
- 1 12-ounce container fresh ricotta cheese, drained in sieve at least 2 hours
- 1 cup finely grated parmesan cheese (about 3 ounces)
- 2 tablespoons (packed) golden brown sugar
- 2 teaspoons plus 2 tablespoons sea salt
- 1/2 teaspoon freshly ground nutmeg
- 2 ¾ cups (about) all purpose flour
- 1 cup (2 sticks) unsalted butter
- 1 tablespoon brown sugar
- ¼ teaspoon cinnamon
- 1/3 cup chopped pecans

Direction

- Line large baking sheet with parchment paper. Place sweet potatoes on plate; microwave on high until tender, about 5 minutes per side. Cut in half and cool. Scrape sweet potato flesh into medium bowl and mash; transfer 3 cups to large bowl. Add ricotta cheese; blend well. Add Parmesan cheese, brown sugar, 2 teaspoons salt, and nutmeg; mash to blend. Mix in flour, about 1/2 cup at a time, until soft dough forms.
- Turn dough out onto floured surface; divide into 6 equal pieces. Rolling between palms and floured work surface, form each piece into 20-inch-long rope (about 1 inch in diameter), sprinkling with flour as needed if sticky. Cut each rope into 20 pieces. Roll each piece over tines of fork to indent. Transfer to baking sheet.
- Bring large pot of water to boil; add 2 tablespoons salt and return to boil. Working in batches, boil gnocchi until tender, 5 to 6 minutes. Transfer gnocchi to clean rimmed baking sheet. Cool completely. (Can be made 4 hours ahead. Let stand at room temperature.)
- Preheat oven to 300°F. Melt butter in heavy large saucepan over medium-high heat. Cook until butter solids are brown and have toasty aroma, swirling pan occasionally, about 5 minutes.
- (Reserve ¼ cup of the melted butter, Add 2 teaspoons brown sugar and 1/8 tsp. cinnamon to ¼ cup of the melted butter, add half of this mixture to the last minute of sautéing of each batch.)
- Transfer half of remaining butter to large skillet set over medium-high heat. Add half of gnocchi. Sauté until gnocchi are heated through, about 6 minutes. Empty skillet onto rimmed baking sheet; place in oven to keep warm. Repeat with remaining butter and gnocchi.
- Cover with foil and return baking sheet to oven until ready to serve.
- Divide gnocchi and sauce among shallow bowls. Sprinkle with chopped pecans.
- Bon Appétit
- December 2005

320.   Sweet Potato Ravioli With Lemon Sage Brown Butter Recipe

Serving: 8 | Prep: | Cook: 60mins |Ready in:

Ingredients

- 1 (1-pound) sweet potato
- 2 tablespoons grated fresh parmesan cheese
- 1/2 teaspoon salt, divided
- 1/4 teaspoon ground cinnamon
- 1/8 teaspoon ground nutmeg
- 24 wonton wrappers
- 1 large egg white, lightly beaten
- 6 quarts water
- cooking spray
- 3 tablespoons butter
- 1 tablespoon chopped fresh sage
- 1 tablespoon fresh lemon juice
- 1/8 teaspoon freshly ground black pepper
- sage sprigs (optional)

Direction

- Preheat oven to 400°.
- Pierce potato several times with a fork; place on a foil-lined baking sheet. Bake at 400° for 40 minutes or until tender. Cool. Peel potato; mash. Combine potato, cheese, 1/4 teaspoon salt, cinnamon, and nutmeg in a small bowl.
- Working with 1 wonton wrapper at a time (cover remaining wrappers with a damp towel to keep them from drying), spoon 1 tablespoon potato mixture into center of each wrapper. Brush edges of dough with egg white; bring 2 opposite corners to center. Press edges together to seal, forming a triangle. Repeat procedure with remaining wonton wrappers, potato filling, and egg white.
- Bring 6 quarts water to a boil. Add 8 ravioli; cook 2 minutes or until done. Remove ravioli from pan with a slotted spoon. Lightly coat

cooked wontons with cooking spray; keep warm. Repeat procedure with remaining ravioli.

321.   Szechuan Sesame Noodles Recipe

Serving: 6 | Prep: | Cook: 15mins |Ready in:

Ingredients

- 8 ounces thin dried Asian noodles or linguine
- 4 tablespoons oriental sesame oil
- 4 tablespoons chopped peanuts
- 2 tablespoons finely chopped peeled fresh ginger
- 3 large garlic cloves, minced
- 6 tablespoons bottled teriyaki sauce
- 2 tablespoons fresh lime juice
- 1 teaspoon chili-garlic sauce
- 1 1/2 cups thinly sliced green or red onions
- ~~~~
- Optional:
- snow peas
- red bell pepper, sliced
- cilantro

Direction

- Cook noodles in large pot of boiling salted water until tender but still firm to bite. Drain; return noodles to same pot. Mix in 1 tablespoon oil and peanuts.
- Heat 3 tablespoons oil in heavy small skillet over medium-low heat. Add ginger and garlic; stir 10 seconds.
- Add teriyaki sauce, lime juice and chili sauce; simmer 30 seconds.
- Mix sauce and onions into noodles. Season with salt and pepper.
- Serve warm or at room temperature.

322. TAMMYS Cheesy Chicken Spaghetti Recipe

Serving: 8 | Prep: | Cook: 30mins | Ready in:

Ingredients

- 4 chicken breast OR 5 chicken breast fillets. YOU CAN ALSO USE DARK MEAT IN THIS RECIPE. WE PREFER WHITE MEAT.
- 2 CANS OF chicken broth
- 3 chicken BULLION CUBES
- 1 bell pepper DICED
- 2 onions DICED
- 2 CUPS OF green onions DICED
- 1 CUP celery DICED
- parsley
- seasoningS OF YOUR CHOICE
- 1 CAN OF Rotel tomatoes
- 1 CAN OF cream of mushroom soup
- 1 CAN OF cream of chicken soup
- CAN ALSO USE 1 CAN OF cream of celery soup (IF YOU DONT HAVE THE CELERY TO DICE)
- 1 LG. BOX OF VELVETTA cheese
- LARGE PKG. OF spaghetti
- mushrooms OR mushroom pieces & STEMS (OPTIONAL)
- olives (OPTIONAL)

Direction

- BOIL THE CHICKEN WITH SEASONINGS, PARSLEY, BROTH AND OR BULLION CUBES AND HALF OF YOUR DICED ONIONS, CELERY AND BELL PEPPER. COOK UNTIL TENDER. DEBONE OR CUT CHICKEN IN TO BITE SIZE PIECES. SAVE BROTH WHEN CHICKEN IS DONE.
- SAUTEE REMAINING VEGETABLES & MUSHROOMS (IF YOU CHOOSE TO ADD MUSHROOMS) AND SET ASIDE.
- BOIL SPAGHETTI
- IN A LARGE POT COMBINE THE ROTEL TOMATOES, SOUPS, CHEESE (CUT INTO BITE SIZE PIECES), SAUTEED VEGETABLES AND MUSHROOMS. COOK LOW SO

CHEESE WON'T BURN. IF THIS MIXTURE IS THICK ADD CHICKEN BROTH TO YOUR DESIRED CONSISTENCY.
- ADD CHICKEN
- ADD SPAGHETTI
- ENJOY THIS NOW OR PLACE IN A BAKING OR CASSEROLE DISH TOP WITH SHREDDED CHEESE. BAKE UNTIL CHEESE IS MELTED.
- THIS IS MARVELOUS WITH GARLIC BREAD, SALAD AND A VEGETABLE OF YOUR CHOICE.
- YOU CAN ALSO USE LIGHT, LESS FAT, LESS SODIUM, ETC... TO MODIFY THIS DISH FOR YOUR DIET

323. TGI Fridays Bruschetta Chicken Pasta Recipe

Serving: 4 | Prep: | Cook: 45mins | Ready in:

Ingredients

- Chicken Breasts:
- Four 4 oz. chicken breasts (grill right before serving)
- **
- season both sides of chicken breasts with salt and black pepper. Grill 3-4 minutes per side
- for grill marks or until the chicken breasts reach 165ºF.
- ***
- garlic Bread:
- 1 stick of butter (1/4 pound)
- 1/8 teaspoon salt
- 1/8 teaspoon black pepper
- 1/8 teaspoon garlic powder
- ++++++++++++++++++++++++++++++++++++++
- Melt butter in microwave and stir to combine seasonings.

- Drizzle your favorite bread with garlic butter and bake at 350° until crispy and golden brown (approximately 4 minutes).
- **
- Pasta:
- 1 lb. angel hair pasta (can cook and chill ahead of time)
- 2 tablespoons salt
- ***
- Boil pasta in ½ gallon of water with salt until al dente. Drain and transfer to a bowl. If cooking
- ahead of time, shock in an ice bath to cool, remove from water and toss with 2 Tbsp. of salad oil.
- ***
- fresh tomato Sauce:
- 6-8 medium-size roma tomatoes
- 2 tablespoons olive oil
- 1/4 teaspoon salt
- 1/8 teaspoon black pepper
- 2 cloves of minced garlic
- 10 fresh basil leaves
- 1/2 cup plain tomato sauce
- ***
- Balsamic Glaze:
- 1 cup balsamic vinegar
- 1 tablespoon sugar

Direction

- Bring to a boil in small sauce pan and turn down flame to a simmer. Reduce by 75% until sauce turns to a thick syrup and hold at room temperature.
- Wash, core and dice tomatoes to 1/4" pieces, save juices and place in a small bowl.
- Wash, dry and cut basil leaves into thin strips.
- Add to tomatoes along with salt and pepper and hold for 2 hours before using.
- Heat a heavy bottom sauce pan under medium-low flame.

- Add 2 Tbsp. olive oil and heat oil for 20 seconds.
- Add any remaining garlic butter from bread to sauce pan.
- Sauté 2 cloves of garlic sliced into thin coins in oil for 45 seconds on each side until soft and tender - do not brown garlic.
- Increase heat, add tomato mixture and stir.
- Add 1/2 cup of plain tomato sauce to pan and bring to a light boil. Add pasta to sauce pan and toss with fresh sauce (sauce should just coat pasta).
- Transfer to a service platter or plate individually and garnish with balsamic glaze.
- Slice chicken breast into strips on a bias (45 degree angle) and place on top of pasta.
- Garnish with fresh chopped parsley.

---

324. Taco Pasta Salad Recipe

Serving: 6 | Prep: | Cook: 20mins | Ready in:

Ingredients

- 1 pound ground beef
- 1 (1.25-ounce) package ORTEGA® taco seasoning Mix
- I only use cumin and a small amout of chili powder..
- 1 (16-ounce) package macaroni, cooked, rinsed and drained
- 1 (16-ounce) jar ORTEGA salsa - Homestyle Recipe (Mild)
- I used our HEB store brand.. I find it better.
- 2 cups shredded cheddar cheese
- I mixed with half American and chedder
- 1 cup sliced ripe olives
- Slice your own.. they taste better
- 3/4 cup sliced green onions

Direction

- Cook ground beef and seasoning according to taco seasoning package directions.

- Combine macaroni, salsa, ground beef mixture, cheese, olives and onions; mix well.
- I served with a bed of shredded lettuce and some homemade tortilla chips on side with chopped tomatoes and cilantro.
- Yummmmmmy!
- Serve warm

---

325. Tequila Lime Fettuccine Recipe

Serving: 6 | Prep: | Cook: 10mins | Ready in:

Ingredients

- ½ cup finely chopped fresh cilantro
- 2 tablespoons minced fresh garlic
- 2 tablespoons minced jalapeno pepper (seeds and veins may be removed) skin removed*
- 3 tablespoons unsalted butter (reserve 1 tablespoon for sauté)
- ½ cup chicken stock
- 5 tablespoons freshly-squeezed lime juice
- 2 tablespoons gold tequila, flamed**
- 1½ cup heavy cream
- ¼ medium red onion, thinly sliced
- ½ medium red bell pepper, thinly sliced
- ½ medium yellow bell pepper thinly sliced
- ½ medium green bell pepper, thinly sliced
- 1 pound dry spinach fettuccine or 2 pounds fresh
- 1 ¼ pound chicken breast, diced 3/4 inch
- 3 tablespoons soy sauce
- *to peel a jalapeno, heat about a quarter cup of olive oil in a sauté pan over medium-high heat until the oil shimmers. Add the jalapeno and roll it around until the skin is blistered on all sides. Remove the jalapeno from the pan and robe with a paper towel -- the skin will come right off. Use the olive oil for other dishes -- it is infused with jalapeno flavoring!
- **the fastest way to flame the tequila is to pour it into a wide glass, and light a match. When the flame dies out it is done. Alternately you may use a small sauté pan.

Direction

- Cook 1/3 cup cilantro, garlic and jalapeno in 2 tablespoons butter over medium heat for 4 to 5 minutes. Add stock, tequila and 3 tablespoons lime juice. Bring the mixture to a boil and cook until reduced to a paste like consistency; add cream and reduce by ½ cup. Set aside.
- Prepare rapidly boiling, salted water to cook pasta; cook until al dente, 8 to 10 minutes for dry pasta, approximately 3 minutes for fresh. Pasta may be cooked slightly ahead of time, rinsed and oiled and then "flashed" (reheated) in boiling water or cooked to coincide with the finishing of the sauce/topping.
- Melt remaining butter in a large saucepan over medium high heat
- Add soy sauce, remaining 2 tablespoons lime juice and chicken. Sauté until chicken is partially cooked, about two minutes
- Add onion and peppers, stirring occasionally until the vegetables begin to wilt
- Add tequila/lime cream and bring the sauce to a boil; boil gently until chicken is cooked through and sauce is thick (about 5 minutes). At this point, the sauce should be a deep brown, and quite aromatic
- Add the fettuccine noodles and coat well
- Transfer to serving dish and garnish with fresh cilantro
- Serve family style or transfer to serving dishes, evenly distributing chicken.

---

326. Teriyaki Steak With Noodles Recipe

Serving: 4 | Prep: | Cook: 20mins | Ready in:

Ingredients

- 1 cup teriyaki marinade with pineapple juice
- 1 pound boneless sirloin steak

- 1 package teriyaki noodles
- 1-1/2 cups water
- 1 tablespoon vegetable oil
- 10 ounce box frozen broccoli florets partially thawed

Direction

- Pour marinade over steak in a large plastic bag and turn to coat.
- Cover and marinate in refrigerator about 30 minutes.
- Remove from marinade and discard marinade.
- Grill or broil steak to desired doneness turning once and basting with additional marinade.
- Meanwhile prepare noodles according to package directions adding broccoli during last 2 minutes of cooking.
- Let stand for 2 minutes.
- Serve with sliced steak and garnish with sliced green onions.

327.   Teriyaki Stir Fry Recipe

Serving: 3 | Prep: | Cook: 30mins | Ready in:

Ingredients

- 1/2 Cup hot water(helps the honey stir up easier)
- 1/3 Cup soy sauce
- 1/4 Cup honey(spray measuring cup with cooking spray, the honey comes out easier)
- 3/4 tsp ground ginger or 1 Tbsp. minced fresh ginger
- 1 lb. beef flank steak, or chicken breast, or pork, cut into thin strips **(Place the meat in the freezer for a little bit before slicing. It makes it easier to handle and slice)**
- 2 tsp olive oil
- 2 Cups broccoli
- 1 medium onion, chopped
- 1/2 Cup green pepper, chopped
- 1/2 Cup red pepper, chopped
- 1 Cup fresh mushrooms, sliced

- 1 small can baby corn
- 1 tsp. cornstarch
- Hot cooked rice or noodles, optional

Direction

- In a bowl, mix the first 5 ingredients.
- Pour 1/2 cup into a zip lock bag; add meat. Seal bag, turn to coat.
- Refrigerate for 1 hour. Refrigerate remaining marinade.
- Drain & discard marinade from the meat.
- In a large non-stick skillet or wok, stir fry meat in batches in oil for 2-3 minutes or until no longer pink. Remove & keep warm.
- Add broccoli, onion, peppers, mushrooms & baby corn to the pan; stir fry for 1-2 minutes or until vegetables are tender.
- Return meat to pan.
- Combine cornstarch & reserved marinade until smooth; stir into meat mixture.
- Bring to a boil; cook & stir until thickened.
- Serve over rice or noodles if desired.

328.   Tex Mex Lasagna Recipe

Serving: 6 | Prep: | Cook: 45mins | Ready in:

Ingredients

- 1 pound lean ground beef
- 1 clove garlic minced
- 16 ounce can refried beans
- 1 teaspoon dried oregano
- 2 tablespoons chili powder
- 1/2 teaspoon ground cumin
- 14 ounce can diced tomatoes with juice
- 4 ounce can chopped green chilies
- 10 corn tortillas
- 1-1/2 cups hot salsa divided
- 1-1/2 cups sour cream
- 1/2 cup chopped green onions
- 2 cups grated sharp cheddar cheese

Direction

- Preheat oven to 350.
- Spray rectangular baking dish with cooking spray.
- In large skillet brown ground beef over medium heat then add minced garlic and stir-fry for a few minutes.
- In a large bowl combine cooked ground beef and garlic with the refried beans, oregano, chili powder, cumin, tomatoes and chilies.
- Line baking dish with half of the tortillas then spoon half of the ground beef mixture evenly over tortillas then top with remaining tortillas.
- Spread 1 cup of the salsa in an even layer over the tortillas.
- Add remaining ground beef mixture then bake at 350 for 30 minutes and remove from oven.
- Combine sour cream, remaining salsa and green onions then spread evenly over casserole and top with shredded cheese.
- Return to oven and bake an additional 10 minutes.

---

329.   Tex Mex Spaghetti Pie Recipe

Serving: 8 | Prep: | Cook: 45mins | Ready in:

Ingredients

- 1 tablespoon olive oil
- 2 teaspoons garlic salt
- 1/2 pound ground meat
- 1-1/2 teaspoons chili powder
- 8 ounces spaghetti cooked
- 1 cup salsa
- 4 eggs beaten
- 1 cup shredded cheddar cheese
- salt and pepper to taste

Direction

- Brown ground meat in oil and add garlic salt and chili powder.
- Put meat mixture, spaghetti, salsa, eggs and cheese into a casserole dish.

- Cover and bake at 350 for 30 minutes then uncover and bake 15 minutes longer.

---

330.   Tex Mex Pasta

Serving: 6 | Prep: | Cook: 5mins | Ready in:

Ingredients

- 2 cups uncooked spiral pasta
- 1 pound ground beef
- 1 jar (16 ounces) salsa
- 1 can (10-3/4 ounces) condensed cream of chicken soup, undiluted
- 1 cup shredded Mexican cheese blend, divided

Direction

- Preheat oven to 350°. Cook pasta according to package directions.
- Meanwhile, cook beef in a Dutch oven over medium heat until no longer pink; drain. Stir in the salsa, soup and 1/2 cup cheese; heat through.
- Drain pasta; stir into meat mixture. Transfer to a greased 11x7-in. baking dish. Sprinkle with remaining cheese. Cover and bake until cheese is melted, 15-20 minutes.
- Nutrition Facts
- 1 1-1/2 cups: 585 calories, 28g fat (11g saturated fat), 101mg cholesterol, 1241mg sodium, 46g carbohydrate (6g sugars, 3g fiber), 33g protein.

---

331.   Thai Drunken Noodles Recipe

Serving: 4 | Prep: | Cook: 15mins | Ready in:

Ingredients

- 8 ounces wide ribbon rice noodles
- 1/2 lb pound shrimp,deveined and peeled OR

- 1 cup chicken breast,diced
- 2 cloves garlic,minced
- 1 shallot,sliced
- 1/2 cup chopped red bell pepper
- 1/2 cup green pepper,chopped
- 1 cup chopped onion
- 1/2 cup cabbage,chopped
- 1 tomato,diced
- 1 egg,beaten
- 1 cup fresh basil,reserve shredding until ready to use
- oil for frying
- dry roasted unsalted peanuts
- cilantro for garnish,optional
- 1 lime,for garnish,cut in wedges
- 2 Tbls oyster sauce
- 1 tbls rice vinegar
- 1 Tbls Asian fish sauce
- 1 Tbls palm sugar,or regular brown or white
- 1 Tbls lime juice
- 1 Tsp ground chili flakes or Sambal chili sauce

Direction

- Soak rice noodles in warm water for 15 minutes. Note: If they soak longer don't worry. I have done it at least an hour ahead.
- Combine all ingredients listed below lime wedges, stir to mix, set aside.
- In a lightly greased hot pan, add egg, swirl to create a thin layer on pan, hold over heat, and turn heat down return pan to burner. Do not overcook, only a few minutes. Roll up omelette, remove from heat, cut into thin strips.
- In a wok fry shallots and garlic in appx.5 Tbsp. hot oil over medium high heat. Add chicken and or/tofu careful not to brown garlic remove from heat if oil too hot. Add vegetables, stir fry about 2 minutes, add shrimp, stirring frequently. Add noodles, toss well. Add oyster sauce mixture. Toss to coat well, add tomatoes. Cook another minute or two stirring well. Remove from heat. Place noodle/veg/chicken mix in a large bowl. Add basil, toss to mix.

- Serve garnished with chopped peanuts, lime wedges, cilantro and a few sprigs basil. Serve soy sauce on side. Enjoy
- NOTE: This recipe originally called for fresh Sen Yai noodles, unavailable in my area. I replaced with dry rice noodles but I have used regular extra wide egg noodles with good results. Cook them underdone/al dente, rinse with cold water and drain, reserve until ready to stir fry, it is still very good with these.

332. Thai Prawn Noodle Soup Recipe

Serving: 4 | Prep: | Cook: 30mins | Ready in:

Ingredients

- 3C chicken stock, try my homemade recipe.
- 2c water
- 3 stalks of lemongrass
- 3T fish stock, vietnamese or thai
- 10-12 kaffir lime leaves
- 1T canola oil
- 3 cloves garlic, minced
- a thumb-sized piece of ginger, minced (about as much as the garlic when said and done.)
- 1 large shallot, finely diced
- 1/2t crushed thai chillies
- 20 raw prawns
- 1/4 package of rice stick noodles
- 2 limes, 1 1/2 juiced and 1/2 into wedges for garnish
- 1 handful of cilantro leaves only

Direction

- Bring to a simmer the water, chicken stock, fish sauce, lime leaves and lemon grass (bruised). Allow it to simmer for at least 20 minutes.
- In a pot large enough to accommodate the stock sweat the shallots, garlic, ginger and chillies until shallot is translucent - about 5 minutes. Don't let the garlic brown!

- Strain the broth into the pot with the garlic and etc. Bring to a boil.
- Ideally you want to cook the noodles and prawns so they finish at the same time. In my case the noodles were about 6 minutes. So I cooked the noodles for 4 minutes, turned it down to a simmer and added the prawns which take about 2 minutes.
- When prawns and noodles are done take the soup off the heat. Stir in lime juice. Taste for salt, depending on your fish sauce you may need to add some.
- Ladle soup into bowls garnish with a healthy amount of cilantro and a lime wedge.

333. Thai Spicy Noodles Recipe

Serving: 4 | Prep: | Cook: 10mins | Ready in:

Ingredients

- 1/2 pkg. spaghetti noodles, about 1 inch bundle (I like the thin spaghettini)
- 1 T cornstarch
- 1 T each fish sauce and freshly squeezed lime juice
- 1 1/2 tsp. sugar
- 2 skinless boneless chicken breasts
- 1 jalapeno pepper or 2 tsp. chopped pickled peppers
- 1 red pepper
- 1/2 c baby carrots
- 4 oz snow peas or sugar snap peas
- vegetable oil
- 2 tsp. chopped garlic
- 2 tsp. bottled minced ginger or 1 tsp. freshly grated ginger
- 10 oz chicken broth
- 2-3 tsp. curry powder
- 2 green onions, sliced

Direction

- Cook spaghetti until al dente. Drain but do not rinse.
- In small bowl, stir cornstarch with fish sauce, lime juice and sugar until dissolved. Slice chicken into thin strips. Core and seed jalapeno, then finely chop. Chop red pepper. Slice baby carrots in half. Peel and discard strings from snow peas.
- Lightly coat a large saucepan with oil and add chicken, ginger, jalapeno, garlic. Stir often until chicken is light brown, 3-4 min. Pour in chicken broth. Using wooden spoon, scrape up and stir in any brown bits from pan bottom. Stir in cornstarch mixture, then pour into pan. Stir until well mixed. Add red pepper, carrots and snow peas. Sprinkle with curry. Stir often until snow peas are bright green and sauce bubbles, 3 min. Add noodles and stir constantly until hot, 1 min. Remove from heat and stir in onions. Serve with lime wedges.

334. Thai Esque Peanut Noonoos Recipe

Serving: 4 | Prep: | Cook: 15mins | Ready in:

Ingredients

- 1 lb angel hair pasta OR rice noodles
- 2 cups broccoli slaw mix (optional)
- 1 cup chopped tofu (I used Wild Woods Baked Thai SpouTofu)
- Finely sliced scallions
- Chopped peanuts (optional)
- Sauce:
- 2 tbsp crunchy peanut butter
- 2/3 c rice vinegar
- 2 tbsp hoisin sauce
- 1 tbsp brown sugar
- 1 tbsp fresh ginger, minced
- 1 tsp cayenne pepper
- 1 tsp crushed red pepper flakes
- Few splashes tamari
- Few splashes wok oil

- Small splash sesame chili oil

Direction

- Cook pasta according to package directions and drain.
- In medium bowl, mix sauce ingredients.
- Toss sauce and broccoli slaw mix (if using) with pasta while still warm. Garnish with scallions and peanuts if desired.
- Serve warm or chilled.

---

335.   The Blue Macaroni And Cheese Recipe

Serving: 6 | Prep: | Cook: 20mins | Ready in:

Ingredients

- 2 1/2Cup milk
- 2 bay leaves
- 450g macaroni = 1 lb.
- 4T (1/2 stick) butter
- 3T flour
- 1Cup medium cheddar
- 3T Parmesan grated
- 1Cup blue cheese, crumbled
- 1/2Cup bread crumbs, preferably fresh

Direction

- Preheat the oven to 400°F.
- Bring a large salted pot of water to a boil.
- In a small saucepan heat the milk with the bay leaves over medium-low heat. When small bubbles appear along the sides, turn off the heat.
- Under cook the pasta by two minutes.
- Drain it, rinse it quickly to stop the cooking, and put it in a large bowl.
- In a saucepan over medium-low heat, melt the butter; once it starts to foam add the flour and cook, whisking until the mixture starts to brown. Remove the bay leaves from the milk,

and add about 1/4 cup of the milk to the hot flour mixture, whisking continuously.

- Once it is smooth add a bit more milk and continue until all milk is combined. Stir in cheddar. Taste for seasoning, remember.
- Add the sauce to the noodles, stir in the Parmesan and adjust for seasoning. Fold the blue cheese in. turn the pasta into a casserole dish to with breadcrumbs and bake until bubbling and the crumbs turn brown, about 15 minutes.
- You can broil it at the end if the crumbs aren't browning.

---

336.   Theresa Bs Cajun Rice Dressing Recipe

Serving: 10 | Prep: | Cook: 30mins | Ready in:

Ingredients

- 1-1/2 lb ground chuck hamburger meat (YOU CAN ALSO USE DEER MEAT OR turkey)
- 1 tsp cayenne pepper
- 2 cups cooked rice
- 1 can cream of mushroom soup
- 1 can of French onion soup (OR CREAM OF ONION)
- 2 stalks celery diced
- 2 yellow onions diced
- 1/2 cup chopped parsley
- 1 cup green onions (bottom & tops)
- 1/2 cup bell pepper diced
- seasonings: salt, pepper and garlic (to your taste)
- a little water
- OPTIONAL: YOU CAN ALSO ADD crawfish tails, COOKED eggplant, chicken GIZZARDS OR oysters TO THIS RECIPE (SHE DONT BUT SOME DO)
- .

Direction

- Cook rice (YOU CAN THROW IN ONE BEEF BULLION CUBE INTO YOUR RICE WHILE COOKING)
- Sautee all vegetables
- Warm soups
- Salt and pepper meat, brown in a little shortening over medium high heat, stirring constantly, keeping meat scraped from bottom and sides of pan.
- Add sauté vegetables
- Add small amount of water;
- Add soups
- Add cooked rice and stir gently.
- Cover and let stand until ready to serve. Serve hot. BLACK PEPPER MAKES THIS DISH, NOT TOO HOT AND NOT TOO MILD, SO BE CAREFUL. WORK WITH THE RECIPE. KEEP TASTING AS YOU ARE COOKING.

337.   This Is The One Baked Macaroni And Cheese Recipe

Serving: 6 | Prep: | Cook: 60mins | Ready in:

Ingredients

- 1 pound uncooked elbow macaroni
- 1/2 cup butter
- 1/2 cup flour
- 1-1/2 cup milk
- 1-1/2 cup sour cream
- 1 tsp salt
- 1/2 Tbsp pepper
- 10 oz bar sharp cheddar cheese, grated
- panko bread Crumbs
- butter for Crumbs

Direction

- Preheat oven to 350°F.
- Cook macaroni in salted boiling water according to package directions. Drain and rinse with cold water. Pour into a 3-qt. casserole.

- In a saucepan, melt butter and stir in flour. Gradually stir in milk and sour cream. Add salt and pepper.
- Cook over low heat, stirring constantly, until sauce bubbles and thickens.
- Reserve 1 cup grated cheese for the top of the casserole. Toss macaroni with remaining cheese.
- Pour sauce over macaroni and mix thoroughly. Sprinkle with reserved cheese.
- Bake for 1 hour, or until bubbly and brown.
- Serve immediately.
- Notes: Use sharp or a mix of Gruyere and white cheddar.
- Asiago cheese is also nice in mac and cheese dishes.
- Sliced ripe tomatoes and buttered bread crumbs would be a nice addition.
- Mix in the additional shredded cheese before adding the tomatoes.
- Can add ham and onions for a heartier dish.

338.   Three Cheese Manicotti Recipe

Serving: 8 | Prep: | Cook: 35mins | Ready in:

Ingredients

- 1/4 cup chopped onion
- 1 clove garlic, minced
- 1 tablespoon cooking oil
- 1 14-1/2-ounce can tomatoes, cut up
- 1 8-ounce can tomato sauce
- 1 teaspoon sugar
- 1 teaspoon dried oregano, crushed
- 1/4 teaspoon dried thyme, crushed
- 1 small bay leaf
- 8 dried manicotti shells
- 2 beaten eggs
- 2 cups shredded mozzarella cheese (8 ounces)
- 1-1/2 cups ricotta cheese or cream-style cottage cheese
- 1/2 cup grated parmesan cheese

- 1/2 cup snipped fresh parsley
- 1/2 teaspoon dried oregano, crushed
- Dash pepper

Direction

- For sauce, in a 2-quart saucepan cook onion and garlic in hot oil until tender. Add undrained tomatoes, tomato sauce, sugar, the 1 teaspoon oregano, the thyme, and bay leaf. Bring to boiling; reduce heat. Simmer, uncovered, for 20 to 25 minutes or until thickened. Remove from heat; discard bay leaf.
- Meanwhile, cook pasta according to package directions; drain. Rinse shells in cold water.
- For filling, in a medium mixing bowl stir together eggs, half of the mozzarella cheese, the ricotta or cottage cheese, Parmesan cheese, parsley, the 1/2 teaspoon oregano, and dash pepper. Spoon filling into manicotti.
- Pour half of the tomato mixture into a 2-quart rectangular baking dish. Arrange stuffed manicotti in the baking dish. Pour remaining sauce over shells. Sprinkle remaining mozzarella cheese atop.
- Bake the stuffed manicotti, covered, in a 350 degree F oven for 35 to 40 minutes or until heated through. Makes 8 servings.
- Make-Ahead Tip: Prepare as above, except do not bake. Cover and chill in the refrigerator for up to 24 hours. Bake as above.

339. Tomato And Artichoke Pasta Recipe

Serving: 4 | Prep: | Cook: 15mins | Ready in:

Ingredients

- 1 28 oz. can whole, peeled tomatoes (drained from liquid and chopped)
- 1 medium onion (diced)
- 8 marinated artichoke quarters (diced)
- 4 garlic cloves (minced)
- 1 tbsp. dried oregano
- 1 tbsp. dried basil, or about five leaves of fresh chopped basil
- 1/2 tsp. red pepper flake
- 1 tbsp. vodka (optional)
- 1/2 cup parmesan cheese
- 1/4 cup heavy cream
- 1/4 cup olive oil
- 1 cup pasta water
- salt
- pepper

Direction

- In large pot, boil water and cook pasta. (Note: if you cook pasta completely before beginning sauce, reserve one cup of the starchy pasta water)
- In a large pan over medium-high heat, add the oil. Once the oil begins to shimmer, add the red pepper flakes and allow them to cook for 1 to 2 minutes until the oil has a subtle orange hue. The red pepper is infusing with the oil to give everything a nice spicy heat. (Note: We like spicy food, so we add a whole teaspoon to ours. This is a good place to adjust how much kick you want in the dish, so feel free to experiment to make it work for you.)
- Add the onions and artichokes, lightly salt them and let cook for about 4 minutes. You are looking for the onions to become slightly translucent as they cook.
- Add the tomatoes and cook for about 3 minutes.
- Add the garlic and cook for another 4 minutes. At this point, you should a rough mixture of cooked base coming together for the rest of the sauce. It should have a bit of liquid, but not much.
- Add the cracker pepper, basil and oregano, stir and continue to cook for another 2 minutes.
- Add the vodka and stir in. This step is optional. I believe vodka contributes to a more flavorful sauce, but really, it is not essential. After adding it, let it cook for 1 minute.
- Turn down the heat to medium-low. Add the cream. This will make it a nice pink sauce. At this point, you are waiting for your pasta to

cook. If you haven't already put the pasta on, now is the time.

- Once the pasta is cooking or is near ready, add the Parmesan cheese to the sauce. You want it to melt into the mixture, so you may need to turn up the heat to medium and stir vigorously.
- Add the cooked pasta to the pan with the finished sauce. Add about a cup of the reserved pasta water. Turn off the heat. Toss the pasta to coat and let sit for about 1 minute. Serve. Enjoy!
- Note: The pasta water is important for three things. First, the sauce you have in the pan is thick and the water will loosen it up. Second, the water should have a nice salty flavor that will help to round out the seasoning. Finally, the starch from the pasta has seeped into the water. Therefore, the pasta will have a nice flavorful adhesive quality that will make it work well with the pasta.

---

340. Tortellini Italian Fatty Recipe

Serving: 57 | Prep: | Cook: 120mins | Ready in:

Ingredients

- bacon
- italian sausage
- prosciutto
- roasted red tomatoes
- Greek olives in an Italian herb seasoning
- tortellini
- grated cheeses - mozzarella, parmesan, romano, & Asiago
- paul newmans roasted garlic sauce
- Organic baby spinach
- Itlaian seasonings
- minced garlic and onion

Direction

- I flatten out 1lb of Italian sausage. I use a gallon zip lock baggie and then cut the sides down. This helps with rolling the fatty after the filling is put in.
- After the sausage is flattened out I put the mince garlic and onion on, then I laid out the spinach leaves roasted red tomatoes and olives, and then added the cheeses, than laid out the cooked tortellini (I used a 3 cheese tortellini) next came the shaved Prosciutto.
- At this point I roll this up into a log. And on a layer of saran wrap I have a basket weave of Bacon laid in place. I place the Fatty on the bacon and using the saran wrap, I roll and re-roll until it has tightened together. Place in the fridge to cool and set up while I get the smoker to temp.
- I smoke this at 225 degrees for approx. 2 hrs. to an internal temp of 155 - 160. Let rest a bit before eating.
- I prefer these much better the next day, but that's true with most smoked foods.
- A fatty can be stuffed with any combination of flavors you wish. Hope you enjoy this.

---

341. Tuna Casserole Recipe

Serving: 8 | Prep: | Cook: 20mins | Ready in:

Ingredients

- 1 (16 oz) package egg noodles
- 1 (6 oz) can tuna, liquid removed
- 1 (10.75 oz) can condensed cream of mushroom soup
- 1 (10 oz) package frozen green peas, defrosted
- 1/4 cup milk
- 1/4 cup butter
- 1 cup cheddar cheese, shredded

Direction

- Boil a large pot of lightly salted water, then add the pasta. Cook until 'al dente'. In the final 3 minutes of cooking, add the peas; drain.

- In the same pot, melt the butter over a medium heat. Now, stir in the tuna, mushroom soup, milk, and cheese. Mix well until the cheese is melted, and the mixture becomes smooth. Add the pasta and peas and stir until evenly coated.

342. Tuna Noodle Casserole Recipe

Serving: 9 | Prep: | Cook: 20mins | Ready in:

Ingredients

- 2 (6 oz) cans tuna, liquid removed
- 1 (16 oz) package pasta, tri-colored variety
- 3 (10.75 oz) cans condensed cream of mushroom soup
- 1 cup broccoli, chopped
- 1 red bell pepper, chopped
- 2 carrots, sliced
- 3 stalks celery, diced
- 1/2 onion, diced
- 2 tbsp cheddar cheese, shredded

Direction

- Boil a large pot of lightly salted water, then add pasta. Cook for 8-10 minutes or until 'al dente'. Now, drop in the broccoli, and carrots and boil for no more than 5 minutes before removing pasta, then drain. Preheat oven to 350 degrees F.
- Combine the tuna, pasta, soup, broccoli, bell pepper, carrots, celery, and onion into a large bowl, and mix well. Evenly place the mixture in a 9x13 inch baking dish, and add the cheese on top. Bake for 20 minutes, then serve.

343. Turkey Tetrazzini Recipe

Serving: 8 | Prep: | Cook: 90mins | Ready in:

Ingredients

- 8 ounces thin spaghetti, broken into 3-inch lengths, cooked, rinsed, and drained
- 1 1/2 cups shredded cheddar cheese, divided
- 1/4 cup parmesan cheese, divided
- 2 to 3 cups diced cooked turkey
- 2 tablespoons diced pimientos, if desired
- 1 tablespoon butter
- 4 ounces sliced mushrooms
- 1/4 chopped cup onion
- 1 can cream of mushroom soup
- 1/2 cup chicken broth
- 1/4 cup dry sherry
- salt and pepper, to taste

Direction

- Combine spaghetti with 1 cup Cheddar cheese and half of the Parmesan cheese.
- Add turkey and pimientos. In a skillet, melt butter and sauté mushrooms and onions just until tender; add to the turkey mixture along with remaining ingredients.
- Gently stir to combine ingredients; place in a greased casserole and sprinkle with remaining cheeses.
- Cover with lid or foil and bake at 350° for about 45 minutes, or until hot and bubbly.

344. Tuscan Carbonara Recipe

Serving: 4 | Prep: | Cook: 25mins | Ready in:

Ingredients

- 1 pound spaghetti
- salt
- 1/2 pound pancetta or bacon, diced
- 1 medium onion, finely diced
- 5 large egg yolks
- 1/4 cup heavy cream
- 1 cup grated parmigiano-Reggiano
- Freshly ground black pepper

Direction

- Cook the spaghetti al dente (firm but not hard), in a large pot of boiling salted water according to package directions.
- Meanwhile, fry the pancetta and onion over medium-low heat in a large, straight sided skillet until the pancetta is crispy and the onion has softened. Turn the heat off.
- In a medium mixing bowl, whisk together the yolks, cream and grated cheese. When the spaghetti is ready drain and toss it into the skillet with the pancetta and onion. Quickly pour the egg mixture over the spaghetti and toss everything together well to combine. The residual heat from the skillet, onions and spaghetti will be enough to cook the eggs and make a creamy sauce. Direct heat from the stovetop will make an overcooked, scrambled egg, lumpy mess. Season the spaghetti with salt and pepper and serve immediately.
- Cook's Note: You can also make this dish using any pasta shape you like. Try penne, fusilli, shells or cavatappi for a twist on the classic.

345. Tuscan Chicken Slow Cooker Pasta Weight Watchers Recipe

Serving: 8 | Prep: | Cook: 270mins | Ready in:

Ingredients

- 1 lb boneless skinless chicken breasts, cut into small chunks
- 1 15 oz can kidney beans, drained and rinsed
- 1 15 oz can tomato sauce
- 1 15 oz can diced tomatoes, undrained
- 1 4 oz can sliced mushrooms, drained (I used fresh)
- 1 small green pepper, chopped (optional)
- 1 small onion, chopped
- 2 stalks celery, chopped (optional)

- 3 cloves garlic, minced
- 1 cup water
- 1 T italian seasoning
- 6 oz uncooked whole wheat spaghetti, broken in half (DON'T use more - it'll soak up all the liquid & turn the whole thing into a gooshy mess!)

Direction

- Place all ingredients, except spaghetti, in slow cooker.
- Cover and cook on low for 4 hours, or until vegetables are tender (Note: I cooked it 8 hours & it still tasted wonderful)
- Turn setting to high, stir in spaghetti and cover.
- Stir after 10 minutes.
- Cover and cook until pasta is tender, about 20 minutes more (but check it after 10 minutes - if the pasta gets mushy it'll spoil the whole dish!).
- Yields 1 1/2 cups per serving.

346. Tuscan Orzo Salad Recipe

Serving: 8 | Prep: | Cook: 240mins | Ready in:

Ingredients

- 1lb orzo pasta, cooked to package directions, drained, and rinsed in cold water
- 1 small green pepper, diced
- 1 small red pepper, diced
- 1 small orange or yellow pepper, diced
- 3-4 green onions, chopped
- 1/2 cup pitted kalamata olives, chopped
- 1/4 cup capers
- 1/2 cup Italian or Tuscan dressing(oil/vinegar based)--mine follows
- 1/2 cup asiago cheese, shredded or grated
- dash of crushed red pepper flakes(this can be omitted if you use the following dressing recipe)

- 1/2 cup fresh parsley
- ***Tuscan Dressing***
- 1 cup dressing quality olive oil
- 1/4 cup red wine vinegar
- juice from 1/2 lemon
- 1T total of mixed dried herbs(ie parsley, oregano, basil, and please include some rosemary)
- 1t dried red pepper flakes
- 1 clove garlic, finely minced
- 1t toasted sesame seeds, finely ground
- 1/2t celery seed, ground
- dash of onion powder
- salt and fresh ground pepper

Direction

- Blend all dressing ingredients, if using, in food processor, and set aside.
- Combine all remaining ingredients, but dressing and parsley, and toss to combine.
- Add dressing and parsley and, toss again.
- Refrigerate a few hours. Serve cold

---

347.   Tuxedo Chicken Recipe

Serving: 4 | Prep: | Cook: 20mins | Ready in:

Ingredients

- 6 cups (12 ounces) bow tie pasta (farfalle)
- 4 skinless boneless chicken breasts (about 1 1/3 pounds)
- 1 tablespoon of butter
- 1/2 cup of chopped onion
- 2 cups frozen chopped broccoli
- 1 container (8 ounces) of reduced fat sour cream
- 1 cup half and half
- 1 tablespoon Dijon mustard
- 2 teaspoons of worcestershire sauce
- 1/4 teaspoon garlic powder
- We liked it topped with romano/parm grated cheese

Direction

- Cook pasta according to directions
- Melt butter on medium low in a 12 inch skillet
- Add chopped onion and cook until soft about 3 minutes
- Slice the chicken into 1/2 inch strips
- Raise heat to medium high and add chicken cook until no longer pink in the center.
- Meanwhile, place broccoli in a microwave safe dish and microwave 3-4 minutes until warm
- Remove the chicken from the skillet with a slotted spoon and set aside
- Reduce the heat to medium low & stir in sour cream and half and half into the chicken juices to blend well
- Add mustard, Worcestershire, and garlic powder.
- Stir well and continue to cook until the sauce is slightly thick about 2 minutes (do not boil)
- Return the chicken to the skillet and add the broccoli then raise the heat to medium high and bring the sauce almost to a boil
- Reduce heat to low and simmer to blend the flavors 1-2 minutes
- Drain the bowties and place on a serving plate and top with the chicken mixture
- Serve

---

348.   Ultimate Baked Macaroni And Cheese Recipe

Serving: 12 | Prep: | Cook: 30mins | Ready in:

Ingredients

- 1 1/2 c. panko bread crumbs
- 9 TBSP. (1 stick plus 1 TBSP) butter, divided, plus more for pan
- 5 1/2 c. whole milk
- 1/2 medium onion, cut into large chunks
- 2 bay leaves
- 1/4 tsp. fresh grated nutmeg
- 1/4 tsp. fresh cracked black pepper

- 1/4 tsp. cayenne pepper
- 2 tsp. kosher salt
- 1/2 c. flour
- 3 c. grated sharp cheddar cheese, divided
- 2 c. grated monterey jack cheese, divided
- 1 1/2 c. grated Italian cheese blend, divided
- 1 1/2 c. grated swiss cheese, divided
- 1 c. grated parmigiano Reggiano, divided
- 16 oz. uncooked large elbow macaroni

Direction

- Preheat oven to 375 degrees F. Butter a 3-quart casserole dish; set aside.
- Place bread crumbs in a small bowl. Melt 3 TBSP. of the butter; drizzle over bread crumbs. Toss well with a fork to coat crumbs evenly. Set aside.
- In a medium saucepan, heat milk, onion, bay leaves, nutmeg, black and cayenne peppers, and salt over medium heat. Stir frequently. Just as you begin to see tiny bubbles form around the edge of the pan, reduce heat to low and continue heating milk for 15 minutes, stirring frequently. Remove from heat and cover; let sit at least 30 minutes.
- While milk sits, prepare the pasta. Bring a large pot of water to a boil; salt well. Add pasta and cook according to package directions, removing pasta from the heat about 2 minutes before directions suggest. You are looking for the pasta to still have a little bite or chewiness to it. Drain pasta well and rinse with cool water. Rinsing removes some of the starch from the pasta and helps keep the cheese sauce from getting grainy while baking. Drain pasta well and set aside.
- In a large bowl, toss together the cheeses: 2 c. of the sharp cheddar, 1 c. of the Monterey Jack, 3/4 c. of the Italian blend, 1 c. of the Swiss, and 1/2 c. of the Parmigiano. Set aside.
- Using a fine mesh sieve over a large bowl, pour milk through sieve to filter out the onion, bay leaf, etc. Discard solids.
- In a large pot (use the pasta pot - less to clean) melt remaining 6 TBSP. of butter over medium heat. When butter bubbles, add flour. Whisk

together well and cook, stirring, 1 minute (this is your roux).
- Slowly pour the warmed and strained milk into the roux while whisking constantly. Continue cooking, whisking constantly, until the mixture bubbles and thickens.
- Remove sauce from the heat and add the cheeses you mixed in the bowl. Whisk well to blend; sauce should be smooth. Add rinsed and drained macaroni, stir well to combine.
- Empty pot into prepared baking dish. In the bowl you used to mix the first batch of cheese, mix the remaining cheeses: 1 c. sharp Cheddar, 1 c. Monterey Jack, 3/4 c. Italian blend, 1/2 c. Swiss, and 1/2 c. Parmigiano. Toss well to combine and sprinkle over the top of the macaroni and cheese sauce.
- Sprinkle buttered bread crumbs over the top of the cheese. Bake, uncovered, for 30 minutes, or until bubbly and topping is golden. Remove from oven and cool for 5 minutes before serving.

---

349.   Ultimate Meaty Spaghetti Sauce Recipe

Serving: 12 | Prep: | Cook: 180mins | Ready in:

Ingredients

- 1 lb. ground beef
- 1 lb. bulk mild Italian sausage
- 1 medium onion, chopped
- 3 ribs celery, chopped
- 1 green pepper, seeded and chopped
- 3 large cloves garlic, minced or sliced
- 1 tsp. dried oregano
- 1 tsp. dried basil
- 1/2 tsp. dried marjoram
- 1/2 tsp. dried thyme
- pinch dried rosemary
- 1/2 tsp. dried red chili flakes
- 1 bay leaf
- 1/2 tsp. fresh cracked black pepper

- pinch kosher salt
- 2 - 14.5 oz. cans tomato sauce (plus one extra can - 'in case')
- 2 - 14.5 oz. cans Italian stewed tomatoes
- 1 - 6 oz. can tomato paste
- 2 TBSP. brown sugar
- 1 - 12 oz. can sliced mushrooms, drained
- 1 - 14.5 oz. can black olives, drained and sliced

Direction

- In large stock pot, cook beef, sausage, onion, celery, green pepper, and garlic until meats are browned. Drain off fat.
- Add oregano, basil, marjoram, thyme, rosemary, chili flakes, bay leaf, black pepper, and pinch salt. Sauté for 1 minute to release some of the essence from the herbs and spices.
- Add tomato sauce. Using scissors, cut up stewed tomatoes in can, or use a food processor. Add to meat mixture with tomato paste. Stir well to combine. If sauce is too thick, add additional can of tomato sauce. Add brown sugar.
- Simmer covered for 2 1/2 hours, stirring occasionally. Add mushrooms and olives. Simmer uncovered for at least another 1/2 hour. Remove bay leaf before serving. Serve over pasta, or use in baked dishes, such as ziti or lasagna.

350. Veal Paprikas Recipe

Serving: 4 | Prep: | Cook: 45mins | Ready in:

Ingredients

- 1 lb. stew veal in 1/2-inch cubes
- 1 large yellow onion, chopped
- 3 T. bacon grease, lard or oil
- 2 T. Hungarian paprika (Spanish has comparatively no flavor)
- 1 14-oz. can diced tomatoes, drained
- 1 red bell pepper, seeded and chopped
- 10 mushrooms, sliced

- 2 T. each: heavy cream and sour cream
- 1 t. flour
- 1 recipe noodles (noodles.html">Egg noodles) or spaetzle (http://bondcrecipes.blogspot.com/2007/07/sptzle.html)

Direction

- If using noodles, make them first (spaetzle are so fast and easy you can whip them up while the veal is cooking).
- Sauté the onions over medium heat, stirring frequently, until they begin to soften. Cover, reduce the heat to low, and cook another five minutes.
- Stir in paprika, veal, and tomatoes. Add about 1/4 cup water, cover, and cook over low heat for an hour, until the veal is tender.
- Add the bell pepper and mushrooms, stir, cover again and cook for 15 minutes, until the peppers are softened.
- Mix heavy cream, sour cream and flour, then stir into the paprika. Cook a minute, just to get the "flour" taste out, and serve.

351. Vegan Mac And Cheese Recipe

Serving: 4 | Prep: | Cook: 12mins | Ready in:

Ingredients

- 1 lb noodles (I prefer spiral because the sauce sticks to them so well)
- 2 cloves garlic
- half of an onion diced into very small pieces
- 1 cup nutritional yeast (a yellow cheese like flakes that can be found in most "Whole Foods" stores - DO NOT BE CONFUSED WITH bread YEAST - THEY ARE TOTALLY DIFFERENT)
- 1 cup soymilk
- 2 Tbsp margarine
- 1 tsp wet mustard

- 2 pinches chopped basil
- 1 tsp salt
- 1/2 tsp pepper
- oil to coat pan

Direction

- Cook pasta in boiling water, following directions on the box.
- Dice the onion and garlic.
- Lightly cover the bottom of a small pot with oil and fry the diced onion and garlic at medium-low until onion is transparent.
- Pour the nutritional yeast and soymilk into the pot.
- Add the rest of the ingredients, somewhat in the order listed above, while mixing the contents at low heat.
- Continue heating the sauce for a couple minutes, stirring often.
- When pasta is done, strain it and mix with the sauce.
- Enjoy!

---

352.   Vegetarian Hot Pot Recipe

Serving: 5 | Prep: | Cook: 20mins | Ready in:

Ingredients

- 5 1/4 cups vegetable broth, or reduced-sodium chicken broth
- 4 slices fresh ginger, peeled
- 2 cloves garlic, crushed and peeled
- 2 teaspoons canola oil
- 1 3/4 cups shiitake mushrooms, stemmed, wiped clean and sliced (4 ounces)
- 1/4 teaspoon(s) crushed red pepper, or to taste
- 1 small bok choy, cut into 1/2-inch pieces, stems and greens separated
- 3 1/2 ounces Chinese wheat noodles, or rice sticks (see Ingredient note)
- 1 firm tofu, drained, patted dry and cut into 1/2-inch cubes

- 1 cup grated carrots (2 large)
- 5 teaspoons rice vinegar
- 2 teaspoons reduced-sodium soy sauce
- 1 teaspoon toasted sesame oil
- 1/4 cups chopped scallions, for garnish

Direction

- Combine broth, ginger and garlic in a Dutch oven; bring to a simmer. Simmer, partially covered, over medium-low heat for 15 minutes. Discard the ginger and garlic.
- Meanwhile, heat oil in a large non-stick skillet over medium-high heat. Add mushrooms and crushed red pepper; cook, stirring often, until tender, 3 to 5 minutes. Add bok choy stems; cook, stirring often, until tender, 3 to 4 minutes.
- Add the mushroom mixture to the broth. Add noodles, reduce heat to medium-low and simmer for 3 minutes. Add bok choy greens and tofu; simmer until heated through, about 2 minutes. Stir in carrots, vinegar to taste, soy sauce and sesame oil. Serve garnished with scallions.

---

353.   Vegetarian LInguine Recipe

Serving: 6 | Prep: | Cook: 15mins | Ready in:

Ingredients

- 8 ounces of uncooked whole wheat linguine noodles
- 2 medium zucchini, scrubbed and sliced thinly
- 1 lb of white button or crimini mushrooms, sliced
- 1/2 red onion, sliced
- 2 cloves of garlic minced
- 2 tbsp of olive oil
- 1 tbsp of butter
- 1 can of diced tomatoes, (sometimes I use the oregano flavored)
- 1 tsp of dried basil leaves

- 1/2 tsp of salt
- 1/4 tsp of crushed red pepper flakes
- 4 ounces of shredded provolone cheese
- 2 tbsp of shredded asiago cheese

Direction

- Cook the whole wheat linguine according to package directions.
- While cooking the linguine, prep and fix the veggies.
- In a large skillet, heat the oil and butter, sauté the zucchini, mushrooms, red onion and garlic.
- Cook 5 to 7 minutes to soften the mushrooms and wilt the zucchini and onions.
- Add tomatoes, salt, pepper and basil.
- Simmer for 3 minutes.
- Drain the linguine very well and add to the vegetable mixture.
- Sprinkle with both cheeses, toss and serve.

---

354. Vegetarian No Pasta Lasagna Recipe

Serving: 6 | Prep: | Cook: 45mins | Ready in:

Ingredients

- 10 roma tomatoes, halved and seeded
- 1 tbsp olive oil
- salt and pepper
- 1/2 cup diced shallots
- 1 10.3-oz package low-fat silken tofu (eg. Mori-Nu)
- 1/2 cup low-fat cottage cheese
- 1 tbsp dried oregano
- 2 tsp paprika
- 4 cloves garlic
- 1/4 cup fresh basil leaves
- 1 head romaine lettuce
- 250g water-packed artichoke hearts, drained and chopped
- 3/4lb asparagus, trimmed and blanched

- 1 cup grated part-skim mozzarella

Direction

- Preheat the oven to 250°F. Line a baking pan with parchment paper or foil.
- In a bowl, combine the tomatoes and half of the oil. Season generously with salt and pepper.
- Place the tomatoes in the pan, cut side down. Bake about 2 hours, and allow to cool before skinning.
- Soften the shallots in a skillet in the remaining oil over medium heat. Cool slightly.
- In a food processor, combine tofu, cottage cheese, herbs and spice, garlic and sautéed shallots. Puree smooth and remove to a mixing bowl.
- Fold in the artichokes, season with salt and pepper and set aside.
- In a pot of boiling salted water, blanch the lettuce leaves for 1 to 2 minutes, then shock in a bowl of ice water.
- Drain and dry thoroughly with a clean tea towel. Set aside.
- Heat the oven to 350°F.
- Spread half of the tomatoes on the bottom of a 10 x 7" glass dish.
- Cover with a layer of lettuce leaves, then with half the tofu mixture.
- Cover with another layer of lettuce leaves.
- Lay the asparagus on top and add half the mozzarella.
- Cover with yet another layer of lettuce leaves and add the remaining tofu mixture.
- End with a layer of lettuce leaves and sprinkle with the remaining tomatoes and mozzarella.
- Bake 45 minutes. Let stand for 10 minutes before serving.

355. Vietnamese Inspired Noodles With Cilantro And Asaragus Recipe

Serving: 2 | Prep: | Cook: 10mins | Ready in:

Ingredients

- 2 tablespoons vegetable oil
- 2 teaspoons ginger, cut into 1" matchsticks
- 2 cloves garlic, minced
- 2 teaspoons fresh cilantro, minced
- 2 dried thai chillis, ground
- 1 dozen prawns, shells and tails removed and deveined
- 1 bunch asparagus, woody ends trimmed, cut into 1.5" pieces
- 1 lime, juiced
- 2 tablespoons soy sauce
- ⅓ cup chinese cooking wine, or sherry
- 1 green onion, sliced
- 2 small carrots, grated with a peeler
- 1 teaspoon rice wine vinegar
- 2 tablespoons cilantro leaves
- vermicelli noodles

Direction

- Prepare the vermicelli according to the package directions. When draining run under cold water until cool to stop the cooking. Add 1 teaspoon of sesame oil and stir to stop from sticking. Set aside.
- Heat oil in a wok over medium heat. Add ginger, garlic, the minced cilantro, and the chillies and cook for 3 minutes stirring.
- Add prawns and asparagus and cook for 2 more minutes stirring.
- Add 1/2 the lime juice the wine and the soy sauce and cook until the asparagus is just soft and the prawns are pink through.
- Add in the vermicelli and stir until heated through - about 1 minute.
- Remove from heat and toss in the green onion and 3/4 of the carrot.
- Serve garnish with remaining lime juice, carrot, and cilantro leaves.

356. Warm Spinach Feta And Orzo Salad Recipe

Serving: 1 | Prep: | Cook: 10mins | Ready in:

Ingredients

- 1/4 teaspoon salt, plus a large pinch
- 1/4 cup orzo (rice-shaped pasta)
- 2 tablespoons crumbled feta cheese
- 2 teaspoons extra-virgin olive oil
- 2 teaspoons balsamic vinegar
- Freshly ground black pepper
- 1 1/2 cups baby spinach leaves (no stems)
- 2 tablespoons chopped red onion
- 1 heaping tablespoon roasted pistachios

Direction

- In a small saucepan, combine 2 cups water with 1/4 teaspoon salt.
- Bring to a boil over medium-high heat.
- Add the orzo and cook until al dente, about 7 minutes.
- Meanwhile, combine the feta, olive oil, vinegar, a large pinch of salt, and pepper to taste in a medium bowl.
- Drain the orzo through a strainer (not a colander—some of the orzo may escape through the holes!) and add to the bowl.
- Gently stir to coat the orzo with the dressing.
- Add the spinach, onion, and pistachios, and toss once more.

357. White Cheese Chicken Lasagna Recipe

Serving: 12 | Prep: | Cook: 50mins | Ready in:

Ingredients

- 9 lasagna noodles
- 1/2 cup butter
- 1 medium onion, chopped
- 1 clove garlic, minced
- 1/2 cup all-purpose flour
- 1 teaspoon salt
- 2 cups chicken stock
- 1 1/2 cups milk
- 4 cups mozzarella cheese, divided
- 1 cup parmesan cheese, grated
- 1 teaspoon dried basil
- 1 teaspoon dried oregano
- 1/2 teaspoon black pepper
- 2 cups ricotta cheese
- 2 cups cooked chicken. cubed
- 20 ounces frozen chopped spinach, thawed and drained
- 1 tablespoon fresh parsley, chopped
- 1/4 cup parmesan cheese for topping

Direction

- Preheat oven to 350 degrees F (175 degrees C).
- Bring a large pot of lightly salted water to a boil.
- Cook lasagna noodles in boiling water for 8 to 10 minutes.
- Drain and rinse with cold water.
- Melt butter in large saucepan over medium heat.
- Cook the onion in the butter until tender.
- Add garlic and cook 30 seconds more.
- Stir in flour and salt and simmer until bubbly.
- Mix in the broth and milk and boil, whisking constantly, for 1 minute.
- Stir in 2 cups mozzarella cheese and 1/4 cup Parmesan cheese.
- Season with basil, oregano and black pepper.
- Remove from heat and set aside.
- Spread 1/3 of the sauce in the bottom of a 13x9x2" baking dish.
- Layer with 1/3 of the noodles, the ricotta cheese and the chicken.
- Arrange 1/3 of the noodles over the chicken, layer with 1/3 of sauce, the spinach, the remaining 2 cups of mozzarella and 1/2 cup Parmesan.

- Arrange remaining noodles over cheese and spread remaining sauce evenly over noodles.
- Sprinkle with parsley and 1/4 cup Parmesan cheese.
- Bake 35 to 40 minutes.

358. White Clam Sauce Recipe

Serving: 68 | Prep: | Cook: 15mins | Ready in:

Ingredients

- 1 can-25 1/2 oz.-chopped clams
- 4 tsp minced garlic
- 4 oz. butter
- 2 tsp fresh chopped parsley
- 4 oz. olive oil
- salt & pepper
- l med. onion-diced small
- 1 1/2 pounds pasta, your choice

Direction

- Drain clams and reserve juice.
- Sauté onion in olive oil on medium heat.
- Add minced garlic and stir.
- Add clam juice.
- Simmer for 5 minutes.
- Add clams and parsley.
- Turn off heat.
- Add butter.
- Salt & pepper to taste.
- Serve over cooked pasta (your choice).

359. White Lasagna Recipe

Serving: 8 | Prep: | Cook: 55mins | Ready in:

Ingredients

- basil Cream Sauce:
- 3 tbs butter
- 3 tbs all-purpose flour

- 3 cups milk
- 1/2 cup chopped fresh basil (or more if you want)
- 1/2 cup grated parmsan cheese
- 1 clove garlic, minced
- salt to taste
- Filling:
- 1/3 cup pine nuts
- two 10 ounce packages frozen chopped spinach, thawed and squeezed dry
- one 15 oz container ricotta cheese
- 2 cups shredded mozzarella, divided
- 1 1/2 cups Fontina cheese
- 3/4 cup grated parmesan cheese
- 1 egg, beaten
- 1/4 tsp ground pepper
- To finish the dish:
- 12 lasagna noodles
- 1 (more) 10 oz package frozen chopped spinach, thawed and squeezed dry (optional see Tips from DeeDeeC)
- 1 medium zucchini, very thinly sliced (optional see Tips from DeeDeeC)

Direction

- Spray the bottom of 9x13-in baking dish with non-stick cooking spray.
- Basil-cream sauce: in a 2 qt. saucepan, melt the butter over medium heat. Stir in flour until absorbed. Add the milk; cook, stirring constantly, until mixture comes to a boil and has thickened. Remove from heat; stir in the basil, 1/2 cup of parmesan cheese, the garlic and salt. Place plastic wrap on the surface of sauce and set aside. (If you don't it turns brown)
- Filling: over low heat, cook the pine nuts in a dry, small skillet until all the nuts are at least partially browned. Chop. (I don't brown mine, I just put them in the food processor)
- Place pine nuts in a large bowl. Add the spinach, ricotta, 1/2 cup of the mozzarella, the Fontina, 3/4 cup parmesan, the egg, and pepper. Stir to combine and set aside.
- Cook the noodles according to package and drain.

- Preheat oven to 375.
- Thinly spread 1 cup of the basil-cream sauce in the bottom of baking pan. Place a layer of noodles over the sauce. Use 4 noodles per layer.
- Spread 1/2 of the ricotta filling over the noodles. Spread 1/2 of the remaining basil-cream sauce over the cheese.
- Top with more noodles and spread with remaining ricotta filling.
- Top with remaining noodles and spread remaining sauce over noodles.
- Bake 30 minutes. Sprinkle with remaining 1 cup mozzarella; continue baking 20 more minutes. Remove and let stand about 15 mins.
- Tip: I actually like to use a little more spinach (one more package.) I like to have a layer of spinach (not mixed into the cheese filling) just under the 2nd and 3rd layers of noodles. OR Sometimes I use very thinly sliced zucchini.

---

360.   Whole Wheat Chick Pea Pasta Recipe

Serving: 2 | Prep: | Cook: 10mins | Ready in:

Ingredients

- 1 tsp red pepper flakes, or to taste
- 2 cloves of garlic
- 2 tsp of oil
- 1 16 oz package of frozen broccoli
- 1 16 ox can of chic peas (garbanzo beans)
- 1/2 cup finely grated parmesan.
- 4-6 oz of dried whole wheat pasta
- 1/3 cup of pasta water

Direction

- Have pot of boiling water for pasta ready.
- Heat oil in pan over medium heat for 3 minutes. Add red pepper flakes, stir and let simmer for 30 seconds.
- Add garlic, stirring, until fragrant - about 30 seconds.

- Add the package of frozen broccoli and let it sit, resist the urge to stir, for about 3 minutes.
- Add pasta to boiling water.
- Stir the broccoli once, and reduce heat to medium-low. Cover and cook for about 5 minutes more, until the broccoli is heated through.
- Add the chick peas and cook for two minutes until heated through.
- Take 1/3 cup of water from pasta and add to the chick pea mixture.
- Drain the pasta.
- Bring Water in chick peas to a boil and reduce by half over medium heat, about 2 minutes.
- Toss pasta in with chick peas, add parmesan cheese and lots of fresh cracked pepper.
- Plate and Serve!

361.   Wild Mushroom And Fennel Risotto Recipe

Serving: 4 | Prep: | Cook: 35mins | Ready in:

Ingredients

- A few splashes of olive oil
- A chunk of butter
- An onion, chopped
- 1 fennel bulb, chopped
- Some fennel seeds and roasted garlic powder
- A generous handful of fresh shiitakes, sliced
- A smaller handful of dried morels, soaked for ~20min, reserve liquid and slice morels
- 1 cup white wine, (take a few sips off the top, then pour yourself a real glass)
- 1 ½ cups arborio rice
- About 4 cups of stock, combination of reserved morel liquid, chicken stock and water
- Lots of freshly grated parmesan

Direction

- Heat olive oil and butter in a large pan.
- Add onion, fennel, mushrooms, fennel seeds and garlic and stir occasionally until soft.

- Add rice and mix in well.
- When rice is fully coated, add wine and stir until wine is almost completely absorbed.
- Begin adding stock, about ½ cup at a time, allowing each previous ½ cup to absorb before adding the next one. At this point you will almost have to stir continuously.
- When your rice looks slightly creamy but is still a little al dente to the taste, add the parmesan and mix it in.
- Then eat it!

362.   Yakisoba Recipe

Serving: 4 | Prep: | Cook: 20mins | Ready in:

Ingredients

- 1 cup thin noodles
- 1/2 lb. round steak, sliced very thin
- 2 medium onions, cut in thin wedges
- 2 mediu carrots, sliced very thin
- 1 red bell pepper sliced, vey thin
- 1/4 head cabage, sliced in strips
- 2 cups fresh or 1 cup canned bean sprouts, drained.
- 2 tbsp. oil (to fry

Direction

- Cook and drain the noodles according to package directions.
- Heat the oil in a wok, and brown meat, add vegetables in order as given above. Stir frying each a few minutes, and add noodles last and cook just long enough to heat through vegetables should be crisp- tender. May be served on rice or alone. Pass soy sauce

363.   Cheeseburger Calzones Recipe

Serving: 8 | Prep: | Cook: 13mins | Ready in:

Ingredients

- 1 pound ground beef
- 1 med onion, chopped
- 1 small green pepper, chopped
- 1 jar pasta sauce (your choice)
- 1 small can mushroom slices, drained
- 1 cup shredded cheese
- 1/2 cup sliced black olives
- 1 pkg refrigerated large flaky biscuits (8 biscuits)

Direction

- Preheat oven to 375 degrees. In skillet, brown hamburger with onion and green peppers. Drain. Stir in 1 cup pasta sauce, mushrooms, black olives, and cheese.
- Press each biscuit into a 6 inch circle. Place 1/2 cup beef mixture on each circle, fold edges to close. Seal completely by pressing a fork along the edges.
- Place on cookie sheets.
- Bake 13 minutes or until golden brown.
- Heat remaining sauce and pour over calzones on the plate.

364.   Korean Cold Kimchi Noodles Recipe

Serving: 2 | Prep: | Cook: 5mins | Ready in:

Ingredients

- 1 cup of kimchi, finely sliced
- 2 tbs of sesame oil
- 2 tbs of gojuchang (korean chilli paste)
- 1 teaspeoon of sugar
- 1 teaspoon of vinegar
- 1 teaspoon roasted sesame seed

Direction

- Cook Japanese or Korean soba until al dente
- Mix kimchi, sesame oil, chilli paste, sugar and vinegar
- Mix noodle with kimchi mixture, mix well
- Sprinkle with sesame seed, serve

365.   Lemon Cream Farfalle With Salmon And Capers Recipe

Serving: 2 | Prep: | Cook: 10mins | Ready in:

Ingredients

- 1/2 lemon plus zest- or more to taste if you like
- 1/2 cup Greek yogurt
- 1 can of salmon
- 2 Tbsp capers
- 1/2 pound fafalle (butterfly) pasta aka bowtie
- salt

Direction

- Cook the pasta accordingly to package directions in salted water, drain and transfer to a large bowl.
- In a small bowl, add some lemon juice and lemon zest to the yogurt and stir well.
- Stir the lemon-y yogurt into the pasta.
- Divide into two bowls.
- Flake the salmon and divide between the bowls.
- Sprinkle 1 tablespoon of capers on each dish.
- Enjoy~!

Index

A

Apple 3,14

Artichoke 7,161,163,165,182

Asparagus 3,6,7,15,16,34,35,125,157

B

Bacon 3,4,5,6,7,19,54,104,128,163,183

Basil 3,4,22,34,53,193

Bay leaf 71

Beans 91

Beef 3,4,5,6,7,18,25,26,38,56,57,63,79,80,85,89,138,159

Bread 96,173

Broccoli 3,13,20,30,39,41

Broth 6,147,167,168

Butter 3,4,5,6,7,32,38,58,87,111,138,140,148,152,169,170,171,172,187

C

Cabbage 3,5,6,10,32,91,131

Capers 3,8,27,195

Caramel 3,35

Cauliflower 3,36

Chard 4,73,157,158

Cheddar 4,69,73,75,104,119,120,184,187

Cheese 3,4,5,6,7,8,11,19,27,28,31,37,38,62,64,69,72,75,76,85,101,102,104,114,116,119,130,162,164,165,168,180,181,186,188,191,195

Cherry 103

Chicken 3,4,5,6,7,8,12,29,31,32,33,37,38,39,40,41,42,43,44,45,46,47,48,51,56,60,62,65,75,77,87,89,92,96,100,105,106,115,117,118,121,122,140,144,145,149,153,154,160,161,162,173,185,186,191

Chinese cabbage 71

Chives 3,28

Cinnamon 7,169

Crab 4,52

Cream 3,4,5,6,7,8,13,15,39,40,53,54,65,84,101,122,124,125,128,134,144,155,167,192,195

Crumble 22,99

D

Dijon mustard 29,40,76,104,130,150,186

E

Egg 4,7,37,66,68,85,91,169,188

F

Farfalle 4,8,69,195

Fat 4,5,6,7,39,59,99,100,120,121,128,183

Fennel 4,8,69,194

Feta 5,7,104,157,165,191

Fettuccine 3,4,5,7,9,11,70,98,175

Fish 4,48

Fontina cheese 193

French bread 50

Fruit 120

G

Garlic 4,6,7,15,65,74,91,93,114,122,128,133,140,150,152,160

Gin 48

Gnocchi 6,7,133,134,169,170,171

Gouda 3,24

Grain 120

Gratin 3,40

Conclusion

Thank you again for downloading this book!

I hope you enjoyed reading about my book!

If you enjoyed this book, please take the time to share your thoughts and post a review on Amazon. It'd be greatly appreciated!

Write me an honest review about the book – I truly value your opinion and thoughts and I will incorporate them into my next book, which is already underway.

Thank you!

If you have any questions, **feel free to contact at:** *author@cuminrecipes.com*

Vicky Roy

cuminrecipes.com

Printed in Great Britain
by Amazon